The urban crisis

Edited by **Burton A. Weisbrod** & **James C. Worthy**

The urban crisis

Linking Research to Action

Northwestern University Press   Evanston, Illinois

Northwestern University Press
Evanston, Illinois 60208-4210

Copyright © 1997 by
Northwestern University Press.
Published 1997. All rights reserved.

Printed in the United States of America

ISBN 0-8101-1389-9 (cloth)
ISBN 0-8101-1390-2 (paper)

Library of Congress Cataloging-in-Publication Data

The urban crisis : linking research to action / edited
by Burton A. Weisbrod and James C. Worthy.
p.   cm.
Includes bibliographical references and index.
ISBN 0-8101-1389-9 (cloth : alk. paper). —
ISBN 0-8101-1390-2 (paper : alk. paper)
1. Urban policy — United States — Congresses.
2. Urban poor — Employment — United States —
Congresses.   3. Metropolitan government — United
States — Congresses.   I. Weisbrod, Burton Allen,
1931–   . II. Worthy, James C.
HT123.U7437   1997
331.13'0973'091732 — dc20   96-41992
                                          CIP

Contents

Acknowledgments

The Metropolitan Assembly that gave rise to this book is part of the series of continuing efforts of the Center for Urban Affairs and Policy Research at Northwestern University to bridge the gap between researchers and the world of public policy. We are grateful for the help of many people in supporting, organizing, and administering the conference and for preparing the material for publication. David H. Mortimer, vice president of the American Assembly, provided highly useful advice and counsel in planning the event. Rebecca Riley, vice president of the John D. and Catherine T. MacArthur Foundation, provided funding that was indispensable, as well as strong support for the concept of developing a research agenda that could advance solutions to the enormous problems of our cities within a metropolitan context. An Advisory Committee, whose members are listed below, helped develop the overall strategy for the Assembly. The interchange of ideas that gave rise to the research agenda was materially advanced by the group discussion leaders, Northwestern professors Fay Lomax Cook and Myron Roomkin, both faculty fellows at the Center for Urban Affairs and Policy Research. Drafting the research agenda that grew from the 2-day Assembly was advanced by rapporteurs Kanika Kapur and James Fenelon, Ph.D. candidates in Northwestern's departments of economics and sociology, respectively. Audrey Chambers and Annie Fitzpatrick provided valuable staff support for the conference. We thank all of these people, whose roles were individually and collectively essential to the success of this agenda-setting process.

Metropolitan Assembly Participants

Assembly Organizers
  Burton A. Weisbrod, *Northwestern University*
  James C. Worthy, *Northwestern University*
Mayors and Managers Associations
  Rita Athas, *Executive Director, Northwest Municipal Conference*
  David Bennett, *Executive Director, West Central Municipal Conference*
  Lynn Montei, *Executive Director, DuPage Mayors and Managers Conference*
  Beth Ruyle, *Executive Director, South Suburban Mayors and Managers Association*
Community Colleges and State Universities
  Paul N. Thompson, *President, William Rainey Harper College*
  Wim Wiewel, *Special Assistant to the Chancellor, University of Illinois, Chicago*
Elected Officials
  Lawrence Christmas, *President, Oak Park, Illinois*
  Paul R. Soglin, *Mayor, Madison, Wisconsin*
  Ronald Wietecha, *Mayor, Park Ridge, Illinois*
Appointed Officials
  Mary Sue Barrett, *Chief of Policy, Office of the Mayor, City of Chicago*
  Curt Johnson, *Chief of Staff, Office of the Governor, State of Minnesota*
  Vincent Lane, *Chairman, Chicago Housing Authority*
  Phillip Peters, *Executive Director, Northeastern Illinois Planning Commission*
  M. J. Peterson, *First Deputy Director, Mayor's Office of Employment and Training, City of Chicago*
  Julie S. Putterman, *Assistant Commissioner, Department of Planning and Development, City of Chicago*
Business, Civic, and Community Organizations
  Jean Allard, *President, Metropolitan Planning Council*
  Scott Bernstein, *Director, Center for Neighborhood Technology*
  Myer Blank, *Senior Research Associate, The Civic Federation*
  James W. Compton, *President, Chicago Urban League*
  Denis Detzel, *Managing Director, Eastlake*
  Bertrand Goldberg, *President, Bertrand Goldberg Associates, Inc.*
  Lawrence Howe, *Executive Director, The Civic Committee, Commercial Club of Chicago*
  Kent Lawrence, *Lawrence, Kamin, Saunders & Uhlenhop*
  Craig Lewis, *Vice President, South Shore Bank*

John Lukehart, *Vice President, Leadership Council for Metropolitan Open Communities*

James D. Nowlan, *Executive Director, Illinois Tax Foundation*

Alexander Polikoff, *Executive Director, Business and Professional People for the Public Interest*

William A. Sampson, *President, Chicago United*

Otto A. Silha, *Chairman, City Innovation*

Daniel Solis, *Executive Director, United Neighborhood Organization*

D. Garth Taylor, *Executive Director, Metro Chicago Information Center*

Foundations

Michael Marcus, *Senior Staff Associate, Chicago Community Trust*

Rebecca Riley, *Vice President, MacArthur Foundation*

Media

Neal R. Peirce, *Contributing Editor, National Journal*

Patrick Reardon, *Urban Affairs Editor, Chicago Tribune*

Scholars

Marcus Alexis, *Northwestern University*

Howard Chernick, *Hunter College*

Fay Lomax Cook, *Northwestern University*

Greg Duncan, *University of Michigan*

Michael H. Ebner, *Lake Forest College*

Dennis Epple, *Carnegie Mellon University*

Jeffrey Fagan, *Rutgers University*

Roberto M. Fernandez, *Stanford University*

Bernard Frieden, *Massachusetts Institute of Technology*

Joseph Gyourko, *Wharton School, University of Pennsylvania*

Lawrence Lavengood, *Northwestern University*

David Merriman, *Loyola University*

Andrew Reschovsky, *University of Wisconsin–Madison*

Myron Roomkin, *Northwestern University*

James Rosenbaum, *Northwestern University*

Jerome Rothenberg, *Massachusetts Institute of Technology*

George Tolley, *University of Chicago*

John F. Witte, *University of Wisconsin–Madison*

Advisory Committee

Jean Allard, President
Metropolitan Planning Council

Donald Haider, Professor
Northwestern University

Vincent Lane, Chairman
Chicago Housing Authority

Donald S. Perkins, Trustee
Northwestern University

Julie S. Putterman, Assistant Commissioner
Department of Planning and Development City of Chicago

Rebecca Riley, Vice President
John D. and Catherine T. MacArthur Foundation

Charles H. Shaw, Chairman
The Shaw Company

Burton A. Weisbrod & James C. Worthy

Prologue

Decaying infrastructure, dilapidated housing, dysfunctional schools, racial tensions, violence in the streets, broken families — the litany of urban poverty in the 1990s goes on and on.

Why do these and a host of other problems besetting our cities and the people who live in them keep growing? What should we do about them? Why do the efforts to find solutions by both government and the private sector prove so ineffective?

From September 30 to October 2, 1994, Northwestern University's Center for Urban Affairs and Policy Research, in cooperation with the American Assembly, convened a Metropolitan Assembly composed of 60 experts from research, government, business, community organizations, and journalism to examine these questions. This effort followed the April 1993 American Assembly of Columbia University, which addressed these and related questions at a conference on the "Crisis of the Cities." That conference, chaired by the Honorable Henry Cisneros, Secretary of Housing and Urban Development, generated the book *Interwoven Destinies: Cities and the Nation*, which highlighted many critical urban problems and pointed to the limitations of our knowledge base.

The Northwestern University Metropolitan Assembly, supported by a grant from the John D. and Catherine T. MacArthur Foundation, was conceived and organized not to "solve" these problems but to identify and assess the state of knowledge about them and the causes from which they arise. More particularly, the goal was to identify the critical matters on which inadequacies of knowledge have been obstacles to the formulation and effective execution of public and private solutions, and from this to develop a research agenda for the years ahead that would aid in understanding why society finds it so difficult to alleviate, let alone solve, the festering problems of urban life. We believed that there were — and are — critical gaps in knowledge that are major barriers to successful attacks on urban problems.

Numerous explanations have been offered, and at least as many cures proposed, for our deteriorating cities — hardly a secure foundation for public policy. As a step toward providing a more adequate foundation, the

1

Metropolitan Assembly sought to test whether a diverse group of people knowledgeable about various facets of urban difficulties but distinct in their outlooks could reach consensus on what is known and what still needs to be learned if society is to deal successfully with the urban crisis.

Realistic understanding of the causes for today's urban problems and effective ways for dealing with them is important not only for the specialists but also for the general public. To an extent untrue of many other issues of contemporary society, very large numbers of people have knowledge of urban problems, gained either from direct personal involvement or from the newspapers and television. Relatively few people know much about or are much concerned with issues such as monetary policy or regulatory reform, but many have strong feelings about schools, welfare policy, and public housing. Information derived from personal experience or from daily news accounts is anecdotal, and however true and vivid it may be in terms of the facts in individual cases, its limited scope impairs its value as a base for shaping public policy. Moreover, its highly emotional content inevitably portrays an overly simple picture of complex social realities, further inhibiting its value for policy-making purposes.

Unfortunately, attitudes and opinions based on anecdotal rather than systematic evidence can strongly influence the course and character of public and private action. Nor will superficial general observations suffice. A heavy responsibility thus rests on the shoulders of urban scholars to develop and broadly disseminate systematic accounts of the realities of the problems with which they deal. An equally grave responsibility rests with policy makers to be sure their actions are based on reliable factual information seen in realistic perspective.

In light of the urgent need for better informed public opinion, urban scholars can no longer be content with publishing the fruits of their scholarship in the learned journals of their specialized fields; rather, they need to give attention to means by which the results of their work can be more widely disseminated among policy makers and the public at large. Because this is not the place to make any attempt at spelling out what such means might be, our purpose here is merely to call attention to a matter that urgently needs attention.

In planning the Assembly, we anticipated that the group discussions might generate either of two types of findings. One was that today's urban problems are so complex that even the experts do not know what to do about them, and public and private inaction, even "gridlock," reflects that reality. By this diagnosis, the problems, while serious and even tragic, are beyond any practical means of remediation, given the present state of knowledge. A second possible answer was that despite the complexity of the problems, our knowledge base is sufficient to at least alleviate if not actually solve them, but for some reason the political system has failed to mobilize the resources and efforts needed.

Whether society's failure to stem our urban ills results from either of these circumstances, the effect is the same: public policy that accomplishes little. Depending on which is paramount, however, the implications for ways to break the bottlenecks are quite different. Lack of agreement on what actions will work and at what cost implies a need for research on the cost-effectiveness of alternative mechanisms for attacking the problems. By contrast, agreement on proper mechanisms implies a need for research on why public and private agencies have failed to use effectively the knowledge that is already available.

Unfortunately, there may be sharp disagreement between the research community and the policy-making community on whether, for any given issue, the problem is lack of knowledge or failure to use the knowledge we have. There may be broad agreement, but certainly not unanimity, among urban scholars that an anticrime "three strikes and you're out" law is bad public policy, but prevailing opinion among political leaders may be that this is the way to go. The Metropolitan Assembly addressed this problem and others by giving responsible members of both the research- and action-oriented communities an opportunity to reason together.

The deliberations of the Assembly did in fact generate substantial agreement on the major problems and the questions that must be answered in order to deal with them. These questions are presented later in this volume in "An Urban Research Agenda." They make it clear that while there is a significant body of knowledge about what approaches to take to various problems, there are also major gaps in the knowledge base. And while there is agreement on the effectiveness of certain kinds of public and private action, there is a great deal that still needs to be learned. The Research Agenda makes these needs explicit. It also makes clear that knowledge gaps extend to our efforts to distinguish between reasons for inaction: lack of knowledge of what to do, or difficulties of mobilizing governmental and private-sector resources.

To give sharper focus to the work of the Assembly, proceedings were organized around the central theme of employment and its linkages with other urban problems, such as schooling and the world of work, or welfare reform and employment. Limiting the focus in this way made sense because opportunities for adequately remunerative employment are central to most of the major problems faced by the modern urban community.

To maximize the sessions' productivity and to start deliberations on a common factual base, six background papers were commissioned from nationally recognized scholars and were distributed in advance to serve as the core of the Assembly discussions. Following the Assembly, the papers were edited for inclusion in this book for wide circulation to the scholarly, policy-making, civic, business, and journalistic communities. In September 1996, several of the papers were updated to reflect changes in policy and new legislation.

The papers are of two sorts. Four address the links between the employment market and schools, welfare programs, crime, and the "spatial mismatch" between residential patterns and the transportation systems that connect workers with jobs.

It was also recognized that much of the difficulty of dealing with urban problems may arise from organizational failures. Thus, there are two papers on organizational weaknesses: one addresses the obstacles confronting governments in a metropolitan region as they attempt collaborative activities to surmount narrow jurisdictional concerns, and the other examines the obstacles confronting government and private-sector efforts to collaborate effectively. Specifically the six papers and their authors are as follows:

Papers on Connections between Jobs and Urban Problems

1. "Welfare Reform and Employment: What We Know, and What We Still Need to Know," by Professor Greg Duncan, then of the University of Michigan and now of Northwestern University.
2. "Legal and Illegal Work: Crime, Work, and Unemployment," by Professor Jeffrey Fagan, then of Rutgers University and now of Columbia University.
3. "Spatial Mismatch: Housing, Transportation, and Employment in Regional Perspective," by Professor Roberto M. Fernandez, Stanford University.
4. "Schools and the World of Work," by Professor James Rosenbaum, Northwestern University.

Papers on Organizational Coordination

5. "Urban Fiscal Problems: Coordinating Actions among Governments," by Professor Howard Chernick, Hunter College, and Professor Andrew Reschovsky, University of Wisconsin–Madison.
6. "Public-Private Partnerships and the 'Crisis' of Local Government," by Professor Jerome Rothenberg, Massachusetts Institute of Technology.

The authors of papers 2, 3, and 4 are sociologists; the others are economists. All were asked to summarize the present state of knowledge in their specific problem areas, to note the important public policy–relevant issues on which they believed there is substantial professional consensus, and to identify key gaps in knowledge that constitute serious obstacles to the development of cost-effective public policy. They were also asked to consider the relevance of race as well as the significance of a metropolitan regional focus, and the extent to which the causes and cures for selected central city problems are inseparable from events in the various suburbs.

In addition to the papers commissioned to provide a structured framework for Assembly discussions, there were two other features of the program. One was an address by the Honorable George Latimer, Director of the Special Actions Office of the U.S. Department of Housing and Urban Development, who placed the event in national perspective. The other was a panel discussion in which three influentially positioned users of research outlined their views on the role of urban academic scholarship in the dynamic processes of contemporary urban society. The panelists were Jean Allard, at that time president of the Metropolitan Planning Council of Chicago, Vincent Lane, at that time chairman of the Chicago Housing Authority, and Neal Peirce, syndicated columnist of the *Washington Post* Writers Group. These four individuals added depth and richness to the deliberations of the Assembly.

Since the commissioned papers were distributed in advance, each was introduced at the Assembly by a discussant identified with a governmental, community, or civic organization—this in the spirit of seeking to bridge not only disciplinary gaps, but of equal importance, gaps in the perspectives of the research- and action-oriented communities. To move the discussion toward a consensus on questions to be included in the public policy agenda, discussants were encouraged to be critical of the analysis and identification of issues as outlined by the academic papers' authors.

All of these papers make clear that "the cup of knowledge is both half full and half empty." When it comes to the design and implementation of public policies toward urban problems, there is a great deal of research to build upon. While the debate continues about how to attack the problems of crime, for example, the evidence is powerful that criminal behavior, particularly when it involves lucrative activities such as drugs or theft, is affected by job opportunities, or lack of opportunities, in legal activities (Fagan). Similarly, the evidence is strong that manpower training programs can impart valuable skills to workers, and in the process reduce welfare rolls and increase earning power and productivity. The evidence is equally strong, however, that the costs are high—indeed, generally higher than the cost of the welfare payment alternative, as people with little education and few skills cannot be converted easily into well-paid productive workers (Duncan).

The centrality of employment to the panoply of urban problems points to another set of relationships about which a great deal is known: the critical link between the schools and job opportunities. If students see a close connection between their efforts in school and the availability of well-paying postschooling jobs, they are likely to be far more diligent in their studies and in their school deportment (Rosenbaum). The evidence from Germany and Japan is instructive, but the sociocultural differences from the United States suggest the need for better understanding of the advantages and disadvantages of linking schools and employers in the design of curricula, systems for grading students, and job placement.

While schools and job training are instrumental in providing job skills, translating those skills into productive employment requires more. Residential housing opportunities, locations of job opportunities, and the means of transportation connecting them are essential ingredients. It is commonplace to assume that the relocation of jobs from central cities to suburbs has caused a "spatial mismatch" for which the solution is either an improved transit system or a reversal of the exodus of jobs. Perhaps that is so, but there is mounting evidence to the contrary: that employment has left the central city precisely to escape the problems and the low-skilled, mostly black, labor force (Fernandez). Insofar as this is so, efforts to reverse the job flow are unlikely to be effective, and improvements in transportation will lead to still greater dispersion of jobs. Understanding this problem is fundamental to dealing with its manifestations.

It is increasingly clear that the set of problems involving creation of job skills and motivation of students to learn, along with cutting crime, dealing with hardship cases through welfare programs, and linking jobs to residential patterns, is difficult, and perhaps impossible, for any one community or local government to attack successfully. A planning and implementation process that encompasses at least a metropolitan area is needed, but the obstacles to its organization and effective functioning are formidable (Chernick and Reschovsky). The first step appears to be documentation and recognition of the forms and extent of interdependence of the local governments in a metropolitan area. Can a clearer, more compelling case be made that the self-interest of suburban communities dictates their participating in the funding and administration of central city schools, police, and other services?

When the role of public policy in solving urban problems is considered, there is an all-too-common tendency to think of the role of governments:

local, metropolitan region, state, or federal. This is too limited. In a basically private enterprise economy, the vast majority of job opportunities are private, and therefore the declining job opportunities in central cities are the accumulated result of many separate private decisions. This suggests at least a potential role for governments to reverse the process. Evidence is growing that neither government nor private enterprise alone is an effective mode for breaking the nexus of urban job decline. Cooperation between governments and the private sector, through joint ventures and otherwise, has shown considerable promise in overcoming impediments to urban revitalization, and such cooperation has taken a variety of forms (Rothenberg).

When we, or any of the authors of the surveys, refer to "evidence" regarding the costs and effectiveness of some particular mechanism for urban restructuring—even when we refer to *strong* evidence—we do not mean that there is unanimity of research findings or absolute certainty of the consequences of a given policy initiative. Neither do we mean that the same results will hold for all population age groups, for cities of all sizes, or for every part of the country. The state of knowledge is clearly inadequate for such confidence and generality to hold. But that should not be a deterrent to active public policy built on findings from research. Insistence on "complete" knowledge is counterproductive, leading to perpetual inaction and thus maintenance of the status quo. There can be no assurance that the next launching of a space vehicle will be flawless, no assurance that the next foreign policy intervention will be successful, no warrant that a new environmental protection measure will actually work, no guarantee that a new drug will be entirely safe as well as effective. Certainty is neither possible nor worthwhile as a goal; its cost is too high. When serious problems exist, as they certainly do in the context of urban decay and poverty, the cost of insistence on ever-better information is the continuation of poor schooling, lack of opportunity, failure of young people to take advantage of opportunities that are available, family disintegration, crime, and poverty.

It is just as important to recognize the preponderate weight of research evidence as it is to recognize its lack of certainty. Caution and action need to be balanced. The six surveys of the state of research highlight what is "known" with reasonable confidence about each relationship. The research agendas focus on what the authors and other Metropolitan Assembly participants see as *what needs to be known* to advance urban public policy. Both are important.

The spirit of consensus building, together with the goal of identifying the knowledge limitations that now handicap effective urban policy making, continued throughout the 2 days and evenings of discussions as the participants, divided into two groups, were led through the six topics by skilled discussion leaders, both affiliated with Northwestern University's Center for Urban Affairs and Policy Research: Professor Fay Lomax Cook (School of Education and Social Policy) and Professor Myron Roomkin (J. L. Kellogg Graduate School of Management).

Following these discussions, a tentative list was drafted of the major research questions on which substantial consensus appeared to have been reached. These lists were circulated to the authors for their reactions, and revised lists were thereupon submitted to all Assembly participants for further comment. The results of this interactive process are presented in "An Urban Research Agenda."

As organizers and editors, we hope this agenda and the accompanying chapters will prove useful in helping focus the attention of the scholarly, the action-oriented, and the research-funding communities on the problems most critically in need of reliable factual knowledge for the formulation of more effective public policies, and on practical means for integrating the efforts of various stakeholders in reversing the deterioration of our cities.

PART I

Connections between Urban Problems and Jobs

Greg Duncan

Welfare Reform and Employment
What We Know, and What We Still Need to Know

Introduction

Few urban problems inspire more emotion than welfare "dependence." Vivid in countless television programs and magazine articles are images of three-generation black welfare families, languishing in dilapidated public housing projects, raising children who, if male, are destined to live (and perhaps die as a result of) a life of crime and, if female, will themselves soon become welfare-dependent mothers.

The popularity of President Bill Clinton's pledge to "end welfare as we know it" by imposing a 24-month limit on the duration of receipt fed off public resentment toward welfare recipients, as have many provisions of the welfare reform legislation passed in 1996.

The debate and legislated reforms make countless assumptions about the characteristics and motivations of current and prospective welfare recipients and about the neighborhoods and labor markets in which they reside. The extent to which these assumptions are supported by systematic, as opposed to anecdotal, evidence is one of the topics addressed in this study.

The main purpose of this essay is to identify unmet evidentiary needs that are critical in formulating welfare reform policies directed at promoting both the employability and the actual employment of current and future recipients.

I begin with a review of the demography and dynamics of welfare caseloads. I show that while many welfare experiences are short-lived and most recipients are much more employable than case study accounts would suggest, there does indeed exist a sizable group of mostly younger,

Terry Adams, Dorothy Duncan, and Burton Weisbrod made a number of helpful comments on the essay. Support from the National Institute for Child Health and Human Development through its Family and Child Well-Being Research Network is gratefully acknowledged.

less educated recipients for whom, barring explicit training and employment efforts, long-term welfare dependence is very likely.

I next discuss the nature of the labor markets in which welfare-to-work transitions will take place. The good news here is that, in contrast to European countries, the U.S. labor market has generated and will probably continue to generate jobs for women with modest levels of formal schooling. The bad news is that most of these jobs pay very little and offer little chance for advancement. A look at the skills of welfare recipients shows that while many can and do get jobs, a substantial minority have very few skills employers would likely value.

Although we have no recent experience to draw from in assessing the likely effects of the proposed time limits on the receipt of welfare, states in the 1980s engaged in a great deal of experimentation with welfare-to-work programs. I review the results of these experiments, which show that many are cost-effective, although none was successful in promoting permanent employment for the vast majority of people in the programs, and most of the women making successful transitions from welfare to work continue to live below or, at best, slightly above the poverty line.

After reviewing key elements of Clinton and Republican welfare-reform proposals, I focus on key gaps in our knowledge about welfare recipients and their experiences.

The Demography and
Dynamics of Welfare Caseloads

SUMMARY: There is no "typical" welfare experience; rather, there is a mixture of experiences, many quite short but some very long. Recipients are also heterogeneous; some of them can and undoubtedly will find work, while for others employment is unlikely without additional training. Caseload records show that most recipients are white, have a high school degree, do not live in public housing, are well past their teenage years, and are not responsible for very young children. Most welfare experiences are sufficiently short that a majority of first-time recipients will never accumulate the 24 months of receipt that would trigger the termination of benefits in Clinton's welfare-reform proposal or the 60-month limit in some Republican proposals. However, an important minority of recipients do conform to the stereotype of teen-mother-turned-long-term-recipient. It is these individuals on whom most of the welfare reform debate needs to center.

TABLE I: *Various Characteristics of the AFDC Caseload across Time*

	1969	1975	1979	1986	1990	1992
% of all U.S. children who live in AFDC families	8.7*	11.8	11.0	11.2†	11.9	13.0
No. of child recipients, in millions	6.1*	8.0	7.1	7.1†	7.9	9.2
% of AFDC cases with mothers under age 20	7	· · ·	· · ·	3	8	· · ·
% of children in AFDC families under age 3	15	· · ·	· · ·	22	24	· · ·
% of AFDC recipients who are black	45	· · ·	· · ·	41	40	· · ·
% of AFDC recipients living in public housing	13	· · ·	· · ·	10	10	· · ·

Source: Committee on Ways and Means (1993), tables 15, 21, 26, and 31.
* 1970 figure.
† 1985 figure.

Who are welfare recipients and to what extent do their qualifications and family situations make them attractive to potential employers? Information gleaned from welfare caseload records and published in the Committee on Ways and Means (1993) *Green Book* provides the snapshot of welfare recipients shown in table 1.

There was a marked increase in the prevalence of receipt around 1970 and then little change until the early 1990s. After an increase from about 9 percent to 12 percent in the early 1970s, only in the early 1990s did the fraction of American children living in recipient families change by more than 1 percentage point. The recession of 1990–91 helped drive the caseload to 9.2 million children by 1992. Projections forecast a continuing increase to more than 9.5 million children in 1993 (Committee on Ways and Means 1993, table 26).

The characteristics of recipient families have changed over these years, usually in the direction of greater employability:

- Fewer than one in 10 welfare recipients is under age 20 (table 1, row 3), although a substantial number of older recipients were under age 20 when they first started receiving welfare (Ellwood 1986).

- Somewhat more cases involve very young children now than before (table 1, row 4), although such cases still constitute only about one-quarter of the total caseload.
- The fraction of cases involving blacks (table 1, row 5) or families living in public housing (row 6) has declined somewhat. Blacks are persistently overrepresented among AFDC recipients throughout this period, although they never constitute a majority of the caseload. Only one in ten welfare recipients lives in public housing.

These facts — especially the relatively high schooling levels and absence of very young children — would appear to bode well for the potential employment prospects of welfare recipients. However, it is crucial to bear in mind that families observed in these caseload statistics are a heterogeneous lot, with these average characteristics masking the extremely diverse nature of welfare experiences and qualifications.

A useful picture of recipients' experiences is provided by a focus on the total length of welfare experiences, from beginning to end. This reveals the extent of short-term receipt — for example, how many and what kinds of individuals ever starting to receive welfare complete their receipt within, say, 1 or 2 years, as well as the more important question of long-term receipt — how many and what kinds of recipients are still receiving assistance 5, 10, or even more years after starting to receive it.

Ellwood (1986) takes a comprehensive look at the welfare experiences of first-time recipients by estimating the total number of years — regardless of pattern — first-time recipients can expect to receive welfare over the 25-year period following the point of first receipt. He estimates that:

- 30 percent of first-time recipients can expect to receive welfare for only 1 or 2 years, while another 30 percent can be expected to receive it for 8 or more years. Most exits (46 percent) are related to demographic events such as marriage or the loss of eligibility because children either left the household or became too old, although a significant minority (26 percent) can be linked to employment.

Thus, even in the absence of welfare-to-work or other intervention programs, a substantial share of recipients will permanently end their receipt of welfare by marriage, work, or other means within a fairly short time.

TABLE 2: *Duration of Welfare Receipt and Prevalence of Long-Term Receipt by Characteristics of Recipients at the Time They First Started to Receive AFDC*

Recipient Characteristics at Beginning of Receipt	Average No. of Years of AFDC Receipt	% with More Than 10 Total Years of AFDC Receipt
Age:		
Under 22	8	33
22–30	7	26
31–40	5	15
Over 40	5	16
Marital status:		
Never married	9	39
Divorced	4	14
Separated	7	24
Age of youngest child:		
Under 3	8	32
3–5	7	24
6–10	5	11
Over 10	5	12
Disability status:		
No disability	7	25
Disability limits work	7	25

Source: Ellwood (1986), table IV.1.

On the other hand:

• There are enough long-term recipients to warrant concern about who they are and what might be done to shorten the likely length of their welfare receipt.

Ellwood attempts to identify recipients most likely to have very long periods of receipt. He finds, not surprisingly, that young mothers are the most likely long-term recipients. Table 2 reproduces some of his figures, showing, by various characteristics of first-time recipients (i) the average number of years of receipt, and (ii) the fraction in each group who can be expected to receive welfare for 10 years or more.

TABLE 3: *Employment Qualifications of 25-Year-Old Women, by Receipt of Welfare in the Previous 12 Months*

	% of Continuous Welfare Recipients	% of Nonrecipients
Less than high school degree	52	10
High school degree	35	44
College degree or more	0	22
Bottom quarter of aptitude test	72	22
Above average on aptitude test	12	51

Source: Burtless (1994), table 2.

Three correlated characteristics are most closely associated with long periods of receipt—young mothers, never-married mothers, and young children. Four in 10 never-married mothers, one in three very young mothers, and one in three mothers with young children have welfare "careers" that last at least 10 years. These fractions are considerably higher than those associated with other characteristics. Thus, not surprisingly:

- Concern over long-term welfare receipt should focus first and foremost on young, never-married recipients.

Burtless's (1995) analysis of the employment qualifications of 25-year-old recipient women provides a pessimistic picture. Table 3 presents some of Burtless's information on the formal schooling and aptitude scores of a national sample of young women, some of whom were continuous recipients in the prior 12 months and the rest of whom had received no welfare during that time. The differences are stark.

Burtless found that a majority of these young welfare recipients lacked a high school diploma. Fully 72 percent of recipients scored in the bottom quarter of a general comprehensive aptitude test. Thus, in contrast to the encouraging prospects for welfare-to-work transitions for many recipients, the data show very little in the characteristics of young recipients that potential employers might find attractive.

Evidentiary needs.
Considerable research has been devoted to describing the nature of welfare experiences and recipients. Sources such as the *Green Book* pub-

lish annual updates on caseload characteristics. Needed are updates on the dynamic elements of welfare experiences, tracking, for example: (i) the fractions of women and children who have recently begun to receive welfare for the first time, (ii) the fractions of recipients who had started their receipt at various points in the past who voluntarily stop receiving welfare during a given year, and (iii) the events associated with the beginnings and endings of welfare experiences. As welfare reform is instituted, there will be substantial need for information on its performance.

Demand-Side Labor Market Developments

SUMMARY: Although the labor market prospects of low-skilled workers have worsened over the past 20 years, men rather than women have borne the brunt of these changes. Most women with few labor market skills have been and will probably continue to be able to find jobs. The key problem is that the jobs they find provide few opportunities for advancement or decent pay. Skill upgrading is the most promising longer-run solution.

The employment prospects of welfare recipients are a function of the skills recipients bring to the labor market as well as the demand for those skills by local employers. Drawing upon Blank's (1995) excellent analysis of demand-side issues in the context of welfare reform, this section reviews developments in the labor market prospects of low-skilled female workers.

Over the last 2 decades, almost all Western economies have witnessed dramatic changes in the comparative economic fortunes of high- and low-skilled workers. Technological changes have increased the demand for and earnings of more experienced and educated workers at the expense of less skilled workers. In contrast to the European experience, the U.S. economy has generated millions of new jobs during this period. Most relevant to the debate over welfare reform is the fact that the demand for low-skilled female labor has remained fairly strong and prospects for continued employment opportunities are good. The fundamental labor market problem of welfare recipients is not jobs *per se* but rather the earnings and career trajectories of these jobs.

Blank (1995) presents national data on labor force activity and wages of workers at various skill levels between 1979 and 1992. Of particular importance here is how the least educated men and women have done. Table 4 summarizes several key results.

Men and women have shown very different trends in their involvement

TABLE 4: *Labor Force Involvement and Earnings of Men and Women, by Schooling Level, 1979 and 1992*

Education Level	Labor Force Participation: % of All Individuals in Group Who Are Working or Actively Looking for Work				Low Wages: % of Working Men and Women Earning Less Than $5 per Hour	
	Men		Women			
	1979	1992	1979	1992	1979	1992
Less than high school degree	76	70	43	43	7	24
High school degree	90	87	60	67	4	11
College degree or more	93	92	71	80	2	3
All education levels	86	84	58	67	4	10

Source: Blank (1994), tables 3 and 7, based on tabulations from the Current Population Survey.

in the labor force. The fraction of men who are either working or looking for work has fallen for all groups of men, with the fall especially large among men with the lowest schooling levels. As of 1992, fully 30 percent of adult, male, high school dropouts were not in the labor force, a figure that was one-quarter higher than its 1979 level. Fewer female high school dropouts were in the labor force at either time, but there was no decline in the labor force activity of female dropouts. Among women with either high school or college degrees there was a sharp jump in labor force participation. When coupled with the fact that the extent of unemployment was slightly lower among women than men at all schooling levels (data not shown in table 4), the picture that emerges is one of a labor market that has proved capable of generating substantial numbers of additional jobs for women workers, including women with modest schooling levels.

The picture of earnings paid is bleak for the kinds of jobs held by low-skilled men and women. Table 4 also shows what fraction of adults earned very little (under $5 per hour in 1992 dollars) as well as the fraction who earned a wage capable of providing a full-time worker with an income somewhat above the poverty line ($10 per hour). The fraction of low-wage jobs more than doubled (from 4 percent to 10 percent) between

1979 and 1992, with the increases especially marked (e.g., such jobs more than tripled for high school dropouts) for the kinds of jobs held by workers with the lowest schooling levels. There was a concomitant drop in the fraction of jobs held by high school dropouts that paid at least $10 per hour.

Not all workers fared badly with respect to wages. College graduates had jobs that provided wage increases that more than kept up with inflation over this period. Taken as a whole, the 1980s witnessed a dramatic jump in inequality, with higher-skilled jobs paying well and low-skilled jobs paying very little. Although the earnings of low-skilled female workers did grow slightly faster than those of their male counterparts, they still earned less than low-skilled male workers and lost ground relative to higher-skilled workers of either sex.

Evidentiary needs.

What is most depressing on the demand side of the labor market is not so much the initially low wages commanded by welfare recipients but rather the fact that there are no discernible job ladders, either within or across firms, that might lead to higher-paying jobs. Entry-level jobs provide a valuable screening function in the labor market as well as at least some basic training in the world of work. However, the skills and productivity workers gain with experience are not recognized by other employers; indeed, employers probably have incentives to minimize the mobility of their most productive workers. We know very little about how low-wage labor markets operate and how the career mobility of workers might be enhanced.

Lessons from the Various Welfare-to-Work Experiments

SUMMARY: In contrast to most policy areas, there is good information, based on well-designed, randomized experiments, regarding the effects of various job search and training programs on the earnings and employment of AFDC recipients. By and large, it shows statistically significant but substantively modest effects of many interventions, with the size and duration of the benefits usually depending (in a positive direction) on the cost of the intervention.

Few areas of public policy have been the subject of more experimentation than the relationship between welfare receipt and work. In the 1970s the welfare "reforms" most hotly debated were cash grants with few restrictions, which were feared for the massive exodus of workers from the labor force they might induce. Tens of millions of dollars were spent on formal experiments in which families were randomly allocated to "treatment" groups, which were eligible to receive various versions of the new cash grant program, and a "control" group, which was eligible to receive only the existing mixture of benefits.

Random allocation is the key element here; there are countless examples of new programs that have allowed administrators discretion in selecting participants. A natural tendency of administrators is to "cream" the pool of potential participants by selecting the ones most likely to benefit from the program. Although the success of these programs may be very real for the participants, it provides no reliable indication of whether more typical participants might benefit, or whether these programs could be exported successfully to other locations.

During the 1980s, the Reagan administration encouraged states to experiment with various welfare-to-work programs. A wide variety of such programs were set up as true random experiments (Gueron and Pauly 1991). Some involved quite minimal assistance, with an average of only a few hundred dollars spent per recipient in teaching them to search for jobs. Other programs provided more extensive training, with costs running into the thousands of dollars per recipient.

In evaluating the value of these programs, one reasonable criterion is analogous to a business's evaluation of whether an investment is profitable — that is, whether the benefits of the program exceed its costs. The costs consist mostly of the administrative time spent in facilitating the job search or providing training. Benefits are measured by the increased earnings of participants that can be attributed to the program.

The extent to which the government recaptures some of the increased earnings in the form of income taxes, Social Security payroll taxes, or reduced spending on welfare benefits is irrelevant in this calculation because a societal evaluation of "profit" presumes that the increased earnings reflect an increased worker productivity. The extent to which the government captures some of the increased earnings in the form of taxes or reduced welfare spending is irrelevant to a societal accounting that values a more productive economy regardless of the division of the additional slices of the pie that that productivity creates.

In terms of this standard of profitability, most of the programs, especially the costlier job-training programs, were indeed profitable. (Programs that stressed only community service without a training or search component were the least successful.) However, in no case did the programs result in virtually all or even most of the recipients making successful, long-term transitions into the labor force. For example, the program set up in San Diego is considered to be one of the most successful. In it, some $850 was spent per recipient for a combination of education, job training, and assistance in job search. Enrollment in the San Diego program was high, in part because of extensive efforts, enforced by sanctions, to maximize participation. The high enrollments are important, since they imply that the results reflect the experiences of both the most employable cases, who are most likely to enroll in these programs, as well as the least-likely-to-enroll difficult cases. By the second year, the San Diego program had raised the earnings of the experimental group over the treatment group by 29 percent, with the difference persisting into the third year of the experiment. But the base for this increase is low — some $2,250 per year, so that in terms of dollars, the increase amounted to only about $650 per year.

As indicated by its title, the Teen Parent Welfare Demonstration focused on the hardest-to-employ segment of the caseload — teen parents in three inner-city areas, including the South Side of Chicago (Maynard 1993). The young mothers received relatively extensive support services to promote formal schooling and, when appropriate, job training. As with the San Diego program, extensive outreach, coupled with sanctions, produced very high participation rates (around 90 percent). When compared with mothers in the control group, mothers in the experimental treatment group were considerably more likely to be enrolled in school (42 percent vs. 29 percent). Employment rates of the experimentals were about 5 percentage points higher, and earnings were somewhat higher ($20 per month) as well.

As is clear from these figures, a general problem with these programs is that most recipients who succeeded in securing long-term employment did so at quite low wages. When coupled with the fall in AFDC benefits that the increased earnings produced, the total family incomes of these women as workers were little different from their total incomes as welfare recipients — both were typically below the poverty line. Although most women making the transition to work are pleased with the change, it must surely be discouraging at some level to see that their families' incomes had not been improved much by the employment. Whether this lack of monetary incentives will at some point discourage them in their efforts to gain and keep paid employment remains to be seen.

Evidentiary needs.

Although expensive and time-consuming to run, the remarkable investments in randomized evaluations of welfare-to-work programs in the 1980s have provided us with a great deal of reliable information about the payoffs to various kinds of job search and training programs. Roughly speaking, they show that these programs can be cost effective and that the payoffs are more or less in line with the size of the investments. State administrators have a great deal of well-documented experience to draw from in designing programs such as these.

Were time limits and possible public-sector jobs to be part of the next round of welfare reform (see the next section), then there would be urgent needs for program-design information to assist administrators.

Welfare Reform Proposals

SUMMARY: In a radical departure from previous versions of welfare reform, Clinton's proposal imposes a 24-month limit on the duration of receipt of benefits, after which a private- or possibly a public-sector job would provide earnings rather than a welfare check. Republican-led legislation passed in 1996 will end the entitlement status of welfare programs, provide great freedom for states to design their own programs, have no public-sector job guarantee, and, in certain circumstances, elimininate benefits for young mothers and immigrants.

President Clinton's proposed welfare reform constituted a dramatic departure from previously attempted reforms and a major political gamble. Most of its stated goals — making work more attractive than welfare, curbing the epidemic of teen out-of-wedlock births, increasing the financial responsibility of fathers — are supported by almost all sides in the welfare debate. Although tame when compared with the welfare reform proposals in the Republican's "Contract with America," the most controversial part of Clinton's proposal was the 24-month limit on the period of receipt of welfare benefits. With numerous qualifications and phase-in provisions, the period of time that a new welfare recipient can continue to receive benefits is limited to 24 months, after which point the recipient will be expected to work, if necessary at a "temporary subsidized job."

Welfare reform legislation passed in 1996 goes far beyond Clinton's proposals in (i) ending the entitlement status of welfare programs, which means that states running out of money would not be required to provide benefits to qualified families; (ii) freezing federal funding of welfare programs; (iii) providing block grants to states for funding welfare programs, with very few restrictions on how states should spend the money; (iv) limiting the total duration of receipt to 60 months; and (v) denying benefits to noncitizens.

There are many complications to these proposals that need not concern us here. Most important for the welfare-to-work transitions are the following:

- In contrast to "workfare" programs where participating recipients received the full amount of welfare benefits, working mothers in Clinton's public employment would be paid only for the hours actually worked. Most jobs would pay the minimum wage for between 15 and 35 weekly hours of work. There are no provisions at all for public employment in the 1996 legislation.
- In the Clinton proposal, child care is guaranteed during training and work programs and for 1 year after the transition to private employment. Child-care guarantees in the 1996 legislation are left up to the states.
- Any nondraconian proposal to "end welfare as we know it" by imposing time limits must struggle with the fact that it is considerably more expensive in the short run to provide training and, if necessary, jobs for recipients than to give them checks. Most education and training programs have proved their worth, but they are costly, and the political climate does not permit much to be spent on them. Earlier versions of the Clinton proposal called for nearly $20 billion in new spending over 5 years, but opposition to tax increases forced this figure down to $9.3 billion over 5 years. The 1996 legislation provides no significant funding of education and job-training programs. States are required to have 50 percent of recipients working 30 or more hours per week by 2002, but there is no explicit appropriation for assisting the states in providing training or employment.

Sadly, the process of "ending welfare as we know it" has provided little, if any, help to welfare recipients for their welfare-to-work transitions.

Crucial Gaps in Our Knowledge of How to Enhance Welfare-to-Work Transitions

We have noted in previous sections some of the information gaps regarding welfare recipients and their experiences, the labor markets in which employment transitions would occur, and the design and payoffs of government programs that would assist recipients in making welfare-to-work transitions.

We have argued that information needs in these areas are relatively modest, since the evidence gathered, analyses conducted, and experiments run over the last 15 years have told us a great deal about the nature of the problems and the benefits of the kinds of welfare-to-work programs undertaken by program administrators during the 1980s.

A persistent, although perhaps minor, problem is that the circumstances and backgrounds of current recipients will always differ in some ways from those of the past recipients based on whom policy decisions have been drawn. Some of these differences (e.g., schooling levels, family structure) can be measured and factored into the analysis. But if important unmeasured differences exist, then prescriptions based on old information may be flawed. Obviously, more recent information is always preferable.

A more important problem is that the 1996 welfare reform calls for major changes in policy for which we have no experience on which to base evaluations. It is claimed that various provisions will "send a message" to young people who will then think twice about having children out of wedlock or dropping out of high school. There is no good way to test the validity of this assertion. Most programs targeted on at-risk adolescents and teen mothers have proved ineffective in preventing either first or (in the case of the Chicago-based Teen Parent Welfare Demonstration mentioned earlier) subsequent pregnancies and births. The insensitivity of teen out-of-wedlock birthrates to large differences in the generosity of welfare benefits across states and across time also suggests that welfare reform of the kind contemplated in Congress will have at best minor impact on such births, but that judgment is also based on little direct evidence. When and if welfare reform is enacted, there will be a need for timely information about its possible effects on the employment and other behavior of recipients.

THE BIGGER PICTURE

The most optimistic view based on existing evidence is that (i) many welfare recipients will succeed in getting and keeping jobs with no assistance from work-related programs of any kind; and (ii) a significant and cost-effective fraction of harder-to-employ recipients can be helped into the labor force by existing programs, provided that the pubic is willing to invest in these programs; but (iii) although cost-effective, existing programs still leave large numbers of recipients without jobs; and (iv) few of the transitions, even to permanent employment, translate into permanent transitions out of poverty or near-poverty.

If we take as a more comprehensive goal of welfare "reform" the facilitation of successful transitions to decent standards of living, then the need for information changes a great deal:

Pregnancy prevention.

Once a never-married teenager has a child, there is a 77 percent chance that she will receive welfare within 5 years (Gleason, Ranfarajan, and Schochet 1994). Although spending money on teen mothers' education, job training, and job search has been shown to produce modest, positive effects on their labor market prospects, a far better strategy would be to prevent the pregnancy in the first place. We know very little about how best to do this. In contrast to education and training programs, experiments with pregnancy-prevention programs have not shown most of them to be cost effective (Kirby 1994). The fact that welfare reform calls for no spending for pregnancy-prevention programs is a reasonable response to our apparent inability to design programs that work.

Proponents of welfare reform provisions that would not increase benefits if recipient mothers bore additional children or would simply deny benefits altogether to teen mothers assume that the level of welfare benefits affects women's decisions about getting pregnant and bearing children. However, countless studies have failed to turn up evidence that out-of-wedlock childbearing, particularly among blacks, is influenced at all by the generosity of benefits (Moffitt 1992). And studies focused explicitly on whether the generosity of incremental benefits for additional children affects fertility behavior of recipients reach a similar conclusion (Robins and Fronstin 1993). This leads us to conclude that all but the most draconian welfare-reform proposals would have no substantial effects on the rate of out-of-wedlock childbearing.

If neither manipulation of welfare benefits nor focused pregnancy-prevention programs has an appreciable effect on out-of-wedlock childbearing, what does? This is a key question that cannot be answered with the existing information and analysis.

One promising line of inquiry might be to focus less on the alleged benefits to a teenager bearing a child out of wedlock and more on the cost side. The economic benefits — welfare benefits for the most part — of bearing a child out of wedlock are so readily apparent that they have come to dominate the debate over teen childbearing.

Some costs are obvious (e.g., food and clothing), while others are more subtle. What does a teenager forgo if she has a child, and how have those costs changed over time? Bearing a child too early might cause a teenager to give up opportunities for additional schooling and a promising career. Moreover, having a child before marriage might reduce the chance of a later marriage or might restrict in undesirable ways the set of possible marriage partners.

Evidence on labor market trends presented earlier suggests that, in terms of earnings, career opportunities of even high school–graduate women have deteriorated badly over the past 20 years, thus lowering one element of the cost of teenage childbearing.

Marriage opportunities have deteriorated even more sharply, especially among blacks and urban blacks in particular (Wilson 1987; Duncan and Hoffman 1991). The dismal situation of minority males may well be a key component of successful integration of welfare recipients into mainstream jobs and, more generally, mainstream society. Males were the big losers in the welfare-reform proposal — all that remains that relates to fathers are punitive provisions for paternity establishment and child support. While these provisions deserve support, they beg the more important issues of how to promote the labor market success of fathers and integrate fathers back into the lives of their children.

Understanding whether any of the cost and benefit considerations is important to prospective teen mothers and fathers requires additional research on their knowledge and expectations. What little research that has been done thus far on expectations has treated them as a yes-no proposition — either people expect to be married by, say, age 25, or they do not; or they expect to have a decent-paying job, or they do not. A more reasonable approach is to measure expectations on a continuous scale. This has been done successfully in a number of surveys and is a promising path for understanding more about adolescent decision making.

Effects of employment versus home time on children.
Although welfare programs are designed ostensibly to assist children, most of the debate over their design concerns the behavior of the mother and absent father. The effects of welfare reforms on the development of children and adolescents ought to be a central issue in the debate over those reforms.

Increasingly, evidence suggests that, among components of a family's socioeconomic status, income level is one of the most important determinants (and possibly *the* most important determinant) of the physical (Miller and Korenman 1994) and cognitive (Duncan, Brooks-Gunn, and Klebanov 1994) development of children. The generosity of welfare benefits clearly affects the level of family income. Whether growing up in a welfare-recipient family has an independent and adverse effect on the life chances of children is an important and as yet unresolved research question. Several past studies have found such intergenerational linkages (Gottschalk 1992; Duncan and Yeung 1995).

Would limits on welfare duration benefit children? In studying this question, it is important to keep in mind the entire range of changes that such policies might bring about. The total amount of income might change, exerting an independent effect on the family's ability to provide a home environment that would promote beneficial outcomes for the children. However, in the absence of large increases in the generosity of wage-enhancing programs like the Earned Income Tax Credit (EITC), the *level* of family income is the aspect of the families of recipient-turned-worker mothers least likely to change much with welfare reform.

Substantial increases in maternal employment will have much larger effects on the amount of time mothers have to supervise or monitor the behavior of their adolescent children. Is mothers' time spent at home productive in the sense that children are better off when there is more of it? There is mixed evidence on the detrimental effect of maternal employment on the development of children and adolescents, but little of it is focused on the low-income mothers who will be affected most by the reforms. We need more information about how the mandatory-employment provisions of welfare reform are likely to affect children.

Public opinion.
Public opinion has always been of two minds about supporting programs for low-income families (Cook and Barrett 1992). "Welfare programs" always get low marks, while at the same time considerable support is offered for programs that would help the poor develop skills needed for self-sufficiency.

One view of the emerging consensus surrounding welfare reform is that it shows that the only form of assistance that the public is willing to support is one that imposes the same norms and expectations regarding maternal employment for the welfare population that hold for the general population. We now have compelling evidence to suggest that a large-scale training program would bring substantial numbers of current recipients into the labor force and, if coupled with a fairly generous wage subsidy to low-wage families and strict child support, would lift many of their families out of poverty.

Will the public support the tens of billions of dollars needed for large-scale implementation of truly comprehensive programs? Preliminary evidence from the welfare reform debate is not promising. A number of additional taxes were suggested to secure financing for a more ambitious version of the welfare reform bill, but virtually all were defeated with hardly a ripple of public reaction. Is public opinion really unsupportive of any form of welfare reform, perhaps believing that the government is unable to implement an efficient set of programs? Or is the public simply misinformed about the efficacy of any kind of training or employment programs? We have few answers to key questions about how to mobilize public opinion to support effective programs.

Do today's urban neighborhoods doom reform efforts?

Most people presume that neighborhoods exert important effects on children, even independent of the family conditions under which children are raised. On the basis of research in Chicago, William Wilson (1991) writes of the many ways in which neighborhood-level poverty, dependence, female family structure, and, especially, pervasive joblessness among adult men so dominate the climate of neighborhood life that little else seems to matter.

The evidentiary basis for such neighborhood effects is, at best, thin. There is little doubt that children growing up in inner-city as opposed to suburban neighborhoods are much less likely to be successful, self-sufficient adults, but the key question is whether this is due to the resources and other conditions of the *families* in which they are raised or to the *neighborhood* and *labor market* conditions in which they find themselves. The question is crucial, since family-resource problems can be addressed, at least in theory, with family-based tax and transfer strategies, while correcting neighborhood-based problems poses a much more formidable set of policy problems.

The literature on neighborhood effects does not provide a clear answer. Most intriguing is a study by James Rosenbaum and his colleagues (1991) of low-income black families from low-income public-housing projects in Chicago. As part of the Gautreaux Housing Program court case, nearly 4,000 families were involved in a subsidized program that arranged for private housing, much of it in Chicago suburbs, but some of it in the city of Chicago itself. Since participants were assigned to the first available housing and were not allowed to choose between city and suburb, their locations approached the experimental ideal of randomized assignment. Rosenbaum reports an impressive series of positive differences, both in the employment outcomes for adults and in developmental outcomes for their children, for the families assigned to the suburban locations. However,

Rosenbaum's analysis is limited to families who remained in their suburban locations and thus suffers from its own form of selection bias.

The Department of Housing and Urban Development has just begun an ambitious six-city (including Chicago) Gautreaux-type intervention in which random subsets of housing-project families are given assistance in moving to low-poverty, presumably mostly suburban, neighborhoods. Called "Moving to Opportunity," this intervention should provide an important replication test for the dramatic improvement in the lives of both mothers and children found in Rosenbaum's analysis.

Although Rosenbaum's results suggest that neighborhoods may exert powerful effects on children and adolescents, other evidence indicates that neighborhoods do not totally overwhelm other factors. As mentioned before, experimental interventions focused on teen mothers living on the South Side of Chicago and other inner-city areas showed the same pattern of modest but significant effects on employment and earnings as experiments based in "better" neighborhoods. This indicates that inner-city neighborhoods do not necessarily doom intervention programs. Consistent with this conclusion are nonexperimental studies (e.g., Brooks-Gunn et al. 1993; Clark 1993) comparing children and adolescents in a variety of family and neighborhood settings. They find many examples of successful children and adolescents even in the worst neighborhoods. Much remains to be learned about the nature of neighborhood effects.

Suppose for a moment that neighborhood-based as opposed to family-based conditions were found to be the crucial determinants of the opportunity structure of children. Two kinds of intervention strategies might be contemplated — a Gautreaux-type intervention based on promoting mobility out of inner-city neighborhoods, and a "Marshall Plan" approach directed at restoring the economic and social vitality of poor neighborhoods. To be effective, either would have to be implemented on a scale much larger than anything attempted thus far. Indeed, the sheer scale of operation would raise a myriad of implementation questions.

The Gautreaux program is small enough to be invisible to most residents of the receiving areas. If a Gautreaux-type dispersal program were implemented on a much larger scale, then there would surely be enormous problems of enlisting suburban communities to participate. Similarly, the scope of truly effective revitalization programs would have to be much larger than current efforts. If, as Wilson believes, male joblessness is the dominant problem in inner-city neighborhoods, then perhaps our experiments should be with massive public employment programs, targeted initially on a small number of trial neighborhoods, and then expanded if successful. Since virtually all of the large-scale intervention program experiments to date have been directed at individuals and families rather than neighborhoods, we lack even the most rudimentary knowledge about large-scale implementation issues.

Labor market mobility.

It is fitting to conclude our "big picture" section on information needs by returning to the topic of labor market mobility. Despite the prevalence of high school diplomas among welfare recipients, the frequent employment transitions of many recipients who receive no special help, the capacity of the economy to generate jobs for women with modest skills, and the many examples of economically successful welfare-to-work intervention programs, the sad fact is that the vast majority of what we judge to be "successful" welfare-to-work transitions provide family incomes that differ little from welfare-based income levels (Jencks 1992). The kinds of jobs welfare recipients can secure typically pay little more than the minimum wage. Even when augmented by the EITC, the effective wage for a family with two children increases only to $6 per hour.

Expanding once again the generosity of the EITC is one possible solution. As with any other income maintenance program, the EITC has a built-in trade-off between the number of workers covered and the abruptness of the "phasing out" of the benefit for above-minimum-wage workers. Opting for greater coverage increases costs, but halting benefits too abruptly generates work disincentives.

More difficult solutions include upgrading the formal skills of current and future generations of workers and enhancing the labor market mobility of low-skill workers. In both cases, skill upgrading is the key. In the former, the emphasis is on formal schooling; in the latter, less formal on-the-job training. Interventions such as the Teen Parent Welfare Demonstration have had their greatest success in school enrollment, although even here the enrollment rates in the experimental treatment group were less than 50 percent. Virtually nothing has been learned from intervention programs about enhancing the career mobility of welfare recipients who made successful transitions into the labor force. This may be the most important gap in our knowledge of welfare-to-work transitions.

REFERENCES

Blank, Rebecca. 1995. "Outlook for the U.S. Labor Market and Prospects for Low-Wage Entry Jobs." In *The Work Alternative: Welfare Reform and the Realities of the Job Market.* Washington, D.C.: Urban Institute Press.

Brooks-Gunn, J.; G. J. Duncan; P. K. Klebanov; and N. Sealand. 1993. "Do Neighborhoods Influence Child and Adolescent Behavior?" *American Journal of Sociology* 99(2):353–95.

Burtless, Gary. 1995. "The Employment Prospects of Welfare Recipients." In *The Work Alternative: Welfare Reform and the Realities of the Job Market.* Washington, D.C.: Urban Institute Press.

Clark, Rebecca. 1993. "Neighborhood Effects on Dropping Out of School among Teenage Boys." Mimeograph. Washington, D.C.: Urban Institute.

Committee on Ways and Means. 1993. *1993 Green Book, Background Material and Data on Programs within the Jurisdiction of the Committee on Ways and Means.* Washington, D.C.: U.S. Government Printing Office.

Cook, F. L., and E. J. Barrett. 1992. *Support for the American Welfare State: The Views of Congress and the Public.* New York: Columbia University Press.

Duncan, G. J.; J. Brooks-Gunn; and P. K. Klebanov. 1994. "Economic Deprivation and Early-Childhood Development." *Child Development* 65(2):296–318.

Duncan, G. J., and S. D. Hoffman. 1991. "Teenage Underclass Behavior and Subsequent Poverty: Have the Rules Changed?" In *The Urban Underclass,* edited by Christopher Jencks and Paul Peterson, pp. 155–74. Washington, D.C.: Brookings Institution.

Duncan, G. J., and J. Yeung. 1995. "Extent and Consequences of Welfare Dependence among Children." *Child and Youth Services Review* 17(½):1–26.

Ellwood, D. 1986. "Targeting 'Would-Be' Long Term Recipients of AFDC." Report prepared for the Department of Health and Human Services. Mathematica Policy Research, Princeton, N.J.

———. 1988. *Poor Support, Poverty and the American Family.* New York: Basic Books.

Gleason, P.; A. Ranfarajan; and P. Schochet. 1994. "The Dynamics of AFDC Spells among Teenage Parents." Paper presented to the Econometrics Society Meetings, Boston, January 1994.

Gottschalk, P. 1992. "The Intergenerational Transmission of Welfare Participation: Facts and Possible Causes." *Journal of Policy Analysis and Management* 11(2):254–72.

Gueron, J., and E. Pauly. 1991. *From Welfare to Work.* New York: Russell Sage Foundation.

Jencks, Christopher. 1992. "Can We Put a Time Limit on Welfare?" *American Prospect*, no. 11 (Fall):32–40.

Kirby, D.; L. Short; J. Collins; D. Rugg; L. Kolbe; M. Howard, B. Miller; F. Sonenstein; and L. Zabin. 1994. "School-Based Programs to Reduce Sexual Risk Behaviors: A Review of Effectiveness." *Public Health Reports* 109(3).

Maynard, Rebecca, ed. 1993. "Building Self-Sufficiency among Welfare-Dependent Teenage Parents." Princeton, N.J.: Mathematica Policy Research.

Miller, J., and S. Korenman. 1994. "Poverty and Children's Nutritional Status in the United States." *American Journal of Epidemiology* 140(3):233–43.

Moffitt, R. 1992. "Incentive Effects of the U.S. Welfare System: A Review." *Journal of Economic Literature* 30(1):1–61.

Robins, P. K., and P. Fronstin. 1993. "Welfare Benefits and Family-Size Decisions of Never-Married Women." Institute for Research on Poverty Discussion Paper no. 1022–93, Madison, Wis.

Rosenbaum, James. 1991. "Black Pioneers — Do Their Moves to the Suburbs Increase Economic Opportunity for Mothers and Children?" *Housing Policy Debate* 2(4):1179–1213.

Wilson, W. J. 1987. *The Truly Disadvantaged: The Inner City, the Underclass, and Public Policy.* Chicago: University of Chicago Press.

———. 1991. "Studying Inner-City Social Dislocations: The Challenge of Public Agenda Research." *American Sociological Review* 56(1):1–14.

Jeffrey Fagan

Legal and Illegal Work

Crime, Work, and Unemployment

There are conflicting notions on the relationship between crime and unemployment among young men and women in urban areas. Much of the literature before 1980 was based on fairly simplistic concepts of criminality and also about how people divide their time between legal and illegal work. For example, economists emphasized labor market participation and income returns as measures of employment, but paid little or no attention to the returns from illegal activities. The economic lives of unemployed people were sideshows in this literature, and the extent to which their incomes included returns from both crime or *licit* informal economic activities was poorly understood. Criminologists also ignored crime as illegal work. They generally focused on the underlying causes of crime and unemployment, attempting to model the two behaviors, establish their causal order, and determine their relationship to proximate individual-level causes such as family background and peer networks. Accordingly, efforts to explain the relationships between crime and work, or the effects of unemployment on criminal involvement, resulted in limited tests of theory and a generally disagreeable literature.

These questions have been revisited more closely in recent years with the growing involvement of young men and women in expanded street-level drug markets, the intensification of poverty and racial segregation, and the economic restructuring of U.S. cities (Fagan 1992; Hagan 1993*a*, 1993*b*; Freeman 1995). In the past, analyses of crime and the labor market usually addressed the effects of unemployment or other labor market conditions on crime, and results typically went in the expected direction (Freeman 1983; Witte and Tauchen 1994). The recent growth of illegal income opportunities, in a context of declining wages and job losses in inner cities, has increased the potential returns from crime and perhaps altered the basic economic calculus for many young people. Thus, labor market conditions and crime opportunities may influence employment in ways not considered before (Fagan 1992; Freeman 1992; Hagedorn 1994*b*).

Thanks to Richard Freeman for many helpful comments and ideas.

Until recently, researchers often viewed legal and illegal economic activities as mutually exclusive. One view suggests that through processes of self- or social selection, a formidable social and economic wall separates many young men and women from the world of legal work. This separation is the product of several forces that are concentrated in inner-city areas and may account for their persistently higher unemployment rates. Excluded from legal work, their earnings are likely to be heavily skewed toward informal economic activity, and also toward crime incomes.[1] For some, juvenile court records may lead to being labeled as poor risks for hiring, resulting in their exclusion from licit work. Others may be excluded from legal work by poor job skills or low education, a weak labor market, the racial hiring preferences of employers, or spatial mismatches that make jobs inaccessible for urban youths. Many are limited by the cumulative disadvantage from their early involvement in the criminal justice system. These dynamics leave few income options open other than public assistance, the licit informal economy, or illegal work in crime or drug selling. Still other young men may forgo legal work for what they perceive to be more lucrative careers in crime or drug selling. Coupled with declining adult employment rates and incomes, legal work also has been socially devalued (Anderson 1990).

At the core of this view is a presumed divide between legal and illegal economic activity that leads many to choose the latter and forgo the former. Given the alternatives of low-wage payoffs from legal work and the expectation of relatively high returns from income-generating criminal activities, illegal work is a rational choice not unlike choices made among legitimate occupational pursuits (Becker 1968; Viscusi 1986*b*; Freeman 1991). Whatever the origins of the decision to engage in illegal work, the onset of an illegal career is often viewed as narrowing later economic and social options for engaging in legal work, foretelling a lengthy career of illegal pursuits outside the social world of legal enterprise (Hagan and Palloni 1990; Freeman 1992; Sampson and Laub 1993).

EMPIRICAL AND CONCEPTUAL CHALLENGES

Both empirical research and theory challenge a deterministic view of an exclusive relationship between crime and work. Several studies show a fluid, dynamic, and complex interaction between legal and illegal work. Legal and illegal work often overlap both within time periods and over developmental stages. Among young drug sellers, more than one in four are also employed in legal work (Reuter, MacCoun, and Murphy 1990), and legal wages do not necessarily decline as illegal wages increase (Fagan

1992, 1994b).[2] Many drug sellers are only sporadically involved in drug sales, ducking in and out of conventional labor markets at regular intervals (Hagedorn 1994a, 1994b). Ethnographic studies (Sullivan 1989; Williams 1989; Taylor 1990; Padilla 1992; Adler 1993) suggest a blurring of distinctions between legal and illegal work, and a broader conceptualization of work that neutralizes the legal distinctions among licit and illicit income-generating activities. Individuals involved in illegal work may change their evaluations over time of the costs and returns of such work compared to legal pursuits, leading to career "shifts" from illegal to legal sources of income (Shover 1985; Biernacki 1986; Tunnell 1992; Wright and Decker 1994).

Recent theoretical developments also challenge deterministic conceptions of illegal work. In part, economists and criminologists have viewed crime and work as exclusive choices because most study designs are single-period individual choice models that ignore within-individual changes over time (Good, Pirog-Good, and Sickles 1986; Witte and Tauchen 1994). Beginning with Becker (1968) and Ehrlich (1973), crime and legal work have been viewed by economists as the result of rational choices among options that carry both costs and returns. In their simplest form, crime and work are substitutes: each takes time and each produces income. Decisions to engage in one or both behaviors suggest a process akin to an optimization model that reflects the distribution of opportunities and the costs and returns of alternative pursuits (Clarke and Cornish 1985; Stephens and Krebs 1986; Grogger 1994a). Nothing in this framework argues against a vector of income-generating activities that involves simultaneous activities across legal boundaries, constrained by time and the distribution of opportunities, and varying over time.

Life course models present another challenge. In this view, individuals move in and out of activities (roles) that reflect specific developmental stages and the social and economic contingencies attached to each stage (Sampson and Laub 1993). Behavioral trajectories of crime or legal work change as individuals progress through predictable life stages that expose them to changing contingencies and opportunities. These perspectives stand in stark contrast to theories of deviance that attempt to explain involvement in illegal behavior as the product of criminal "traits" that are stable and enduring over the life course (see, for example, Gottfredson and Hirschi 1990). Instead, the active and fluid movement of individuals in and out of illegal work suggests active management of their income-producing choices and a great deal of human perception and agency in their choices.

Accordingly, the relationship between illegal and legal work appears to be fluid and dynamic rather than deterministic. For younger people leaving school, their entry into legal and/or illegal work is influenced by processes of adolescent development in the complex developmental stage of school-to-work transition. This transition is further complicated in inner cities with narrow and highly segmented labor markets, recent unskilled labor surpluses, and expanded illegal markets. For workers already in the workforce, decisions to enter illegal work reflect their experiences in the legal workforce, both economic and social, and a rational economic assessment of the risks and returns from illegal work. The increasing but poorly understood participation of women in illegal work raises additional issues about gender and the dual nature of work.[3]

ISSUES AND QUESTIONS

The interaction of legal and illegal work raises several questions that are the focus of this essay. First, does illegal work draw workers away from legal work? Few studies have examined the extent to which illegal work (especially in drug selling) draws young workers from the legal economy, or whether people doing illegal work are nonparticipants in legal work. To what extent do human capital issues, as well as work opportunities, mediate work-crime relationships? How do regional variables, including the spatial distribution of legal employment and the redistributive functions of illegal markets, influence crime-work relationships? Second, if workers are active decision makers, how often do they "double up" in the legal and illegal economies? To what extent are work and crime mutually exclusive in short periods or across years?

A third set of questions involves the shifts from legal to illegal work and back again. For those who have abandoned the formal labor force for illegal work, what experiences shaped and influenced their decisions? How have those transitions occurred? How do nonworkers view work in an era of declining legal work opportunities? For some, the transition from legal to illegal work may be temporary, raising questions about their experiences in illegal work and the factors that influence their return to legal work. How and why do they decide to return to legal work? Still others may shift back and forth over time. This raises a corollary question about how "dual" careers are managed and the factors that trigger shifts into or out of illegal work.

Three issues conclude the discussion. First, I will assess theories of deviance and criminality to develop new frameworks based on a unified concept of "work." Second, I will identify the methodological issues in studying income-producing careers, and the prospects for using incomes as a dependent variable. Finally, I will analyze these trends to determine the comparative advantages for crime control theory and policy from increasing the returns from legal work versus the potential costs of criminal sanctions for illegal work.

Crime, Work, and Unemployment

Two often disparate literatures inform our understanding of crime and unemployment. Economists view work, whether legal or not, as a rational decision on how to allocate one's time for income production. It suggests that economic costs and incentives have explicit effects on decisions to engage in legal or illegal work. Becker (1968) proposed a time-allocation model in which consumers allocate time between the labor market and crime as a function of wages and criminal returns. Several variables are thought to influence this relationship. First, the expected returns from crime and the expected income from legal work establish the economic prospects of competing alternatives. Second, the returns from illegal work are discounted by the potential costs of criminal sanctions from illegal work. Third, labor market variables influence the perception of the likelihood of legal income, where loose job markets (and high unemployment) drive down wages from legal work. Fourth, the discount from criminal sanctions depends on whether prison is a price worth avoiding. When crime incomes are potentially high, the costs of incarceration may be relatively low compared to forgone illegal wages.[4]

Criminologists tend to divide in their view of crime and work in three ways. While many agree that crime and unemployment are negatively associated, there is strong disagreement on both causal order and the underlying causal mechanisms. Several studies attribute crime to unemployment (e.g., Good, Pirog-Good, and Sickles 1986), while some economists suggest that crime causes unemployment (e.g., Freeman 1992). Some view the negative association between crime and unemployment as spuriously attributable to a common underlying personality trait, such as lapses in self-control (Gottfredson and Hirschi 1990) or strain resulting from the gap between expectations and opportunities (Agnew and White 1992). Others suggest that crime and work are reciprocally related. Early involvement in crime may attenuate occupational attainment, in turn increasing the likelihood of subsequent crime, a sequence that repeats several times over developmental stages (Thornberry and Christenson 1984).

Still others claim that the association is conditional: avoidance of crime is contingent on some quality of employment beyond simple entry into *any* occupational status. For example, Sampson and Laub (1993, p. 304) claim that "employment by itself" does not increase social control, but that work leads to internalized social controls through commitment and stability. Legal work also exposes workers to the social controls of the workplace. Uggen (1992) argues that exposure to high-quality jobs reduces criminal activity, and that stratification in job opportunities affects decisions to pursue criminal activity (see also Rosenfeld and Messner 1989).[5] However, stratification of illegitimate work may also influence the work-crime relationship. Higher positions in illegitimate occupations may constrain mobility toward legal work, as well as reducing its appeal (Matsueda et al. 1992). Thus, both for economists and criminologists, the comparative advantage of legal versus illegal work involves both status returns as well as economic returns. How the two are weighed in decisions about income has rarely been studied.

Conceptual approaches to the crime-work relationship also have differed in how work is operationalized and measured. Measures of labor market attachments have included work participation (job participation, time spent in work, job stability), occupational status, and returns from work. Despite the importance of the net returns of legal versus illegal activities, illegal wages have rarely been studied, nor has status in deviant networks been studied closely (see, for an exception, Matsueda et al. 1992). Also, because crime and legal work are often viewed as trade-offs or time substitutes, there has been little consideration to the simultaneity of crime and work. Accordingly, to analyze trends in the empirical literature, I conceptualize crime and legal work from three perspectives: (*a*) crime and the legal labor market, (*b*) crime, legal work, and illegal wages, and (*c*) the joint distribution of crime and legal work.

CRIME AND UNEMPLOYMENT

While studies at the aggregate level show some connection between labor market variables and crime, they "fail to show a well-defined, quantifiable linkage" (Freeman 1983, p. 106). Freeman reviewed 10 time-series studies and found crime–labor market linkages in nine of them. However, in the three studies that also included deterrence variables, the net effects of labor market variables were weaker than the legal sanction variables. Freeman also reviewed 15 cross-sectional studies and again found weak links using income variables but more positive effects when deterrence variables were included. However, the deterrence studies focused more intensively on legal sanctions and the expected costs of crime, and rarely analyzed the anticipated net returns from crime. This imbalance in models may have produced (artifactually) stronger deterrent effects compared to market incentives (Viscusi 1986*b*).

Analyses with data from the 1980s suggest a clearer positive association between crime and unemployment at the aggregate level. One reason for this may be the declining economic (wage) position of unskilled men (and increasingly, women) throughout the 1980s (Blackburn, Bloom, and Freeman 1990; Moss and Tilly 1991; Corcoran and Parrott 1992). These recent macro-level studies tend to locate unemployment as a cause of crime in a specific causal sequence. Reviewing 63 studies, Chiricos (1987) reported a positive relationship between unemployment and property crime. Using time-series models where unemployment is lagged and therefore presumably antecedent in the causal sequence leading to crime, Cantor and Land (1985) reported a positive effect of unemployment on crime. Land, McCall, and Cohen (1990), focusing on homicide, extended this finding by showing that this relationship is stronger at the intracity level compared to intercity or national levels. The Land, McCall, and Cohen (1990) study also reduced the persistent and extreme collinearity in aggregate measures of crime and unemployment.

Individual-level studies suggest that relationships between crime and unemployment differ when viewed contemporaneously at specific time points, or in sequence over time. Both the contemporaneous and longitudinal behaviors also may be spuriously related to disadvantages in social and developmental contexts. In several studies, adult crime and unemployment are linked in a nonspurious relationship from parental behavior problems through childhood behavior problems to diminished adult employment prospects and involvement in crime (see, for example, Hagan 1993*a*). Unlike the macro-level studies, where changes in aggregate unemployment rates precede increases in crime rates, these individual-level studies posit a causal sequence where crime precedes unemployment in a sequence of developmental stages. However, when temporal units are smaller, it is unclear whether crime or unemployment is the dominant social role and what are the (nonspurious) proximal causes of each behavior. These studies generally lack information on the closely timed sequences of unemployment and crime. Also, as with most literatures, there are potentially confounding artifacts of measurement and study design that must be sorted out.

Research in the United States suggests that there are both contemporaneous and reciprocal effects between unemployment and crime. Good, Pirog-Good, and Sickles (1986) observed employment and arrest records monthly for 300 youths aged 13–18 in a crime prevention program in inner-city Philadelphia. They reported a contemporaneous relationship between crime and employment in the expected (negative) direction, where "employability" had a substantial deterrent effect on crime. But the contemporaneous effects of crime on employment were weaker. Put another way, prior criminal record reduced employability, in turn leading to higher rates of crime.

Using four-wave panel data and a 1945 Philadelphia birth cohort, Thornberry and Christenson (1984) obtained much the same result. Unemployment had significant instantaneous effects on crime, and crime had significant and primarily lagged effects on unemployment. They also found that social class mediated these effects both longitudinally and cross-sectionally: the relationships were strongest for the African-American youths and youths from blue-collar backgrounds. Witte and Tauchen (1984) also used this birth cohort to estimate the effects of wages and employment on crime by employing deterrence variables that were dependent on the individual's level of criminal activity and neighborhood.[6] Both employment (but not wages) and school attendance (but not educational attainment), as well as increased arrest probabilities, exert significant negative effects on crime.

Fagan and Freeman (in press) reanalyzed the National Longitudinal Survey of Youth (NLSY) to assess the effects of crime and legal work in late adolescence on later illegal incomes and crime. The NLSY is a panel study of randomly selected youths ($n = 5,332$) beginning in 1979, with oversamples of minority and poor youths. They found the predicted positive association between crime and unemployment in the 1980 waves. Work and incarceration outcomes in 1983, 1986, and 1989 were then estimated from the cumulative effects of incarceration, crime, and work in the preceding intervals. Controls for demographic and human capital variables at 1979 were included in each model. Crime measures were available only for the 1979 wave, and the proportion of income from illegal sources was computed. Human capital variables included school participation, grade, weeks worked, and test scores from the Armed Forces Qualifications Tests (AFQT) (O'Neill 1990; see also Bushway 1996).

Analyses show that the effects of involvement in crime, detachment from legal work, and human capital at T_0 on future incarceration were stable and consistent over the successive waves. Three models of employment outcomes were developed for each of the three time periods: a dichotomous measure of employment, weeks worked during the year, and legal income. The effects of incarceration were estimated using measures of any incarceration during the preceding years. Adolescent involvement in crime and illegal wages at T_0 also were included. In each model, incarceration produced a significant negative effect on all three work outcomes, and its effects were stronger than any other predictor. Labor force participation and AFQT scores in 1979 were positively associated with work outcomes in the later waves. However, school participation in 1980 was not a consistent predictor of work outcomes in any subsequent period.

These trends suggest that the adverse consequences of incarceration and exclusion from work during adolescence, compounded by human capital advantages or deficits, endured over a 10-year period through middle adult years for both incarceration and employment. For example, Grogger (1994*b*) also used NLSY data to show that arrests early in adulthood reduced future legal wages in the short-term net of either "criminal capital" or human capital variables. However, any disadvantage from arrests in future legal earnings was overtaken by other human capital deficits over a 10-year interval.

Sampson and Laub (1993) reanalyzed data from Glueck and Glueck's *Unraveling Juvenile Delinquency* (1950), a longitudinal study of 500 delinquents and 500 carefully matched controls, and later follow-ups (Glueck and Glueck 1968). The samples were constructed in 1939, and consisted of white males aged 10–17 from several Boston neighborhoods and who had been committed to one of two state juvenile correctional institutions. The controls were recruited from the Boston public schools. Sampson and Laub (1993) found consistent (negative) effects of job stability during early adult years (17–25) on annual adult arrest rates for several crime types, after controlling for juvenile crime rates. Like several other studies, Sampson and Laub (1993, p. 162) claim that "job stability is central in explaining adult desistance from crime." Juvenile incarceration time not only had no significant effect on crime rates as an adult, but its stigmatizing effects may "mortgage" opportunities for and prospects for stable employment in adult life (Sampson and Laub 1993, pp. 165, 168). During middle adult years, job stability during ages 25–32 had a significant negative effect on crime participation during later (32–45) adult years, and no other variable had a larger coefficient.

Studies with ex-offenders also show the significant effects of unemployment on crime. For example, the TARP (Transitional Aid Research Project) was a randomized experiment that tested the effects of income supports for ex-offenders from Texas and Georgia released from prison in 1976–77 (Berk, Rossi, and Lenihan 1980; Rossi, Berk, and Lenihan 1980). There were no significant effects of income supports on short- or long-term returns to prison in either the Texas (Needels 1993) or Georgia (Needels 1994) samples. However, analysis of the pooled experimental and control samples shows that both employment and (legal) earnings have strong significant effects on subsequent crimes following release from prison, even when those wages are sporadic and well below the poverty level. For example, among the Georgia releasees, legal earnings over a 10-year follow-up period had a large and significant effect on criminal desistance but not on the timing (hazard) of return to prison among those who were reincarcerated (Needels 1994). Perhaps most important is the negative effect of crime on earnings: individuals who were not criminally active over the follow-up period earned about 40 percent more than their criminally active counterparts (Needels 1994, p. 34). These effects are likely to be conservative estimates, since this population had relatively low human capital, their employment was sporadic and not well-paying, and their crime rates were quite high both before and after incarceration.[7]

European studies complement research in the United States. For example, Albrecht (1984) used aggregate data from (the former West) Germany to show that the offender rate within the unemployed youth population actually declined from 1977 to 1982 while overall unemployment was rising dramatically. Albrecht further disaggregated the phenomenon between short- and long-term unemployed. While crime rates among the long-term unemployed were unchanged, the crime rates among the short-term unemployed actually fell during this period.

Farrington et al. (1986) used interview data from the Cambridge Study of Delinquent Development, a longitudinal study of 411 adolescent males, to show that crime rates were higher when subjects were unemployed. However, this relationship was conditional on a number of factors. Crime was more likely among only unemployed youths who held attitudes more favorable to offending; those who generally were law-abiding did not commit crimes during periods of unemployment. The crime-unemployment relationship was stronger among youths with histories of low-status jobs. Moreover, only income-generating crimes were more likely during periods of unemployment, but violent crime rates did not change.

Using the concepts of embeddedness and social capital in analyses of the Cambridge data, Hagan (1993a) claims that adult unemployment and criminality are developmental outcomes of adolescent embeddedness among delinquent peers and parental criminality. Hagan (1993a, pp. 486–87) states that "parental criminal conviction interacts with early adolescent conviction to produce later adolescent delinquency and adult unemployment above and apart from other factors." Accordingly, youths who are socially embedded during early childhood in social contexts of peer and parent criminality are likely to be isolated in their adult years from legitimate employment opportunities. Like Sampson and Laub (1993), Hagan's analysis is "deracialized" (Lemann 1991a) and shows that the processes of social embeddedness are generic and occur even in the absence of the aggravating effects of concentrated poverty in the contemporary U.S. context.

In a sample of young males from the Netherlands, Huurne (1988) shows that human capital variables further mediate the effects of unemployment: having a high school degree or coming from a higher social class background mitigates the social consequences of unemployment. Ploeg (1991) obtained similar findings among 300 long-term unemployed Dutch men 20–50 years of age. Unemployed men were unlikely to engage in law violations when they had avoided crime prior to unemployment, but former delinquents did continue their crimes. Like the Farrington et al. (1986) study, Ploeg concludes that unemployment is iatrogenic with respect to crime by engendering feelings of deprivation and injustice that precede crime.

CRIME, WORK, AND ILLEGAL WAGES: MARKET INCENTIVES FOR CRIME

An econometric, rational choice perspective on crime and work suggests that individuals will allocate time to criminal behavior when its returns are higher than other activities, net of perceived punishment costs and estimates of forgone illegal wages. That is, decisions to engage in crime suggest that offenders find the current net benefits of crime to be positive. Not only do labor market variables account for an individual's assessment, but factors including tastes and tolerances for risk, preferences for work, and time allocation also are part of the decision processes (see, for example, Katz 1988; Taylor 1990). Yet, remarkably, few studies have measured illegal wages, and fewer have studied "tastes." Moreover, since reliable official data (e.g., social security records) on illegal wages obviously are unavailable, these studies rely on self-reports of crime frequencies and crime incomes.

Income from All Crimes

Wilson and Abrahamse (1992) estimated illegal wages as the returns from an "average" offense among prison inmates. They used National Crime Victimization Survey (NCVS) data on average losses by victims to estimate the earnings from crime among prison inmates in three states (see Chaiken and Chaiken 1990 for details on the samples).[8] To compute a daily wage from crime, they estimated days free on the street per year after subtracting incarceration time, and extrapolated to a full "work" year. Legal earnings were estimated at $5.78 per hour, after discounting by 20 percent to reflect taxation. Summing across eight crime categories, they reported annualized crime incomes of $2,368 (in 1988 dollars) for burglars and thieves with midlevel offending rates. Drug selling generated the highest returns ($1,014 per year) and business robberies the lowest ($29). For high-rate burglars and thieves, crime incomes were $5,711. Wilson and Abrahamse claim that legal work would actually have paid more than crime for all but one type of offender: auto thieves. For high-rate offenders, crime incomes exceeded work incomes for all crime types. For reasons not stated by the authors, drug incomes (the most lucrative crime category) were omitted in the crime-work wage comparisons. Overall, self-reported crime incomes suggest consistently higher illegal wages compared to estimated legal work incomes across all crime types and for both mid- and high-rate offenders.

Estimates of crime incomes in general adolescent populations were developed by Freeman (1992). A 1989 survey of Boston youths showed self-reported annual earnings that ranged from $752 for infrequent offenders to $5,376 for youths committing crime at least once a week. Hourly rates varied from $9.75 for frequent offenders to $88 for infrequent offenders in the Boston Youth Survey, suggesting a diminishing return from criminal activity. Average hourly wages from crime were $19, and estimated hourly drug wages ranged from $13 to $21. All these estimates, including the lowest rate of $9.75 from crime, exceeded the average legal wage of $7.50 that these young men reported, and substantially exceeded their after-tax take-home pay of $5.60 per hour. Freeman (1992, p. 230) summarizes by stating that the lowest hourly pay rate from crime of $9.75 "is 73 percent greater than take-home pay from a legitimate job, whereas the $19/hour average from crime is over three times the take-home pay."

In a survey of adolescents in three cities (Freeman and Holzer 1986; Viscusi 1986b), crime incomes were $1,607 in 1980 dollars, or $2,423 in 1989 dollars. However, Viscusi (1986a) adjusted these figures by a factor of three for likely underreporting. With this revised income estimate, crime incomes accounted for one-fourth of the total income earned by the young men in the sample. Viscusi's model using the three-city sample also included a crime-versus-legal-income variable. He compared illegal incomes among those who expected to earn such incomes with incomes of respondents with low expected illegal income. He found significant upward positive effects of expected illegal wages on crime incomes, and the effects of these variables in regression equations on crime incomes were roughly twice as large as the influences on the actual crime participation rate. Viscusi (1986b) also compared the differences in legal and illegal incomes as a function of whether the respondent was working or in school. About one in five employed youths and one in eight students committed crimes, but their illegal incomes on average were only a fraction of their total incomes. Because of the skew in crime incomes, crime income was a substantial income supplement for many working youths. Among the NO-JOBSCHOOL group, incomes were evenly divided between legal and illegal sources, but only one-half of this group participated in crime in the study year.

Once again, those participating in crime earned substantially more from crime than from other sources. The results suggest that being in school or holding a job exerts significant downward pressure on crime participation, but only for crimes that have relatively low payoffs. Higher-income crimes such as drug dealing provide stronger economic incentives than the labor market can bear. Yet the mixing of crime and work appears to be a powerful trend. Legal incomes would have to sharply exceed illegal incomes to influence work decisions. Viscusi (1986a, p. 343) claims that equalizing legal and illegal wages would deter only one in six youths who participate in crime.

Fagan and Freeman (in press) analyzed sources (but not amounts) of illegal income using the NLSY 1979 and 1980 waves and detailed measures of the frequency of 11 income-producing crimes. In ordinary least squares models of gross illegal income, little specialization was evident. Coefficients were significant for five crime categories: drug sales (two types), robbery, fraud, fencing, and running numbers (gambling assistance). Incomes from marijuana and "hard drug" sales had the highest coefficients by a factor of two compared to the next strongest predictors. But legal labor force participation also had a significant positive association with illegal income. Consistent with Fagan's (1992, 1994a) study of drug sellers, involvement in multiple social networks from both work and deviant activities seems to expand opportunities for sale of illegal goods and services.

Grogger (1994) also analyzed the NLSY data to determine the effects of legal wages on crime participation.[9] Grogger developed an estimate of illegal wages by multiplying respondents' reports of what fraction of their 1979 income came from crime by their total income estimate for that year.[10] Crime income in 1979 was reported by 274 of the 1,134 respondents in the analysis (24.1 percent); mean income for this group was $1,187, an estimate comparable to Freeman's (1991) estimate of $1,607 for inner-city youths in Boston. Criminal participants worked fewer hours legally than nonparticipants, and earned a lower wage. Hourly market (legal) wages were about 8 percent higher for respondents with no crime income ($4.60) compared to those with criminal income ($4.26).

Grogger estimated a model of legal income using four predictors: market human capital, criminal human capital,[11] nonlabor income, and abilities (the AFQT). Wages increase predictably with skill, experience, and ability, and decline for those with probation sentences within 1 year of interview (about 15 percent lower in the following year, but returning to prearrest trajectories after 2 years). Models estimated for crime income show that criminal human capital has predictably strong, positive effects. Crime incomes increase with lower market (legal) wages, suggesting a rational allocation of time toward the higher-income-producing activity. This finding is confirmed in Grogger's third model, an equation for market labor participation. The effect of legal wages on market hours is large: a 10 percent increase in wages leads to an increase in labor supply of 67 hours, the equivalent of nearly 2 full workweeks (75 hours). And, arrests and convictions have significant negative effects on market participation, as they do over criminal human capital. Finally, for each hour of crime, market labor supply appears to decline by about 1.4 hours.

Young men appear to be particularly sensitive in their time-allocation decisions to market incentives: legal work and criminal participation both are responsive to legal wages and criminal returns in the preceding year. Moreover, illegal wages appear to be quite elastic. Grogger concludes that a 10 percent increase in wages would reduce total criminal hours in the population by about 1.4 percent, with most of the change due to the overall participation rate but some also to the number of hours allocated by legally working men to crime.

Income from Drug Dealing

Estimates of drug dealing income deserve special attention for two reasons. First, drug incomes usually are among the highest-income-producing criminal occupations and show more pronounced effects of the returns from illegal work. Second, the expansion of street-level drug markets in the past decade has provided broader opportunities for illegal work during a time of declining legal wages and work opportunities (Johnson et al. 1990).

A survey of convicted drug dealers ($n = 186$) in Washington, D.C., showed that drug dealing is "much more profitable on an hourly basis than are legitimate jobs available to the same persons" (Reuter, MacCoun, and Murphy 1990, p. viii). The dealers reported net (mean) monthly income of $1,799 from drugs and $215 from other crimes, which projects to an annual crime income of $25,000, and an implied hourly rate of $30 (see also MacCoun and Reuter 1992).[12] Freeman (1992) points out that even if these men had worked full-time for a full year, their illegal pay exceeded $19 per hour. These figures compare poorly with mean legal wages of $1,046 per month, or median legal monthly earnings of $715 for the 75 percent who reported such income. Drug income rates were higher and more skewed for younger respondents aged 18–24. Moreover, drug incomes were far greater than other crime income sources and, unlike the general crime incomes reported by the Boston general adolescent population, did not diminish with frequency.

Drug incomes also exceeded legal (work) incomes by a wide margin in a recent study of drug users and dealers ($n = 1,003$) in two northern Manhattan neighborhoods in New York City (Fagan 1992, 1994b). More than half the males and one-third of the females were involved in drug selling during the 3-year period from 1986 to 1988. Monthly drug incomes ranged from $2,000 for nonsellers to $4,800 for group sellers. After adjusting for average drug expenses of $1,500 per month, net annual drug incomes ranged from $6,000 to $27,600. Over one-fourth of the sellers also had legal incomes, ranging from $150 to $750 per month. These estimates included off-book work and income from a variety of transfer payments and income supports. The percent of total income from legal, taxed wages ranged from 7 percent to 33 percent. Accordingly, like the Washington, D.C., sample of male dealers, legal work and crime were combined by many drug sellers in these two neighborhoods. Fagan (1992, p. 121, n. 18) noted that there remain logical incentives for joint participation in legal work even while earning far higher incomes from drug sales: expanding networks of contacts, expectations of drug selling as a temporary occupation, and an escape route should legal or social pressures push sellers out of the business.

Fagan (1992) also tested whether illegal incomes were substitutes for legal work, and whether "tastes," especially drug consumption, accounted for illegal work. The effects varied by neighborhood. Legal work exerted a significant downward effect on total income in Washington Heights, a vigorous drug market, suggesting that legal work may actually pose an opportunity cost relative to crime incomes. He found no significant effect for human capital on illegal wages, and concluded that the drug sellers and users were unlikely to hold legal jobs at unskilled labor wages. But models of legal work suggested that drug consumption (a proxy for taste/preference variables) did exert significant downward pressures on labor market participation. Nevertheless, workers did have higher education levels, and the two models together indicate that drug selling was a vocation for those who were detached from legal work and unlikely to do well in that context.

Gang members in Milwaukee reported a wide range of drug incomes

(Hagedorn 1994*a*). Three in four of the 236 "founding members" of 14 male gangs (72 percent) had sold cocaine between 1987 and 1991. Of the 90 gang members interviewed, 73 were active drug sellers between 1987 and 1991. About one in four (28.7 percent) claimed they made no more money from drug selling than they could have made from legal work at the going rates for unskilled labor (about $6 per hour). One in five (20.7 percent) earned the equivalent of $7–12 per hour, and one in four (28.7 percent) reported drug incomes in the range of $13 to $25 per hour, or $2,000–$4,000 per month. Few (three of the 73 sellers) reported "crazy money" (more than $10,000 per month) at any time in their drug-selling careers (Hagedorn 1994*a*, p. 202). Mean monthly drug sale income was $2,400, or about $15 per hour, compared to legal monthly incomes of $677.[13]

Most of these studies depend on self-reports of illegal incomes. Accordingly, the validity and reliability of self-reports are crucial factors in estimating returns from crime. While Wilson and Abrahamse (1992) claim strong validity for self-reported crime incomes, both Viscusi and Freeman claim that crime rates and crime incomes are conservative estimates[14] since criminal behavior is seriously underreported, especially for African-American inner-city youths (Hindelang, Hirschi, and Weis 1981). Thompson and Cataldo (1986) directly question the veridicality of self-reports in their criticism of Viscusi's (1986*a*) analysis. What is important in this review is the consistency observed in the effects of incarceration and early criminal involvement on later crime, work, and incarceration, regardless of whether crime and income are measured through official records or self-reports.

Research on returns from illegal work suggests the importance of net returns and illegal market incentives in explaining the relationship between crime and unemployment. Crime, especially drug selling, provides economic incentives for young inner-city males that raise income prospects in ways that legal markets cannot. Freeman, Fagan, and Viscusi found that those with higher illegal incomes did not possess characteristics conducive to success in legal labor markets. They either were detached from legal work, or had been excluded as a result of the accumulation of legal sanctions. Moreover, similar to Hagan (1993*a*), their greater involvement with gangs, organized drug selling, and other illegal activities suggests their social embeddedness in contexts that close them off from conventional opportunities. In samples of both drug dealers and general adolescent populations, illegal and total incomes were highest among those who were most active criminally, and these differed systematically from others with far lower criminal involvement.

Whether individuals "double up" in legal and illegal work addresses several important issues. First, social embedment perspectives (Hagan 1993a) suggest that many youths are excluded from legal work as a result of their earlier involvement in crime and deviant social networks. But active shifting of work and crime occupations suggests greater human agency and job mobility than prior research on crime and work had assumed. Second, the decisions to maximize incomes by crossing legal boundaries suggest opportunities for interventions focused on investments in job skills and wages that could increase legal occupational status if suitable jobs were available. Investments both in skills development and job creation may bear on decisions to straddle the two worlds of work. Third, a high rate of doubling up suggests that an optimizing rather than satisficing model of decision making may be operating. Satisficing models (see, for example, Cornish and Clarke 1986, pp. 181–82) suggest that individuals will select from among the first few alternatives rather than consider a longer set, one of which might provide greater returns. Satisficing may also entail nonmaterial returns, such as excitement or status (Katz 1988). But optimization suggests that these returns are maximized by carefully juggling and analyzing among alternatives. Unfortunately, doubling up has been a relatively neglected question in research on crime and unemployment. We briefly review some of the findings.

Doubling up appears to be quite common among active offenders, including drug sellers earning relatively high illegal incomes. Both the studies of drug dealers discussed earlier suggest doubling up. More than one-fourth of the dealers in the Fagan (1992) and Reuter, MacCoun, and Murphy (1990) studies were involved in work and crime. Illegal incomes were the same regardless of whether these people were also working legally. Among the general population studies, Viscusi (1986a, 1986b) reported that about one in five employed youths committed crimes, one in eight students reported crime in the past year, and one-half of the NO-JOBSCHOOL group committed crimes. Hagedorn (1994a) reported that 75 percent of active gang drug sellers working in 1992 at the time of interview had sold drugs within the past 5 years. Work was sporadic, however; respondents said they had worked only 14 months in the past 36 in legal jobs, and only 25 percent worked in legal jobs more than 24 of the 36 months before the interview. Hagedorn (1994b) suggests that movement between legal and illegal work was common, a decision reflecting a combination of market (legal and illegal) conditions and other legal and social pressures.[15]

Fagan and Freeman (in press) analyzed the NLSY to determine overlaps between crime and work over a 12-year period through 1991. In 1980, the only year when detailed crime information was available in the NLSY, 56.6 percent of those working reported any crime, and 20.6 percent participated in at least one income-producing crime.[16] Using self-reports of *any* income from crime in the NLSY, Grogger (1995) estimated this rate at 25.6 percent. But only 4 percent of those working reported drug sales. Fagan and Freeman also reported rates of legal work among active criminals: 74.4 percent of those involved in crime also worked, but also 33.8 percent of people reporting income-producing crimes also worked. However, 69.2 percent of the drug sellers reported working, a far higher figure than the rates reported by Reuter, MacCoun, and Murphy (1990) and Fagan (1992, 1994*b*). Without detailed information on drug incomes, the motivations for working while selling drugs are hard to explain.

Doubling up and job switching contradicts the perspective of the "formidable wall" that underlies much of the literature on crime and unemployment. It suggests an active process of optimization, where offenders take advantage of economic opportunities that present themselves. Doubling up also reflects the coexistence of conventional and deviant values within individuals, a contradiction noted in delinquency research for decades (see, for example, Cohen 1955, Matza 1964, Sullivan 1989, Fagan 1990; articulated in detail by Anderson 1994 as an adaptive strategy necessary for status and survival). Hagedorn (1994*a*, p. 215) noted that gang members involved in drug selling had long-term attachments to women and most were "unhappily" enduring low-status, low-wage jobs that themselves brought daily slights and personal humiliations. While offenders with criminal histories may face barriers to legal work, those without such barriers face fewer obstacles in "doubling up." Taking a second job is quite common in the United States today, in work as diverse as skilled labor or door-to-door franchise sales. Highly decentralized drug markets offer the chance to earn income through occasional work at hourly rates that are widely perceived to be higher than conventional second jobs. There are few commitments of time and capital, although the risks of injury and incarceration are not trivial.

Crime as Work

The importance of illegal work in developmental sequences leading to adult unemployment and criminality is also evident in ethnographic research on inner-city youth crime. The decline of manufacturing work has limited legal employment opportunities for inner-city youths,[17] and has occurred in contexts of growing and concentrated poverty (Wilson 1987, 1991). The attractions of illegal work are reflected in variables often un-measured in quantitative studies on crime and work, especially tastes and preferences.

The ethnographic literature describes how structural changes in neigh-borhoods and cities have influenced not only the income options and decisions of adolescents but also normative attitudes toward work and the source of status available through social networks and social roles. Struc-tural changes have reshaped the composition of social networks, the sa-lience of informal social controls, and access to nonmaterial sources of social status (Sullivan 1989; Fagan, in press). Fueled by economic re-structuring (Kasarda 1989), the spatial concentration of poverty (Jar-gowsky and Bane 1990), and increasing residential segregation (Massey and Denton 1993), these neighborhood processes are difficult to capture in individual-level quantitative studies but are of obvious importance as mediating processes that explain differences over time and across ecologi-cal units. The continuous effects of these changes across recent genera-tions have contributed to new definitions of work that effectively blur legal boundaries and choices about income.

Recent ethnographic work illustrates how the abandonment of legal work has been accompanied by shifts in conceptions of work among young men and women in poor areas. Anderson (1990, 1994) describes how young males in inner-city Philadelphia regard the drug economy as a primary source of employment, and how their delinquent street networks are their primary sources of status and social control. Similar accounts are offered by Hagedorn (1988, 1994a, 1994b), Taylor (1990), Moore (1992a, 1992b), and Padilla (1992, 1993). Participants in the illegal economies in inner cities are engaged in a variety of income-producing crimes, including drug selling, fencing, auto theft, petty theft and fraud, commercial extortion, and residential and commercial burglary. In diverse ethnic communities in cities far apart, young men use the language of work ("getting paid," "going to work") to describe their crimes.[18] The confounding of the language of illegal and legal worlds of making money seems to signal a basic shift in the social definition of work. For the young men using this language, money from crime is a means to commodities that offer instrumental value as symbols of wealth and status.

Much of this illegal work is organized within ethnic enterprises com-bining shared economic and cultural interests. For gangs in these cities, there is less concern than in the past with neighborhood or the traditional "family" nature of gang life. Moore (1992a) shows how gang members with limited exits from gang life remain longer in the gang, assuming leadership roles and manipulating the gang for their own economic advantage through perpetuation of gang culture and ideology. Chin and Fagan (1994) and Chin (1995) describe the complex economic relationship between street gangs and adult social and economic institutions in three Chinatown neighborhoods in New York City. The adult groups, descendants of the tongs that were the shadow governments in Chinatowns a century ago, are involved in both legal, well-respected social and business activities *and* a variety of illegal businesses that employ street gangs. The gangs guard territories and act as surrogates in violently resolving conflicts and rivalries between the adult groups. Chin (1995) concludes that the gangs prosper economically while functionally maintaining the cultural and economic hegemony of these ambiguous adult leadership groups. Moreover, the gangs are involved in a variety of income-producing activities, especially commercial extortion, that are shielded from legal pressures by cultural processes that tolerate and integrate their activities into the social fabric of everyday life in Chinatown (Chin and Fagan 1994).

Padilla (1992) describes how the new pattern of exploitation of lower-level workers (street drug sellers) in the gang is obscured by appeals by older gang members to gang ideology (honor, loyalty to the gang and the neighborhood, discipline, and ethnic solidarity) combined with the lure of income. Taylor (1990), describing drug gangs in Detroit, and Padilla (1992) also talk about the use of money rather than violence as social control within African-American and Latino drug-selling gangs—if a worker steps out of line, he simply is cut off from the business, a punishment far more salient than threats to physical safety. Drug-selling groups in these two studies superficially are ethnic enterprises, but function more substantively as economic units with management structures oriented toward the maintenance of profitability and efficiency. The institutionalization of these sources of illegal work, and their competitiveness with the low-status and low-income legal jobs left behind after deindustrialization, combine to maintain illegal work careers long after they would have been abandoned in earlier generations.

Patterns of illegal work vary in this literature. Some abandon legal work after a period of employment, others drift in and out of legal work, and a few seem to choose from the outset exclusive "careers" in illegal work. Sanchez-Jankowski (1991, p. 101), for example, claims to have found an "entrepreneurial spirit" as the "driving force in the work view and behavior of gang members" that pushes them to make rational decisions to engage in the profitable world of drug sales or auto theft. Hagedorn (1994b) describes how gang members drift in and out of legal work over time, with decisions closely bundled and often reciprocal. Hagedorn shows that among Milwaukee gang members, income from drug selling far exceeded income from legal work. However, many in the drug economy "appeared to be on an economic merry-go-round" (p. 205), continuing to look for legal work, despite its lower wages, low status, danger, and part-time nature. But for others, the hazards and indignity of low-wage and low-status legal jobs discount the returns from legal work. For example, Bourgois (1989, p. 641) claims that drug dealers who leave legal jobs to embrace the risks and rewards of drug selling are evidence of a "culture of resistance," preferring the "more dignified workplace" of drug selling to the low wages and "subtle humiliations" of secondary labor markets where racism dominates work conditions and social interactions.

Structural changes, especially the decline of manufacturing and unskilled labor, have contributed to the continuity of these views into adulthood. Manufacturing jobs traditionally provided "exits" from gang life and eased the transition from adolescence to adult social roles. Millions of these jobs have disappeared since the 1960s. Hagedorn (1988), Sullivan (1989), Taylor (1990), and Fagan (in press) show how neighborhoods in the past reproduced their employment patterns in succeeding generations through networks of job referrals. Today, what is reproduced is joblessness (Tienda 1989; Wilson 1991).

The changes in the structure of employment shape not only job outcomes for young adults, but the outcomes of early legal problems. Sullivan (1989) tells how early involvement in crime was normative in three ethnically diverse neighborhoods, but the outcomes of arrest varied by neighborhood. White families helped resolve disputes informally, using family support and job networks to soften the potential stigma of arrest. With high rates of joblessness, nonwhite families had few social buffers or job networks between them and the legal system. Not only did they lack access to job networks, but their families were of little help when their income-producing crimes (robberies) evoked official responses. Their disrupted job networks were unable to mitigate legal problems or ease the school-to-work transition, contributing to the continuity of criminality and adverse legal responses. In contrast, youths in predominantly white neighborhoods were able to make sometimes difficult but successful escapes from adolescent crime networks. Hagan (1993b) links this to processes of social embeddedness that truncate future options and amplify the adverse effects of adolescent entanglements in the legal system.

These processes have been institutionalized in many inner-city neighborhoods by the twin processes of deindustrialization and the expansion of drug economies. Fagan (in press) describes the sequence of changes in eight neighborhoods in six cities, from the decline of manufacturing through the disruption of intergenerational job networks and social controls, through the institutionalization of illegal work, especially in drug selling. The growing social isolation, resulting from concentrated poverty and segregation, gives rise to a skewed emphasis on exaggerated displays of material wealth as a source of status (see also Anderson 1990, 1994). Motivations for the perceived higher returns from illegal work are influenced by such tastes for quick "crazy" money (Anderson 1990), and are important components of decisions to engage in illegal work.

The ethnographic literature is consistent with longitudinal and other quantitative studies in several respects. Both literatures reverse the conventional assumptions of macro-level research about the temporal ordering of crime and unemployment: most adolescents were involved in income-generating crimes well before they sought (or considered) the legal labor force. Both in the ethnographic and longitudinal quantitative literatures, the effects of incarceration in early adolescence carried over to adult employment and crime outcomes. The protective influence of human capital variables was evident as well (see, for example, Padilla's description of avoiding gang involvement).

Abandoning Crime for Legal Work

Many offenders drift back and forth over time between legal and illegal work. Hagedorn (1994b), for example, shows how drug dealers move back and forth between legal and illegal work, at times doubling up and at other times specializing. There has been little research on how these changes come about, how often they occur, individual differences in shifts, or the decision processes that result in changes. However, there has been research, much of it based on qualitative life history analyses (Frazier 1981), on desistance from criminality. Many of these studies describe a gradual shift over time from crime careers to relatively mundane conventional careers. Many of these studies describe desistance from criminal careers for people who were deeply embedded in deviant social networks, and who had accumulated many of the social and human capital deficits that seem to predict adverse employment outcomes. What is instructive are the lessons regarding how the decision heuristic changes with advancing age.

Research on "career" robbers and burglars, drug users and sellers, and juvenile offenders describes factors and processes that influence persistent offenders to abandon illegal work.[19] In most cases, desistance centers on a process ascribed to "aging out," where there is a shift in the calculus of rewards and costs of criminality. An accumulation of aversive experiences, changes in personal circumstances, and contingencies in neighborhoods or crime opportunities all may lead to the decision to desist from crime. Greenberg (1977) and Trasler (1979) both conclude that "occupational" criminality may be incompatible with family demands or with holding down a steady (legal) job. Biernacki (1986) shows that desistance from heroin use and attendant crime is contingent on reversing the addict's immersion in the subcultures and social worlds of addiction and, conversely, isolation from more conventional roles and norms. Reestablishing ties with legitimate activities and social networks was far less difficult for those who had not drifted very far, but more difficult for others. Having decided to quit, successful desisters relied on social networks of nonaddicts for support and maintenance of their new roles, as well as access to job contacts and networks.

Fagan (1989) analyzed the desistance literature and identified the sequence of stages leading to decisions to quit and stay away from crime. The decision to quit was often preceded by a series of adverse consequences or social sanctions from illegal work. A combination of pressures — family, legal, health, and a changing view of their former social world — preceded the decision to quit. Some were motivated by the threat of loss of loved ones or children, others by the threats of social sanctions from peers or neighbors, and still others by a desire not to face incarceration (again). Many described how their social supports for illegal work were weaker or disappeared. Some mentioned the physical costs: crime was more difficult to successfully complete, and the anxieties it aroused took an increasing emotional toll (see, for example, Shover 1985; Cusson and Pinsonneault 1986). For some, decisions were "spontaneous," or what they described as instant conversions to another way of life (see, for example, Biernacki 1986; Mulvey 1989).

Adler's (1985, 1993) portrait of drug dealers shows the difficulty of detaching from illicit work that extends beyond the net of legal and illegal returns. Many drug dealers resolved and attempted to leave illegal work but found the conventional world boring. Their return to dealing was motivated less by income than by their "withdrawal" from the excitement of their illegal work. Biernacki also describs the boredom of the "straight" world for many former addicts. Transition from illegal work became episodic, with periods of cessation increasing in length and frequency until becoming final. But the longing for excitement (or psychological and physiological cravings, as described by Biernacki) persisted well after the illegal behavior was abandoned. Other voices in this literature discuss the intrinsic rewards of the "life," while diminishing the salience of its costs. There are important roles of tastes, intrinsic rewards, status rewards, and even emotional thrill (Katz 1988) from illegal work and its social context in the decision to persist in crime. These factors are difficult to control or defeat in the process of desisting from crime, and may play a central role in heuristic processes to persist in illegal work.

These rewards often provide powerful reinforcements. Fagan (1989, p. 408) notes that "with social embedment comes the gratification of social acceptance and social identity. The decision to end a behavior . . . implies withdrawal from the social reinforcement it brings" and fear of social rejection in their new networks. Maintaining the decision to quit illegal work required the construction of new social networks, changes in physical locales, changes in self- and social identity, changes in the functional definitions of crime, substitution of new social roles and behaviors for the old ones (including legal work), new sources of social reinforcement for legal work and a conventional lifestyle, and the development of a strong belief system in the soundness of these changes (Fagan 1989, p. 403).

However, desisters rarely mentioned economic logic in their decision making. Although desistance has been characterized as a predictable process associated with advancing age (Hirschi and Gottfredson 1983; Farrington 1986), no theoretical meaning has been attached to the age curve. Desistance studies suggest that, with age, there are changes in the heuristic processes that offenders use to assess the costs and benefits of crime commission (Clarke and Cornish 1985). Their decisions were unrelated to access to legal work, and were based more on changing perceptions and evaluations of nonlegal social sanctions from illegal work. While they perceived little change in the returns of illegal work, desisters seemed to increase their evaluations of the potential sanction costs of their crimes: loss of loved ones, rejection by social peers, and self-rejection. This changing evaluation of external costs was preceded by internal changes in their self-perceptions.

Accordingly, one consequence of advancing age is a substantive shift in the utility function underlying decisions to engage in illegal work. Evaluation of the costs of illegal work seems to change with age, although perceived returns from illegal work seem undiminished. Because youth participation in crime is highly responsive to legal wages (Grogger 1994b), an alternative explanation suggests that declining crime participation with age may reflect expectations of higher earning potential from legal work. In addition, factors borne out of new social roles (marriage, adult friend, father) and informal social control appear to receive increasing weight with age. Perhaps also the weight accorded to tastes and "thrills" diminishes with age, or is defeated by other emotional states such as anxiety and fear. The revised calculus of illegal work also seems to be shaped by the social contexts of everyday life that offer new social roles, perceptions, and conceptions of work, and by changing self-identity and emotional states.

Unemployment, Work, and Crime: Lessons and Gaps in the Literature

Several trends are evident in these studies, as well as gaps and methodological inconsistencies in the literature. We start the summary with the bad news, because even with these gaps there are important areas where the literatures converge. First, it is difficult to compare single-period, cross-sectional models of individual choices with longitudinal studies. In the single-period studies, crime and work are presented as alternative choices only because of the limited time period measured, overlooking variation over time. Several studies have used data that have at least two time points (e.g., Gottfredson 1985; Good, Pirog-Good, and Sickles 1986), while only a few others (Thornberry and Christenson 1984; Farrington 1986; Viscusi 1986a, 1986b; Freeman 1992; Fagan and Freeman 1994) use panel data extending over several years. Crime and work are events that are likely to occur close in time. The use of annual observations data over lengthy time periods makes it difficult to determine whether crimes occurred during periods of unemployment, underemployment, active employment, or exile from the labor force.

Second, studies of crime and unemployment often omit (legal) deterrence variables that are necessary to compute how individuals discount the returns from legal work based on the potential punishment costs. This is especially important considering that deterrence variables are significant in macro-level studies, often outweighing the importance of labor market variables in the explanation of crime. When included, deterrence usually is measured indirectly using aggregate citywide arrest rates or probabilities (see, for example, Good, Pirog-Good, and Sickles 1986; but see Witte and Tauchen 1994, for an exception), but rarely is it measured as the individual's perceived likelihood of sanctions. This is particularly problematic since crime rates at the neighborhood level and arrest probabilities are not independent (Smith 1986). Accordingly, we are likely to observe both intracity and intercity effects when multicity samples are used, similar to the fluctuations in labor market variables. This suggests the need for careful specification and disaggregation of deterrence variables at the level of neighborhood and city, and the use of hierarchical models to estimate the simultaneous effects of macro-level forces with more proximate neighborhood effects.

Third, estimates of the work-crime association have been confounded with sampling strategies. Comparisons of general population samples that span broad ecological areas create risks of correlation-causation confounding due to the concentration of crime and unemployment in subareas. Research with prison releasees (e.g., Berk, Rossi, and Lenihan 1980; Witte 1980) or intervention program participants (Good, Pirog-Good, and Sickles 1986) may have samples with truncated distributions of human capital variables and concentrations or "ceiling rates" of other risk factors. Similarly, studies that use "street" samples of offenders may effectively control for neighborhood factors but also risk truncated or unmeasured human capital variables (e.g., limited work experiences; see, for example, Fagan 1992). Studies with adult samples may overlook the important events during adolescence that shape later work outcomes.

Fourth, despite the central role of expected returns in economic models of crime and unemployment, illegal wages have been inadequately measured, if measured at all. Returns from legal work have been measured in dollars, occupational status, and labor market participation. But measurement of returns from illegal work is quite rare (see, for exceptions, Viscusi 1986a; Fagan 1992, 1994b; Freeman 1992; Grogger 1994). Other studies use proxies or estimates (Wilson and Abrahamse 1992; Fagan and Freeman in press). Just as labor markets vary across neighborhoods within cities and across cities themselves, so too do illegal markets, especially drug markets (Fagan 1992). Measurement of illegal wages and illegal labor market participation is critical to both sociological and econometric specification of crime decisions and the effects of unemployment. Thus, there are intrinsic weaknesses in estimates of the net utility of legal versus illegal work.

A corollary problem is evident in the measurement of crime. Not only are the economic returns from crime not measured, but the measures of criminal activity themselves vary extensively. The comments of Thompson and Cataldo (1986) reflect the split among economists on whether self-reports or official records provide more reliable measurement of crime. Many researchers hold their noses and use official records of police contacts or arrests, despite their validity problems at the individual level (Elliott and Huizinga 1986).[20] Moreover, the analytic aggregations of crime measures also are quite limited. Many studies use gross, dichotomous measures of *any police contact*, while others use arrests. This distinction is particularly problematic in studies of adolescents since many police contacts are disposed informally. Many studies avoid measures of crime frequency since their distributions often are skewed. Others fail to distinguish types of crime, collapsing instrumental (income-producing) and "expressive" (often violent) crimes into single scales. Yet the distinction between income-producing and other crimes is particularly critical to models specifying actions based on estimates of returns from crime. Official records also seem to be particularly ill suited to measuring returns from illegal work. Using estimators from other data sets for the value of stolen goods or drug income ignores the importance of individual differences in skills on the total income from crime or drug sales.

Fifth, as we discuss in more detail later on, there have been significant changes in legal and illegal labor markets over the 1980s, and in the social processes in inner-city neighborhoods that may affect decisions about crime and work. The percentage of "unskilled" young males in inner cities has grown throughout the 1980s (Mangold 1994). The returns from both legal and illegal work changed significantly throughout the decade, creating the possibility of shifts in the decisions of inner-city youths toward illegal work. So too did tastes and preferences (Fagan, in press). These changes introduce period effects that complicate comparisons of earlier studies with more recent efforts. For example, manufacturing and unskilled labor jobs declined throughout this period (Kasarda 1988, 1992), the types of jobs typically available to youths in economically distressed inner-city neighborhoods. Wages for minority youths remained flat, even in a tight labor market in the mid-1980s (Blackburn, Bloom, and Freeman 1990; Bound and Freeman 1990; Freeman 1992).

A variety of factors complicate access of young African-American males to legal work (Kirschenman and Neckerman 1991; Moss and Tilly 1991) increasing search costs and devaluing the returns from legal work. Arrests and incarceration of young African-American males increased throughout the 1980s as well (Irwin and Austin 1994; Tonry 1995), again posing barriers to legal employment and, according to the crime-causes-unemployment view, decreasing labor force participation. Finally, illegal markets (especially drug markets) expanded contemporaneously with the decline of legal work in inner cities (Fagan 1993), while informal social controls and social capital declined precipitously throughout the preceding decade (Sampson 1987; Wilson 1987; Sampson and Wilson 1994). Accordingly, we may assume that the outcomes of work decisions reflect the growing imbalance between legal and the *perceived* illegal returns in drug markets and other illegal work for inner-city youths. These period-specific effects also suggest that past research may not be applicable in the future. The aggregate effects of high rates of joblessness may create problems of scale that affect individual probabilities of successful outcomes.[21]

FOUNDATIONS FOR THEORY AND RESEARCH

Despite these gaps, there are several consistent themes for building a foundation for theory, research, and policy. First, early involvement in crime and incarceration as an adolescent has negative effects on employment and positive effects on crime in later adult years. Both longitudinal and ethnographic studies place delinquency before unemployment in the sequence of developmental events over the life course. Studies based on data from the United States and England and other European countries consistently identify the legacy of adolescent experiences for future work outcomes. Sampson and Laub (1993) suggest that adolescents "mortgage" their future job stability and work outcomes through adolescent involvement in crime, but that incarceration intensifies these effects over the life course. The importance of family context, especially parental criminality rather than parental unemployment, suggests important leverage points for intervention. The effects of high rates of incarceration for today's adolescents, especially African Americans, may be compounded in the labor market outcomes of their children in another generation.

Second, for many offenders crime does in fact appear to pay. In the few studies that have measured returns from crime, there are calculable market incentives from illegal work. Perhaps more than other types of crime, drug dealing seems to provide substantial earnings above what legal work pays. Careers in illegal work also accord relief from the mundane and often abusive conditions encountered by nonwhites in white-owned businesses. The returns from what Bourgois (1989) terms "Horatio Alger" benefits of illegal work are difficult to calculate, but carry value even in the face of the absence of a net increase in monetary returns.[22] However, the data on illegal wages are extremely limited, and extensive research is needed to analyze the role of market incentives in decisions about legal and illegal work.

Third, human capital and early work experiences are protective factors that help avoid poor job outcomes and illegal work in early adult years. Even in models of work outcomes showing the effects of early crime and incarceration, there are consistent positive effects from human capital variables on legal work outcomes in early adulthood. The measurement of human capital varies widely in crime and unemployment studies, and further research is needed using measures of human capital that are truly independent from work outcomes. The use of AFQT scores provides one such independent measure. The importance of social capital also has been shown, but has received far less research attention (see Sampson and Laub 1993). Human and social capital overlap through job networks and referrals, and in the social embedment of work experiences in social networks where both skills and personal relationships are exchanged.

Fourth, the effects of legal deterrence variables, or the punishment costs of crime, are inconsistent and remain unknown pending further study. In macro-level studies, deterrence variables appear to significantly depress crime rates. In individual-level studies, analyses of deterrence strategies are marked by inconsistencies in conceptualization and measurement. Deterrence rarely is disaggregated by neighborhood or area, even though arrest probabilities vary within and across cities. Measurement usually is limited to the threat of arrest, not of incarceration. Occupational risk also is not included, even in drug selling where injury rates are quite substantial (Fagan and Chin 1990). There are several faces of deterrence, but usually only perceived sanction threat is included. However, incarceration risks may be tolerable or even expected and may be only a minor discount on the net returns from illegal work. A fully specified deterrence model also should include how important these risks are perceived to be, and whether a high risk would actually influence illegal work decisions.

Fifth, there are substantial deterrent influences from nonlegal social sanctions, including threats of loss of family and social opprobrium. These informal social controls operate at the individual level through the social and kin networks of everyday life. Accordingly, their effects are dependent on the structural features of neighborhoods and cities that sustain these networks. When peer, work, residential, and family networks are disrupted, it is more difficult to establish and maintain social controls that operate through neighborhood processes (Sampson and Groves 1989). When they are present, the salience of these informal controls appears to increase with age, even while net market incentives of illegal work remain constant.

Finally, the cultural and social contexts of adolescent life are important factors in determining definitions and conceptions of work that may carry over to adult crime and employment outcomes. The recent ethnographic literature is consistent in describing increasing isolation of inner-city adolescents from the worlds of conventional work. With limited access to legal work, and in segregated neighborhoods with high concentrations of joblessness, alienated views of legal work and diminished expectations for conventional success spread through social contagion and become normative (Tienda 1989). Tastes and preferences are driven by definitions of status dominated by material consumption. Violence substitutes for social control as a means to resolve disputes and attain status (Katz 1988; Sullivan 1989; Anderson 1994), increasing the likelihood either of mortality or incarceration. Legal work at low pay is defined poorly and carries a negative social stigma (Bourgois 1989; Taylor 1990). With intergenerational job networks disrupted, the ability of young people to access increasingly complex labor markets with limited human capital or personal contacts foretells poor work outcomes. What starts as a growing class of unskilled workers in isolated neighborhoods quickly becomes a means for social contagion and rapid detachment from legal work.

Implications for Theory, Policy, and Research

Responding to crime and unemployment requires the development of a theoretical framework for structuring interventions and fashioning policies. We discuss below the prospects for theoretical integration that combines the interests of economists and sociologists. Next, we discuss the design of policies and interventions that build on a conceptual framework to enhance employment outcomes. A research agenda concludes the discussion.

THEORY
Theories of crime and unemployment generally agree on the negative association between the two behaviors, but vary in their specification of causal linkages. We use the framework of Uggen, Piliavin, and Matsueda (1992) to discuss the theoretical implications of the work-unemployment literature. Support for four broad theoretical frameworks is evident in the empirical literature, and the causal mechanisms they specify suggest opportunities for convergence and integration. Choice, opportunity, control, and labeling perspectives have dynamic properties that include both structural elements and the processual elements necessary for a theory of individual development and work outcomes. The development and testing of such a framework is a reachable and logical next step. We briefly review these perspectives and the prospects for theoretical synthesis.

Econometric Choice Models
Economic and choice theories have been the most common basis for empirical research. They portray crime as the result of a decision to seek the (perceived) higher rewards of the illegal labor market compared to the legal market, adjusted for the potential punishment costs of illegal behavior (Becker 1968; Ehrlich 1973). Rational choice theorists (Clarke and Cornish 1985; Cornish and Clarke 1986) extend this model by assum-

ing that offenders in fact do proceed according to a heuristic process, but it includes elements of income satisficing as well as income optimization. Others claim that a process of neutralization is necessary to permit ethical decisions to engage in crime, and that psychic rewards also figure in the decision to engage in illegal work (see, for example, Katz 1988; Grasmick and Bursik 1990). Choice theorists also have used economic choice models to explain deterrence (Miller and Anderson 1986).

There is some support for the economic position in this empirical literature, and choice models have obvious importance in a theoretical model of work decisions. The role of market incentives suggests that crime indeed pays compared to the types of work available to criminal offenders, particularly for drug sales. There are important roles for status and psychic payoffs from illegal work, particularly in social contexts where crime participation is high, labor force participation is low, and crime provides a skewed form of "occupational status." That is, the status and personal costs of legal work motivate selection of legal work. Participation in illegal work also may reflect the proximity of illegal work compared to low-wage legal work, and a choice to minimize search time or circumvent lengthy job queues.

Accordingly, the decision to select illegal work may indeed reflect its net benefits, and structural features of labor markets for urban youths and young adults. If the distribution of opportunities is uneven and skewed away from inner-city urban areas, decisions to seek illegal work may reflect the income satisficing model of decision making (Cornish and Clarke 1986). Moreover, the role of deterrence in economic choice seems clear, yet it has been studied inconsistently. Sociological tests of deterrence often focus on the risks of deviance, discounting the rewards of offending. Even so, there is only weak support for the deterrence components of this model compared to criminal rewards (e.g., Piliavin et al. 1986).

Control Theory

Control theory suggests that crime will occur when individuals have weak social bonds to conventional institutions such as work (Hirschi 1969; Farrington et al. 1986). Work has a controlling effect on crime by providing social and material rewards, and committed workers have greater stakes or investments in legal work. Some conceptualizations of deterrence suggest that when such commitments are present, (psychic and emotional) costs are established if the commitments are broken (Williams and Hawkins 1986). Involvement in work also has controlling effects through the establishment of attachments to coworkers, again raising the prospect of costs when such attachments are broken. Similar processes occur when there is strong commitment to school, and attachments to teachers and student peers. These views suggest a convergence of choice models with control theory (Hirschi 1986; Akers 1990).

Evidence for the control dimensions of work decisions are evident in the Farrington et al. (1986) and Thornberry and Christenson (1984) studies. The mediating effects of law-abiding attitudes with crime avoidance during unemployment periods are offered as evidence of the salience of internal bonds or controls. The positive effects of early work experiences on later work outcomes also suggest an indirect controlling effect of work on crime avoidance. The absence of work also may be interpreted as evidence for the importance of work experiences as controls on criminality. Unfortunately, few studies measure social bonds (commitment, attachment) in research on crime and unemployment. Yet because of their compatibility with the logic of deterrence and choice models, and their support in the empirical literature, control constructs are a necessary part of a theoretical integration.

Opportunity Structures

According to opportunity theories, difficulty in attaining conventional goals — affluence, social status — creates conditions of anomie or strain, leading to criminal pursuits (Cloward and Ohlin 1960; Paternoster and Mazerolle 1994). These themes are evident in the ethnographic literature. Young males and females have turned to a wide variety of informal economic activity, some of it illegal, as stable and well-paying legal jobs became more scarce. Uggen (1993) calls them innovators who reject low-wage legal work and embrace illegal work in pursuit of the twin goals of affluence and social status, while Sanchez-Jankowski (1991) notes their independent spirit of entrepreneurship. Throughout the ethnographic literature, young males in different neighborhoods and ethnic groups report the coexistence of conventional and nonconventional goals, signs that their frustrations with the legal labor market motivate in part their decision to seek illegal work.

Barriers to conventional success may result from job scarcity or access to work that provides status and monetary reward. In some neighborhoods, the distribution of opportunities is such that unemployment is as common as employment among nonwhite adolescents, and there are more illegal than legal opportunities. Wages reflect these persistent trends (Bound and Freeman 1992). Wages for unskilled workers in the United States are far lower than in other industrialized Western countries, and this disparity has grown steadily for nearly 3 decades (Freeman 1994). Legal opportunities appear to be low-status, low-paying, and generally exploited labor (Padilla 1992; Hagedorn 1994*b*), and expansions in the workforce appear to be in "contingent" jobs rather than "permanent" ones (Freeman 1994). The effects of declining wages and opportunities are strongest for unskilled workers, the group of working-age men with the highest crime rates.

In these conditions, detachment from legal work has become normative: illegal activities are defined as "work," and the returns from crime as "getting paid" (Sullivan 1989). Pursuing "conventional" goals through illegal work has become dangerously close to becoming institutionalized in an oppositional culture, just as legal work may become the exception for a "growing underclass of the unskilled" (Wacquant and Wilson 1989; Mangold 1994). Accordingly, the importance of the balance of opportunities for the decision to seek illegal work is another central feature of the crime and unemployment relationship.

Labeling

The exclusion of incarcerated young offenders from legal work is evident in the longitudinal studies of Freeman (1992) and Sampson and Laub (1993). In the labeling perspective, early involvement in the criminal justice system has sustaining negative effects on future behavior. The mechanisms are compounding. Excluded from legal work by criminal records, young offenders in turn may come to define themselves through that label. This may lead to further embedment in deviant networks and a deepening self-concept as an outsider to legal work. Accordingly, the label has both exogenous effects for employers and psychological effects for the individual seeking work.

Such labels may attach and persist even before individuals seek access to legal work. Through parental criminality, adolescents may be embedded in social networks that are outside conventional job networks (Hagan 1993*a*), leading to early criminal involvement and the attachment of a legal sanction that in turn may exclude young people from future legal work.

POLICIES AND INTERVENTIONS

There is obvious intuitive appeal of jobs programs as an intervention to reduce criminality.[23] When offenders can be put to work at sufficient wages to compete with illegal income, logic suggests they will desist from crime. Yet the results of work programs for ex-offenders are disappointing. Even when programs do achieve some success in reducing crime, the negative association between crime and employment is weak (Uggen, Piliavin, and Matsueda 1992). One reason may be the detachment of programs from theoretical foundations that reflect the complex relationships between crime and unemployment. Accordingly, programs may be poorly conceptualized, failing to develop important elements that theory would suggest. Poorly implemented programs may explain poor results. A third reason may be poor theory, even when one is present. There also may be significant effects for subgroups, but such analyses are rarely done or reported. This is potentially important in programs with heterogeneous populations.

Exogenous factors also may undermine the effects of otherwise sound and effective programs. It is a formidable task to develop either preventive or remedial programs in the face of a restructured economy, concentrated joblessness, and growing skill deficits concentrated in urban centers. Questions of scale, the limitations of program technology, and the independent fluctuations of the labor market will combine to limit program effects, no matter how well they are executed. Nevertheless, there are program design components that follow naturally and logically from the above discussion, and strategies that have been field-tested and are worthy of replication. In the discussions that follow, we blend program elements for ex-offender populations with program features that might better suit a younger population prior to incarceration. A more detailed analysis would separate the two; brevity demands they be addressed simultaneously.

Program Design

Programs often differ in their emphasis on improving skills or finding work for participants. Whereas one may emphasize short-term goals, training and skill development programs offer less immediate payoffs and require a leap of faith regarding the availability of suitable jobs. Outcomes of training programs may also vary depending on their emphasis on remediation or new, job-specific (industry-defined) skills. Ancillary services, such as financial aid, transportation, child-care, or job placement services, also may dictate outcomes.

Market incentives for legal work are obvious considerations (see Freeman 1992, 1994; Grogger 1994a, 1994b). Pay scales should be set to meet individual needs and to reflect market wages. The type of work and occupational status are additional considerations. Work outcomes are contingent on job quality, wages, and the status accorded to particular types of work. Placement in unskilled labor, or work for work's sake, may not attend to theoretically important dimensions that the illegal market sometimes fulfills.

Setting also is important (Uggen, Piliavin, and Matsueda 1992). Training in residential settings offers the types of peer support and social reinforcement necessary for younger offenders who may have limited ties to conventional work and social worlds. More motivated older offenders, who have already diversified their social networks, may be better equipped to succeed in training programs that are set in communities and focused more on individuals.

Perhaps most critical is the need to ground interventions in theory. What theory is appropriate? The lessons of the desistance literature provide concrete directions for fashioning programs for ex-offenders. On the assumption that they have sufficient motivation for legal work, the processes of desistance suggest the importance of nonwork services, such as social network supports and remedial services. For younger individuals facing school-to-work or school-to-college transitions, the task is more difficult and complex. The age and social circumstances of participants also may dictate program strategies.

This raises the important issue of interactions between program type and the age of the individual. Quite different interventions could be allocated to younger versus older individuals. For younger people, especially those who have avoided legal sanctions but who face uncertain futures in the labor market, preventive programs will focus on building human capital and school-to-work transitions, combining the development of job skills with job readiness and postplacement efforts to smooth over a potentially rough transition. However, their motivations for legal work may not be as strong as older offenders.

Older individuals have different motivations, shaped by the changing conceptions of work and needs at various developmental stages. Having experienced prison, perhaps they are more willing to discount the returns from illegal work in light of higher punishment costs and (if married) higher commitment costs. Especially for those returning from prison, job placements may be more important than skill development. Yet these individuals face a scary list of obstacles: criminal labels, skill and human capital deficits, and limited access to job networks. They are no doubt at the end of the job queue for a shrinking demand for unskilled labor. Whatever design is planned, ancillary services are necessary for an ex-offender or high-risk population. Their deficits are likely to go beyond issues related to working, and will include such basics as shelter and social supports. Treatment for substance problems may be necessary for ex-offenders, as well as a range of counseling services to respond to the crises of everyday life they may face.

Macro-level interventions are critical, too, particularly in the creation of jobs that are accessible to young people in distressed areas. The "hollowing out" of central cities has removed not only essential services but the jobs that came with them (Wallace and Wallace 1990), advancing the contagion of joblessness. In addition to large-scale training programs, opportunities are needed for creation of local jobs through localized economic development in areas of high joblessness. Community development banks are a possible step in the support of local business. Increased local jobs would have payoffs not only in employment but in offsetting the social contagion of joblessness that undermines commitments to work and the economic logic of legal employment.

Additional policy initiatives should address the issues of enforcement of employment discrimination laws. This involves both initial hiring decisions and termination decisions. Employers are quite open in their racial hiring preferences (Kirschenman and Neckerman 1991). Their biases are based on perceptions of African-American males as making "trouble" through higher wage demands, poor productivity, frequent absenteeism, and conflicts with coworkers and supervisors. However, discrimination in hiring poses a formidable barrier to the development of initial job contacts and the human capital that accrues through employment. Firing decisions also may reflect racial imbalance and bias. Disputes in the workplace between young minority males and white employers are all too common (Ferguson and Filer 1986; Sullivan 1989; Anderson 1989). If there are differential responses to conflict with African-American versus other workers, discrimination laws should be vigorously asserted to avert premature and unfair work termination and the stigma of having been "fired from a job."

FUTURE RESEARCH

Both basic research and policy experiments are necessary to address the problems of crime and unemployment. Basic research is necessary to extend the empirical and theoretical foundations of interventions. Several topics deserve research attention.

Basic Research

Illegal Wages and Illegal Markets. There is little consistent information on the diversity of illegal labor markets and illegal wages. There has been extensive research on drug selling, but drug sellers are involved in a variety of illegal income-generating activities. Research is needed that focuses on the economic lives of people active in illegal markets. Studies are neeeded that examine market incentives for illegal work and the economic and social dimensions of illegal work that compete with the legal labor market. Similarly, research on illegal markets is needed to explain demand for illegal work, especially the social organization of illegal work and its opportunity structures. Basic social processes including recruitment and the flow of capital also will inform knowledge about the competing economic structures of crime.

Models of Decision Making. A fully specified model of decision making will provide necessary information on the cognitive processes leading to decisions to engage in illegal work. Economic choice, opportunity, control, and labeling perspectives should be integrated into a conceptual framework of decision making about work preferences and choices. Prior work experiences should be included to measure the conceptions of work and changes over time in response to experiences in the workplace. Transitions from legal to illegal and back to legal work should be closely analyzed, as should the difficult transitions from school to work and incarceration to work. Samples should include several neighborhoods to assess the mediating influences of peer networks and local economies. A range of informal and formal economic activities should be specified, and data collection points should occur with sufficient frequency to address the close timing of work and crime decisions. Age cohorts should vary as well, recognizing the varying places in the natural histories of crime and work of people at different stages in the life course.

Employer-Employee Relationships. One barrier to employment for unskilled or semiskilled young males at the end of job queues is conflicts in the workplace. These conflicts are the source of frequent absenteeism and the discount on job quality that may influence their decisions to turn to illegal work. Studies on the sources and outcomes of conflicts in the workplace for inner-city youths are needed to help fashion interventions to maintain job stability. This effort may be part of a larger qualitative effort on the work experiences of young males who are at the cusp of decisions regarding legal and illegal work. If conflicts are a source of attrition from the labor force, the origins of and solutions to these conflicts have important implications for maintaining labor force attachments.

Policy Experiments

Prevention. There is an obvious need for prevention experiments that focus on employment or advanced education/training for high-risk youths. Defining high risk is a task recently completed by the National Research Council (1993). They specified neighborhood risks as well as family and individual risks. Prevention efforts are needed to avert initial involvement in crime and the stigmatization of early incarceration. These efforts must also address the problem of job experiences for young males and the social distance of high-risk youths from the social world of legal work.

Extensions of the TARP Experiments. The analyses of the TARP experiments suggest limited effects of supported work programs for ex-offenders, but promising effects in the samples overall for offenders whose human capital "protected" them from failure. Rethinking TARP to incorporate lessons from basic research suggests the possibility of further experiments that include ancillary services as well as financial support and disaggregated interventions for older versus younger offenders.

Hastening Desistance. The cessation of crime with age, and the return of many offenders to legal work at the end of crime careers, suggests opportunities for interventions that broaden and accelerate the processes of desistance. Interventions would be directed at cognitive decisions and processes beginning with cohorts of offenders returning from prison or currently on parole or probation supervision. The interventions might focus on adjusting the assessments of illegal and legal work by introducing additional "costs" and "payoffs" from social sources. The processes of reintegration from illegal work (Biernacki 1986; Adler 1993) require social psychological adjustments to new roles and circumstances. While a portion of this type of intervention may deal with work issues, the lion's share of the effort would be directed at the changes in self- and social identity that accompany the shift away from deviant networks to the more predictable "straight" world.

NOTES

1. Illegal activities are distinguished from the myriad activities of the informal economy, activities that generally involve no *criminal* law violations. See, for example, Bourgois (1989); Taylor (1990); Fagan (1992); Freeman (1992).

2. The "doubling up" of legal work and cocaine sales in the Fagan and Reuter, MacCoun, and Murphy studies indicates that, for many young men, illegal work may be temporary or transitional work that supplements difficult low-wage or otherwise unsatisfactory work. For others, legal work provides options to riskier illegal work, or perhaps broadens markets for sellers of illegal goods or services.

3. Like their male counterparts, many women drug sellers "double up" in drug selling while working legally (Fagan 1994*b*). Some have had long careers of petty hustles and paper frauds, or prostitution work. But many others have not been involved in illegal work until the expansion of the drug economy created new opportunities. Their pathways into illegal work are little understood and likely reflect gender issues in both the licit and illicit economies.

4. This framework is limited in two important ways. First, it assumes that the consumer is risk neutral, and there is no discount on illegal wages from the potential for criminal sanctions. Second, it assumes that the consumer is amoral in the sense that time allocated to crime commission has no more disutility than an hour spent working. We return to this question later in discussing the nonmonetary returns from "lifestyle" and taste variables.

5. Occupations themselves represent a stratification of opportunities, a manifestation of Merton's (1938) concept of "legitimate means."

6. According to Witte and Tauchen (1994), individuals face a deterrence "schedule" or function that relates levels of criminal activity to a probability of arrest. They assume that there are exogenous shifts in the schedule because of differences in police policies or budgets, or changes in the legal code. They also assume that crime and work are not independent and frequently overlap (i.e., they are not substitute uses of time).

7. Witte (1980) obtained similar findings with a cohort of North Carolina prison releasees, even with limited information on employment activities and no data on education. Using length of time for releasees to find a job and the wage of the first job, Witte found that employment and earnings suppressed crime rates.

8. Finding no published estimates of losses from forgery and theft, Wilson and Abrahamse (1992, p. 364) "guessed."

9. Women were excluded from the analyses due to their lower crime participation rates. Males in school or the military were excluded to limit the sample to males for whom the primary alternative uses of time would be market work or crime. Males in jail from 1979 to 1981 (the first 3 years of the panel) were excluded since they were censored from legal work opportunities.

10. Response categories for the percentage of income from crime were set in fourths, ranging from "none," to "about one-fourth," "about one-half," "about three-fourths," to "almost all."

11. Criminal human capital was an index of criminal productivity, and included: prior criminal arrests, prior criminal convictions, family members with criminal records or convictions, and jail sentences during the 10-year analysis interval.

12. Because the income distributions were highly skewed, Reuter, MacCoun, and Murphy also report median net earnings of $721 per month from drug sales, but $2,000 per month among the 37 percent who reported selling drugs on a daily basis.

13. To better illustrate the higher expected returns from drug selling, Hagedorn (1994a, pp. 202–3, table 2) reports that: "The *maximum* amount of money earned monthly by any gang member from legal income was $2,400, the *mean* for gang drug sales" (Hagedorn's emphasis).

14. Wilson and Abrahamse (1992, p. 361) draw on Chaiken and Chaiken (1990) analyses to suggest that self-reports and official records are stable within a factor of 1.5.

15. As pointed out by Hagedorn (1994a, p. 205), doubling up reflects the confusion of street-corner lives depicted by Liebow (1967, p. 219) in an earlier era in Tally's Corner: "Traffic is heavy in all directions."

16. Robbery, sale of cocaine or heroin, sale of marijuana, grand theft, petty theft, shoplifting, frauds and "cons," aid to gambling activities, fencing, burglaries, and auto theft.

17. In the past, manufacturing jobs have provided stable if not spectacular wages for people living in inner cities, and especially for African Americans (Farley 1987).

18. See, for example, Sullivan (1989), Williams (1989), Taylor (1990), Padilla (1992). For example, Felix Padilla describes how gang members in a Puerto Rican

Chicago neighborhood regarded low-level drug sellers in their gang as "working stiffs" who were being exploited by other gang members.

19. See, for example, Mulvey (1989) on juvenile offenders; Trasler (1977) and Shover (1985) on burglars; Irwin (1970) and Cusson and Pinsonneault (1986) on robbers; Adler (1985, 1993) on drug dealers; Biernacki (1986) on opiate addicts who also were involved in a variety of income-producing crimes. See also Fagan (1989) on a conceptual model for spousal assailants.

20. Others are more cautious about using self-reports. Thompson and Cataldo (1986) criticize Viscusi (1986a, 1986b) for exclusively using self-reports. Viscusi failed to detect the absence of muggings, burglaries, and robberies in the self-reports in his sample, and fails to note the typical age-crime relationships found in a wide range of criminological studies (see, for example, Hirschi and Gottfredson 1983; Gottfredson and Hirschi 1990). Yet Elliott and Huizinga (1986), using a general population sample, claim that the extent of underreporting in arrest statistics is overwhelming for nearly all crime types, and the underreporting factor increases with the frequency of self-reported crime.

21. If, for example, crime rates increase beyond some threshold, employers may flee cities or regions for safer environments for their workers. A perception of an unskilled labor force may also motivate employers to relocate their businesses to places with higher productivity, lower wages, more skilled workers, or less troublesome employees.

22. Bourgois talks about how drug workers are willing to work under difficult working conditions, with no benefits and substantial health and safety risks, to escape the racist humiliation they encounter daily in low-wage service and manufacturing jobs.

23. Of course, an alternative policy would focus on reducing the returns from illegal work to match wages for legal work. Current illegal work involves a diverse set of activities, but drug selling appears to be the most lucrative and widespread. Reducing the returns from drug selling would require either a decline in demand (an unlikely prospect given the past 2 decades of drug crises in American cities), or the deregulation of drugs and the substitution of market rules for the legal controls. This has proved to be a politically unpopular option and not feasible in the short run. Experiments with increasing punishment costs over the past decade also have not stemmed participation in violent crime but have been associated with declines in burglary rates. The connection between incarceration rates and property or drug crime rates is tenuous at best, since the bulk of those imprisoned have not been property crime offenders (Reiss and Roth 1993).

REFERENCES

Adler, Patricia. 1985. *Wheeling and Dealing: An Ethnography of an Upper-Level Dealing and Smuggling Community.* New York: Columbia University Press.
———. 1993. "The Post-Phase of Deviant Careers: Reintegrating Drug Traffickers." *Deviant Behavior* 13:103–26.
Agnew, Robert, and Helene Raskin White. 1992. "An Empirical Test of General Strain Theory." *Criminology* 30:475–99.

Akers, Ronald A. 1990. "Rational Choice, Deterrence, and Social Learning Theory in Criminology." *Journal of Criminal Law and Criminology* 82:653–76.

Albrecht, J. J. 1984. "Youth Unemployment and Youth Crime." *Kriminologisch Journal* 101:218–29.

Anderson, Elijah. 1990. *Streetwise: Race, Class, and Change in an Urban Community.* Chicago: University of Chicago Press.

———. 1994. "Code of the Street." *Atlantic Monthly*, May.

Becker, Gary. 1968. "Crime and Punishment: An Economic Approach." *Journal of Political Economy* 76:169–217.

Berk, Richard A; Peter Rossi; and Kenneth Lenihan. 1980. "Crime and Poverty: Some Experimental Evidence from Ex-Offenders." *American Sociological Review* 45:776–86.

Biernacki, Patrick. 1986. *Pathways from Addiction: Recovery without Treatment.* Philadelphia: Temple University Press.

Blackburn, McKinley; David E. Bloom; and Richard B. Freeman. 1990. "The Declining Economic Position of Less Skilled American Men." In *A Future of Lousy Jobs? The Changing Structure of U.S. Wages*, edited by Gary Burtless. Washington, D.C.: Brookings Institution.

Bound, John, and Richard B. Freeman. 1992. "What Went Wrong? The Erosion of Relative Earnings and Employment among Young Black Men in the 1980s." *Quarterly Journal of Economics* 107:201–32.

Bourgois, Philippe. 1989. "In Search of Horatio Alger: Culture and Ideology in the Crack Economy." *Contemporary Drug Problems* 16:619–50.

Bushway, Sharon D. 1996. "The Impact of a Criminal History on Unemployment." Ph.D. diss., Carnegie Mellon University.

Cantor, David, and Kenneth C. Land. 1985. "Unemployment and Crime Rates in the Post–World War II United States: A Theoretical and Empirical Analysis." *American Sociological Review* 50:317–23.

Chaiken, Jan M., and Marcia R. Chaiken. 1990. "Drugs and Predatory Crime." In *Drugs and Crime*, vol. 13 of *Crime and Justice: An Annual Review of Research*, edited by Michael Tonry and James Q. Wilson. Chicago: University of Chicago Press.

Chin, Ko-lin. 1995. *Chinatown Gangs.* New York: Oxford University Press.

Chin, Ko-lin, and Jeffrey Fagan. 1994. "Social Order and Gang Formation among Chinese Gangs." *Advances in Criminological Theory* 6:149–62.

Chiricos, Ted. 1987. "Rates of Crime and Unemployment: An Analysis of Aggregate Research." *Social Problems* 334:187–212.

Clarke, Ronald V., and Derek B. Cornish. 1985. "Modeling Offenders' Decisions: A Framework for Research and Policy." In *Crime and Justice: An Annual Review of Research*, vol. 6, edited by Michael Tonry and Norval Morris, pp. 147–85. Chicago: University of Chicago Press.

Cloward, Richard, and Lloyd Ohlin. 1960. *Delinquency and Opportunity.* New York: Free Press.

Cohen, Albert. 1955. *Delinquent Boys.* Glencoe, Ill.: Free Press.

Corcoran, Mary, and Susan Parrott. 1992. "Black Women's Economic Progress."

Paper presented at the Research Conference on the Urban Underclass: Perspectives from the Social Sciences, Ann Arbor, Mich., June.

Cornish, Derek B., and Ronald V. Clarke, eds. 1986. *The Reasoning Criminal.* New York: Springer-Verlag.

Cusson, Maurice, and Pierre Pinsonneault. 1986. "The Decision to Give Up Crime." In *The Reasoning Criminal*, edited by Derek B. Cornish and Ronald V. Clarke, pp. 72–82. New York: Springer-Verlag.

Ehrlich, Isaac. 1973. "Participation in Illegitimate Activities: A Theoretical and Empirical Investigation." *Journal of Political Economy* 81:521–65.

Elliott, Delbert S., and David Huizinga. 1986. "The Validity and Reliability of Self Reports of Juvenile Delinquency." *Journal of Quantitative Criminology* 2:327–46.

Fagan, Jeffrey. 1989. "Cessation of Family Violence: Deterrence and Dissuasion." In *Family Violence*, vol. 11 of *Crime and Justice: An Annual Review of Research*, edited by Lloyd Ohlin and Michael Tonry, pp. 377–425. Chicago: University of Chicago Press.

———. 1990. "Social Processes of Delinquency and Drug Use among Urban Gangs." In *Gangs in America*, edited by C. Ronald Huff, pp. 183–222. Thousand Oaks, Calif.: Sage.

———. 1992. "Drug Selling and Licit Income in Distressed Neighborhoods: The Economic Lives of Street-Level Drug Users and Dealers." In *Drugs, Crime, and Social Isolation: Barriers to Urban Opportunity*, edited by Adele V. Harrell, George E. Peterson, pp. 99–142. Washington, D.C.: Urban Institute Press.

———. 1993. "The Political Economy of Drug Dealing among Urban Gangs." In *Drugs and Community*, edited by Robert Davis, Arthur Lurigio, and Dennis P. Rosenbaum, pp. 19–54. Springfield, Ill.: Charles Thomas.

———. 1994*a*. "Do Criminal Sanctions Deter Drug Offenders?" In *Drugs and Criminal Justice: Evaluating Public Policy Initiatives*, edited by Doris MacKenzie and Criag Uchida, pp. 188–214. Newbury Park, Calif.: Sage.

———. 1994*b*. "Women and Drugs Revisited: Female Participation in the Cocaine Economy." *Journal of Drug Issues* 24:179–226.

———. In press. "The Dynamics of Crime and Neighborhood Change." Chap. 10 in *The Ecology of Crime and Drug Use in Inner Cities.* New York: Social Science Research Council.

Fagan, J. A., and Ko-lin Chin. 1990. "Violence as Regulation and Social Control in the Distribution of Crack." In *Drugs and Violence*, edited by Mario de la Rosa, Bernard Gropper, and Elizabeth Lambert, pp. 8–39. National Institute of Drug Abuse Research Monograph no. 103. Rockville, Md.: U.S. Public Health Administration.

Fagan, Jeffrey, and Richard B. Freeman. In press. "Crime and Work." In *Crime and Justice: An Annual Review of Research*, vol. 24. Chicago: University of Chicago Press.

Farley, Reynolds. 1987. "Disproportionate Black and Hispanic Unemployment in U.S. Metropolitan Areas." *American Journal of Economics and Sociology* 46:129–50.

Farley, Reynolds, and Walter R. Allen. 1987. *The Color Line and the Quality of Life in America.* New York: Russell Sage Foundation.

Farrington, David P. 1986. "Age and Crime." In *Crime and Justice: An Annual Review of Research*, vol. 7, edited by Michael Tonry and Norval Morris, pp. 189–250. Chicago: University of Chicago Press.

Farrington, David P; Bernard Gallagher; Lyndia Morley; Raymond J. St. Ledger; and Donald J. West. 1986. "Unemployment, School Leaving and Crime." *British Journal of Criminology* 26:335–56.

Ferguson, Ronald, and Randall Filer. 1986. "Do Better Jobs Make Better Workers? Absenteeism from Work among Inner-City Black Youths." In *The Black Youth Unemployment Crisis*, edited by Richard B. Freeman and Harry J. Holzer, pp. 261–98. Chicago: University of Chicago Press and the National Bureau of Economic Research.

Frazier, Charles E. 1981. "The Use of Life Stories in Testing Theories of Criminal Behavior: Toward Reviving a Method." *Qualitative Sociology* 2:122–42.

Freeman, Richard B. 1983. "Crime and Unemployment." In *Crime and Public Policy*, edited by James Q. Wilson, pp. 89–106. San Francisco: Institute for Contemporary Studies Press.

———. 1991. "Employment and Earnings of Disadvantaged Young Men in a Labor Shortage Economy." In *The Urban Underclass*, edited by Christopher Jencks and Paul E. Peterson, pp. 103–21. Washington, D.C.: Brookings Institution Press.

———. 1992. "Crime and the Employment of Disadvantaged Youths." In *Urban Labor Markets and Job Opportunities*, edited by George E. Peterson and Wayne Vroman, pp. 201–38. Washington, D.C.: Urban Institute Press.

———. 1994. *Working under Different Rules.* New York: Russell Sage Foundation.

———. 1995. "The Labor Market." Chap. 8 in *Crime and Public Policy*, edited by James Q. Wilson and Joan Petersilia. 2d ed. San Francisco: Institute for Contemporary Studies.

Freeman, Richard B., and Harry J. Holzer, eds. 1986. *The Black Youth Unemployment Crisis.* Chicago: University of Chicago Press and the National Bureau of Economic Research.

Glueck, Sheldon, and Eleanor Glueck. 1950. *Unraveling Juvenile Delinquency.* Cambridge, Mass.: Harvard University Press.

———. 1968. *Delinquents and Non-delinquents in Perspective.* Cambridge, Mass.: Harvard University Press.

Good, David H; Maureen A. Pirog-Good; and Robin C. Sickles. 1986. "An Analysis of Youth Crime and Employment Patterns." *Journal of Quantitative Criminology* 2:219–36.

Gottfredson, Michael R., and Travis Hirschi. 1990. *A General Theory of Crime.* Palo Alto, Calif.: Stanford University Press.

Grasmick, Harold G., and Robert J. Bursik. 1990. "Conscience, Significant Others, and Rational Choice: Extending the Deterrence Model." *Law and Society Review* 24(3):837–61.

Greenberg, David F. 1977. "Delinquency and the Age Structure of Society."
Contemporary Crises 1:189–223.

Grogger, Jeffrey. 1994. "Criminal Opportunities, Youth Crime, and Young Men's
Labor Supply." Unpublished manuscript. University of California, Santa
Barbara, Department of Economics.

———. 1995. "The Effect of Arrests on the Employment and Earnings of Young
Men." *Quarterly Journal of Economics* 110 (February):51–71.

Hagan, John. 1993*a*. "The Social Embeddedness of Crime and Unemployment."
Criminology 31:465–92.

———. 1993*b*. "Structural and Cultural Disinvestment and the New Ethnographies
of Poverty and Crime." *Contemporary Sociology* 32(May):327–31.

Hagan, John, and Alberto Palloni. 1990. "The Social Reproduction of a Criminal
Class in Working-Class London, Circa 1950–80." *American Journal of
Sociology* 96:265–99.

Hagedorn, John M. 1994*a*. "Homeboys, Dope Fiends, Legits, and New Jacks."
Criminology 32:197–219.

———. 1994*b*. "Neighborhoods, Markets and Gang Drug Organization." *Journal
of Research in Crime and Delinquency* 31:264–94.

Hagedorn, John, with Perry Macon. 1988. *People and Folks: Gangs, Crime and
the Underclass in a Rustbelt City.* Chicago: Lake View Press.

Hindelang, Michael; Travis Hirschi; and Joseph Weis. 1981. *Measuring
Delinquency.* Beverly Hills, Calif.: Sage.

Hirschi, Travis. 1969. *Causes of Delinquency.* Berkeley: University of California
Press.

———. 1986. "On the Compatibility of Rational Choice and Social Control
Theories of Crime." In *The Reasoning Criminal,* edited by Derek B. Cornish
and Ronald V. Clarke, pp. 105–18. New York: Springer-Verlag.

Hirschi, Travis, and Michael Gottfredson. 1983. "Age and the Explanation of
Crime." *American Journal of Sociology* 89:552–84.

Huurne, A. 1988. *Unemployed Youths, Three Years Later.* The Hague:
Staatsdrukkesrij.

Irwin, John. 1970. *The Felon.* Englewood Cliffs, N.J.: Prentice-Hall.

Irwin, John, and James A. Austin. 1994. *It's about Time: America's
Imprisonment Binge.* New York: Wadsworth.

Jargowsky, Paul, and Mary Jo Bane. 1990. "Ghetto Poverty: Basic Questions." In
Inner-City Poverty in the United States, edited by Lawrence J. Lynn, Jr., and
Michael G. H. McGeary, pp. 16–67. Washington, D.C.: National Academy
Press.

Johnson, Bruce D.; Terry Williams; Kojo Dei; and Harry Sanabria. 1990. "Drug
Abuse and the Inner City: Impacts of Hard Drug Use and Sales on Low-
Income Communities." In *Drugs and Crime,* edited by James Q. Wilson and
Michael Tonry. Chicago: University of Chicago Press.

Kasarda, John D. 1988. "Jobs, Migration and Emerging Urban Mismatches."
In *Urban Change and Poverty,* edited by Michael G. H. McGeary and
Lawrence E. Lynn, Jr., pp. 148–98. Washington, D.C.: National Academy
Press.

———. 1989. "Urban Industrial Transition and the Underclass." *Annals of the American Academy of Political and Social Science* 501:26–47.

———. 1992. "The Severely Distressed in Economically Transforming Cities." In *Drugs, Crime, and Social Isolation: Barriers to Urban Opportunity*, edited by Adele V. Harrell and George E. Peterson, pp. 45–98. Washington, D.C.: Urban Institute Press.

Katz, Jack. 1988. *Seductions of Crime*. New York: Basic Books.

Kirschenman, Joleen, and Kathryn M. Neckerman. 1991. " 'We'd Love to Hire Them, But . . .': The Meaning of Race for Employers." In *The Urban Underclass*, edited by Christopher Jencks and Paul E. Peterson, pp. 203–32. Washington, D.C.: Brookings Institution Press.

Land, Kenneth C.; Patricia L. McCall; and Lawrence E. Cohen. 1990. "Structural Covariates of Homicide Rates: Are There Any Invariances across Time and Space?" *American Journal of Sociology* 95:922–63.

Lemann, Nicholas. 1991*a*. "The Other Underclass." *Atlantic Monthly* 268(April):96–110.

———. 1991*b*. *The Promised Land*. New York: Knopf.

Liebow, Elliott. 1967. *Tally's Corner A Study of Negro Street-Corner Men*. Boston: Little, Brown.

MacCoun, Robert, and Peter Reuter. 1992. "Are the Wages of Sin $30 an Hour? Economic Aspects of Street-Level Drug Dealing." *Crime and Delinquency* 38:477–91.

Mangold, Catherine. 1994. "Study Warns of Growing Underclass of the Unskilled." *New York Times*, June 2, p. A10.

Massey, Douglas S., and Nancy Denton. 1993. *American Apartheid: Segregation and the Making of the Underclass*. Cambridge, Mass.: Harvard University Press.

Massey, Douglas S., and Mitchell L. Eggers. 1990. "The Ecology of Inequality: Minorities and the Concentration of Poverty, 1970–80." *American Journal of Sociology* 95:1153–88.

Matsueda, Ross L.; Rosemary Gartner; Irving Piliavin; and Michael Polakowski. 1992. "The Prestige of Criminal and Conventional Occupations." *American Sociological Review* 57(6):752–70.

Matza, David. 1964. *Delinquency and Drift*. New York: Wiley.

Mayer, Jane. 1989. "In the War on Drugs, Toughest Foe May Be That Alienated Youth." *Wall Street Journal*, September 8, p. 1.

Merton, Robert K. 1938. "Social Structure and Anomie." *American Sociological Review* 3:672–82.

Miller, J. L., and A. B. Anderson. 1986. "Updating the Deterrence Doctrine." *Journal of Criminal Law and Criminology* 77:418–38.

Moore, Joan W. 1992*a*. *Going Down to the Barrio: Homeboys and Homegirls in Change*. Philadelphia: Temple University Press.

———. 1992*b*. "Institutionalized Youth Gangs: Why White Fence and El Hoyo Maravilla Change So Slowly." In *The Ecology of Crime and Drug Use in Inner Cities*, edited by J. Fagan. New York: Social Science Research Council.

Moss, P., and C. Tilly. 1991. "Why Black Men Are Doing Worse in the Labor

Market: A Review of Supply-Side and Demand-Side Explanations." Paper prepared for the Social Science Research Council, Committee on Research on the Urban Underclass, Subcommittee on Joblessness and the Underclass. New York: Social Science Research Council.

Mulvey, Edward. 1989. *The Abandonment of Delinquency.* Westport, Conn.: Greenwood.

National Research Council. 1993. *Losing Generations: Adolescents in High-Risk Settings.* Washington, D.C.: National Academy Press.

Needels, Karen. 1993. "The Long-Term Effects of the Transitional Aid Research Project in Texas: Recidivism and Employment Results." Unpublished manuscript. Princeton, N.J.: Princeton University, Department of Economics.

———. 1994. "Go Directly to Jail and Do Not Collect? A Long-Term Study of Recidivism and Employment Patterns among Prison Releasees." Unpublished manuscript. Princeton, N.J.: Princeton University, Department of Economics.

O'Neill, June. 1990. "The Role of Human Capital in Earnings Differences between Black and White Men." *Journal of Economic Perspectives* 4:25–45.

Padilla, F. 1992. *The Gang as an American Enterprise.* New Brunswick, N.J.: Rutgers University Press.

———. 1993. "The Working Gang." In *Gangs*, edited by Scott Cummings and Daniel J. Monti, pp. 173–92. Albany: State University of New York Press.

Paternoster, Raymond, and Paul Mazerolle. 1994. "General Strain Theory and Delinquency: A Replication and Extension." *Journal of Research in Crime and Delinquency* 31:235–63.

Piliavin, Irving; Rosemary Gartner; Craig Thornton; and Ross Matsueda. 1986. "Crime Deterrence and Rational Choice." *American Sociological Review* 51:101–19.

Ploeg, G. J. 1991. *Maatschappelijke positie en criminaliteit.* Groningen: Wolters-Noordhoff.

Reiss, Albert J., Jr., and Jeffrey A. Roth. 1993. *Understanding and Preventing Violence.* Vol. 1. Washington, D.C.: National Academy Press.

Reuter, Peter; Robert MacCoun; and Patrick Murphy. 1990. "Money from Crime." Report R-3894. Santa Monica, Calif.: RAND.

Rosenfeld, Richard, and Steven Messner. 1989. *Crime and the American Dream.* Albany: State University of New York Press.

Rossi, Peter H.; Richard A. Berk; and Kenneth J. Lenihan. 1980. *Money, Work, and Crime: Experimental Evidence.* New York: Academic Press.

Sampson, Robert J. 1987. "Urban Black Violence: The Effect of Male Joblessness and Family Disruption." *American Journal of Sociology* 93:348–82.

Sampson, Robert J., and W. Byron Groves. 1989. "Community Structure and Crime: Testing Social Disorganization Theory." *American Journal of Sociology* 94:774–802.

Sampson, Robert J., and John H. Laub. 1993. *Crime in the Making.* Cambridge, Mass.: Harvard University Press.

Sampson, Robert J., and William Julius Wilson. 1994. "Race, Crime and Urban

Inequality." In *Crime and Inequality*, edited by John Hagan and Ruth E. Peterson, pp. 37–54. Palo Alto, Calif.: Stanford University Press.

Sanchez-Jankowski, M. 1991. *Islands in the Street*. Berkeley: University of California Press.

Shover, Neal. 1985. *Aging Criminals*. Beverly Hills, Calif.: Sage.

Smith, Douglas A. 1986. "The Neighborhood Context of Police Behavior." In *Communities and Crime*, edited by Albert J. Reiss, Jr., and Michael Tonry, pp. 313–42. Chicago: University of Chicago Press.

Stephens, David W., and John R. Krebs. 1986. *Foraging Theory*. Princeton, N.J.: Princeton University Press.

Sullivan, Mercer L. 1989. *"Getting Paid": Youth Crime and Work in the Inner City*. Ithaca, N.Y.: Cornell University Press.

Taylor, C. 1990. "Gang Imperialism." In *Gangs in America*, edited by C. Ronald Huff, pp. 103–15. Newbury Park, Calif.: Sage.

Thompson, James W., and James Cataldo. 1986. "Comment on 'Market Incentives for Criminal Behavior.' " In *The Black Youth Employment Crisis*, edited by Richard B. Freeman and Harry J. Holzer, pp. 347–51. Chicago: University of Chicago Press and the National Bureau of Economic Research.

Thornberry, Terence, and R. L. Christenson. 1984. "Unemployment and Criminal Involvement: An Investigation of Reciprocal Causal Structures." *American Sociological Review* 56:609–27.

Tienda, Marta. 1989. "Poor People and Poor Places: Neighborhood Effects and the Formation of the Underclass." Paper presented at the annual meeting of the American Sociological Association, San Francisco, August.

Tonry, Michael. 1995. *Malign Neglect: Race, Crime, and Punishment in America*. New York: Oxford University Press.

Trasler, Gordon B. 1979. "Delinquency, Recidivism, and Desistance." *British Journal of Criminology* 19:314–22.

Tunnell, Kennth D. 1992. *Choosing Crime: The Criminal Calculus of Property Offenders*. Chicago: Nelson-Hall.

Uggen, Christopher. 1993. "Innovators, Retreatists, and the Conformist Alternative: A Job Quality Model of Work and Crime." Unpublished manuscript. Madison: University of Wisconsin, Department of Sociology.

Uggen, Christopher; Irving Piliavin; and Ross Matsueda. 1992. *Job Programs and Criminal Desistance*. Washington, D.C.: Urban Institute.

Viscusi, W. Kip. 1986*a*. "Market Incentives for Criminal Behavior." In *The Black Youth Unemployment Crisis*, edited by Richard B. Freeman and Harry J. Holzer, pp. 301–46. Chicago: University of Chicago Press and the National Bureau of Economic Research.

———. 1986*b*. "The Risks and Rewards of Criminal Activity: A Comprehensive Test of Criminal Deterrence." *Journal of Labor Economics* 4:317–40.

Wallace, Rod, and D. Wallace. 1990. "Origins of Public Health Collapse in New York City: The Dynamics of Planned Shrinkage, Contagious Neighborhood Decay, and Social Disintegration." *Bulletin of the New York Academy of Medicine* 66:391–434.

Wacquant, Loic D., and William Julius Wilson. 1989. "The Costs of Racial and Class Exclusion in the Inner City." *Annals of the American Academy of Political and Social Science* 501:8–25.

Williams, Kirk, and Richard Hawkins. 1989. "Perceptual Research on General Deterrence." *Law and Society Review* 20:545–68.

Williams, Terry. 1989. *The Cocaine Kids*. New York: Addison-Wesley.

Wilson, James Q., and Allan Abrahamse. 1992. "Does Crime Pay?" *Justice Quarterly* 9:359–77.

Wilson, William Julius. 1987. *The Truly Disadvantaged*. Chicago: University of Chicago Press.

———. 1991. "Studying Inner-City Social Dislocations: The Challenge of Public Agenda Research." *American Sociological Review* 56:1–14.

Witte, Ann. D. 1980. "Estimating the Economic Model of Crime with Individual Data." *Quarterly Journal of Economics* 94:57–87.

Witte, Ann D., and Helen Tauchen. 1994. "Work and Crime: An Exploration Using Panel Data." *Public Finance* 49(Suppl.):155–67.

Wright, Richard; Robert H. Logie; and Scott H. Decker. 1995. "Criminal Expertise and Offender Decision Making: An Experimental Study of the Target Selection Process in Residential Burglary." *Journal of Research in Crime and Delinquency* 32:139–53.

Wright, Richard, and Scott Decker. 1994. *Burglars on the Job*. New York: Cambridge University Press.

Roberto M. Fernandez

Spatial Mismatch

Housing, Transportation, and Employment

in Regional Perspective

The great appeal of the spatial mismatch hypothesis is that it relates the obvious fact of widespread racial residential segregation (see, e.g., Massey and Denton 1993) to employment disadvantages for minorities. Stated simply, the spatial mismatch hypothesis argues that limitations on the residential choices of minorities, particularly the almost total exclusion of African Americans from white suburban areas, inhibit minority access to jobs (especially low-skilled jobs) that have been steadily dispersing from central cities to suburban areas of most metropolitan areas for at least the past 30 years. Consequently, racial barriers in housing are hypothesized to be responsible for a large portion of the low rates of employment and low earnings of minority workers.

In line with the focus of the Metropolitan Assembly, the hypothesis is explicitly about housing and employment prospects in entire metropolitan areas. Also consonant with the goals of the Assembly, the spatial mismatch hypothesis is directly aimed at explaining racial differences in employment. This is especially important in light of the special emphasis that the Assembly has placed on questions of race and diversity. Finally, in light of the location of this meeting of the Assembly, it is useful to consider that, for most scholars, Chicago provides a "pure" case of the issues that are at stake in the spatial mismatch hypothesis. More than for any other region, data from the Chicago metropolitan area have played a key role in the academic and policy debate on spatial mismatch.

In this brief essay, I would like to summarize the extent to which spatial mismatch explanations of minority employment problems can be empirically supported. I will also highlight what is *not* known in this area. I will then summarize and critically discuss various policy alternatives and initiatives that have been proposed to address these problems, underscoring what I think are the most prudent directions to pursue in light of extant knowledge. In keeping with the goals of the conference, I give particular emphasis to *regional* public policy solutions to these problems.

What Do We Know?

Scholars have been studying the spatial mismatch question for almost 30 years. John F. Kain formulated the spatial mismatch hypothesis and began the empirical work in this area in two papers published during the 1960s (see Kain 1964, and the better-known Kain 1968). Of particular interest for this conference is the fact that Kain used data from the Chicago and Detroit metropolitan areas in these early papers. From its very inception, then, Chicago has been prominently featured in scholarship on spatial mismatch. Kain (1968) concluded that racial discrimination in housing markets reduced nonwhite employment in both metropolitan areas, and that continued suburbanization of employment would further exacerbate employment problems for nonwhites in both Detroit and Chicago.

Since this research appeared, a large number of papers have been published both supporting and refuting Kain's central thesis. With a few periods of dormancy, research on this topic has continued throughout the 30-year period, most recently being reinvigorated by the "underclass" debate (see Wilson 1987). Indeed, research on this topic continues today, with scholars taking new approaches purporting to shed light on the spatial mismatch hypothesis (e.g., Zax and Kain 1991; Fernandez 1994; Holzer, Ihlanfeldt, and Sjoquist 1994). Before turning to a review of the literature in this area, I present some data from four northeastern cities — New York, Chicago, Philadelphia, and Detroit — as an illustration of the kind of evidence that has been used to address the spatial mismatch hypothesis.

Tables 1–3 present data which illustrate the major economic and population trends that have formed the basis of the debate surrounding spatial mismatch theory. Table 1 shows that virtually all the job growth between 1970 and 1980 has occurred in the suburban rings of these areas. The city of Chicago lost over 88,000 jobs, while the suburbs gained 630,000 over this period. While the city-suburb disparity in job growth is not as large in the other cities, the trends are all in the same direction. To the extent there has been any net job growth at all in these central cities, it has occurred only in managerial and professional and technical and administrative support jobs.[1] However, the suburban growth in these job categories has far outstripped central city job gains. For Chicago, net job growth for managerial and professional jobs in the suburbs was triple that in the city: 156,000 compared with 51,000. The suburb-city contrast in growth in technical and administrative support jobs was also substantial, 120,000 versus 68,000.

The growth patterns for the final two job categories — clerical and sales and blue-collar — are particularly relevant for the spatial mismatch

TABLE 1. *Change in the Number of Jobs in Selected Central Cities and Suburban Rings, by Occupational Sector, 1970–80*

Metropolitan Area	Managerial and Professional	Technical and Administrative Support	Clerical and Sales	Blue-Collar	Total
New York:					
Central City	90,460	173,780	−187,820	−171,500	−95,080
Suburbs	200,140	210,800	51,060	27,080	489,080
Chicago:					
Central City	51,560	68,400	−89,760	−118,860	−88,660
Suburbs	156,120	120,660	115,360	237,900	630,040
Philadelphia:					
Central City	23,040	35,360	−54,060	−75,200	−70,860
Suburbs	50,280	55,880	36,240	29,500	171,900
Detroit:					
Central City	4,700	15,840	−35,540	−89,860	−104,860
Suburbs	51,860	62,500	43,240	29,320	186,920

Source: Kasarda (1989), p. 29.

TABLE 2. *Population Changes (in Thousands) in Four U.S. Cities, by Race and Ethnicity, 1970–80*

Central City	Total Population	Whites	Non-Hispanic Blacks	Others	Hispanic	% Nonwhite
New York:						
1970	7,895	5,062	1,518	113	1,202	36
1980	7,072	3,669	1,694	303	1,406	48
Change, 1970–80	−823	−1,393	176	190	204	...
Chicago:						
1970	3,363	1,999	1,076	40	248	41
1980	3,005	1,300	1,188	96	422	57
Change, 1970–80	−358	−699	111	56	174	...
Philadelphia:						
1970	1,949	1,247	646	11	45	36
1980	1,688	963	633	28	64	43
Change, 1970–80	−260	−283	−13	17	19	...
Detroit:						
1970	1,511	820	652	9	30	46
1980	1,203	402	754	18	29	67
Change, 1970–80	−308	−418	102	9	−1	...
Total Change, 1970–80	−1,749	−2,794	377	271	396	...

Source: Kasarda's (1985) presentation of U.S. Bureau of the Census, *Census of Population* summary tapes, 1970, 1980.

hypothesis since these are the jobs in which minorities are most likely to be found. Here, too, the data over this time period appear to be consistent with the spatial mismatch story. Central city losses in these job categories have been substantial in all four cities. By way of comparison there has been growth in the number of clerical and sales and blue-collar jobs in the suburbs of all four cities. While the Chicago area has been among the most fortunate of these metro areas in that the suburban job growth in these job categories has been greater than the central city losses,[2] the question remains whether these suburban jobs — precisely those jobs that are most likely to employ minorities — are accessible to minorities.

Table 2 shows the population trends for the four cities over the period 1970–80. Also consistent with the spatial mismatch hypothesis, there has been a general trend for minorities to be concentrated in central cities — the very areas from which jobs have been dispersing. All four central cities have lost population. However, it is whites who have disproportionately left the central city, while minorities have increased their representation there. The city of Chicago showed a net loss of almost 700,000 whites, while blacks and Hispanics showed substantial increases of 111,000 and 174,000, respectively. In percentage terms, the contrast is even more striking. Chicago lost 35 percent of its white population over this period, while non-Hispanic blacks showed a substantial 10 percent increase, and Hispanics posted a huge 70 percent increase. Only Detroit showed a larger percentage decline in the white population, a greater percentage increase in the African-American population, and a greater percentage increase in the nonwhite population.

While the central cities have become increasingly minority in composition, and jobs have been dispersing from central cities, the final piece of the spatial mismatch puzzle concerns the extent to which minorities have also been suburbanizing over this period. Table 3 presents data on changes between 1970 and 1980 in suburbanization for whites and African Americans[3] for the four cities. The numbers reflect the percentage of each metro area population that resides in the suburbs. All four metropolitan areas showed a greater proportion of minorities located in the suburbs. However, with the exception of the Philadelphia metro area, the changes in suburbanization are much lower for blacks than they are for whites. For the Chicago metro area, 72.8 percent of whites resided in the suburbs in 1980 compared with 62.2 percent in 1970. This 10.6 percent increase is 1.85 times the corresponding increase (5.8 percent) for African Americans over the same period. In the New York area, whites suburbanized at four times the African-American rate (with percentage differences of 4.5 for whites vs. 1.1 for blacks), while whites in Detroit suburbanized at a rate

TABLE 3. *Trends in Black and White Suburbanization in 4 Metropolitan Areas with Largest Black Populations, 1970–80*

Metropolitan Area	Whites		Blacks	
	1970	1980	1970	1980
New York	26.9	31.4	7.1	8.2
Chicago	62.2	72.8	10.0	15.8
Philadelphia	67.6	73.5	21.4	26.7
Detroit	77.3	87.8	13.1	15.1

Source: Massey and Denton (1988), pp. 598–600.

over 5 times (5.25) that of blacks (with percent differences of 10.5 for blacks vs. 2.0 for blacks).

The spatial mismatch hypothesis posits that these trends — rapid job growth in the suburbs, slow or negative job growth in the central city, increasing minority representation in the city, and relatively slow black suburbanization — combine to limit minorities' access to the labor market. Whereas these aggregate trends appear quite clearly in the data, it is possible (some would say plausible) that they could be accounted for by other factors (e.g., selective migration; see below), which might lead us to very different conclusions about both the significance of spatial mismatch and the kinds of policies that might be designed to ameliorate minority labor market disadvantages. I now turn to a brief review of the scholarly research literature that attempts to untangle these confounding factors.

There have been three recent, comprehensive reviews of the large empirical literature on the spatial mismatch hypothesis. Two of these (Jencks and Mayer 1990; Holzer 1991) have concluded that while evidence for the hypothesis has been mixed through the 1960s and 1970s, there is better and increasing evidence for the hypothesis in the 1980s. The third review, by Kain himself (Kain 1992), argues that the evidence for spatial mismatch has been compelling all along, and that studies showing no effects are based on poor data, faulty methods, or both. In this long article, Kain (1992) specifically addresses the Jencks and Mayer (1990) and Holzer (1991) reviews, and, study by study, takes issue with their interpretation of the evidence in this area.

Although it would be interesting to get Holzer, Jencks, Kain, and Mayer in the same room to hash out the disagreements in their readings of the literature, it is safe to conclude that they are converging on an interpretation that suggests that spatial mismatch has significant impacts on minority employment. Christopher Jencks, the coauthor of the most cautious of the reviews in terms of policy prescriptions,[4] has continued to follow the research in this area that has come out after his 1990 review. He has noted that recent papers by Ihlanfeldt and Sjoquist (1990) and Zax (1991) strongly support the spatial mismatch hypothesis.[5] Similarly, in a study Holzer coauthored with Ihlanfeldt and Sjoquist (Holzer, Ihlanfeldt, and Sjoquest 1994) after the publication of Holzer's (1991) review, he finds empirical support for the spatial mismatch hypothesis using a national sample of youth. Kain (1992) agrees with both Jencks and Holzer that Ihlanfeldt and Sjoquist's and Zax and Kain's (1991) work is among the most robust in the area.[6]

Since these recent works appear to be the basis of this emerging consensus, it is important to understand what it is about them that is so compelling. I will devote the rest of this section to explaining why they are so important for adjudicating the spatial mismatch hypothesis.

An important problem that has plagued most of the research on spatial mismatch is the issue of selective migration. While it is certainly true that jobs have been moving from the central business districts to the suburbs of major cities (Kasarda 1985, 1988, 1989), so too have people, including African Americans. Therefore, as Jencks and Mayer (1990), Holzer (1991), and Ihlanfeldt (1992) all point out, the divergence in inner-city and suburban black employment rates might be due to selective migration of more employable African Americans to the suburbs. Jencks and Mayer (1990, p. 220) cite the failure to take into account selective migration as "the single most important reason why we have learned so little about this subject in the two decades since Kain first advanced the spatial mismatch hypothesis."

The main way of dealing with selective migration in most research on spatial mismatch is to introduce controls for characteristics that might explain differences between inner-city and suburban residents. The problem, however, is that most studies have had only sparse controls, so it is impossible to be certain that all the relevant variables have been controlled. Therefore, uncertainty overshadows even those studies that have shown the strongest spatial mismatch effects. Of particular concern are variables that might determine suburban residence *independent* of the relatively well measured socioeconomic factors that are sometimes measured in these studies. The implication of not controlling these factors is to *overestimate* the effect of spatial mismatch by attributing unmeasured suburban versus inner-city differences among blacks to spatial mismatch. But there is also a danger of *underestimating* spatial mismatch effects. Good jobs are a cause of suburban residence, and high-income people tend to commute farther because they can afford to do so. Since the hypothesis is that mismatched workers will tend to commute farther than nonmismatched workers, we have the problem that commuting (or, more generally, job accessibility) will be highest for high-income suburban residents, as well as for low-income inner-city residents. This will lead spatial mismatch effects to be downwardly biased.

The recent work of Ihlanfeldt (Ihlanfeldt 1988, 1992; Ihlanfeldt and Sjoquist 1990, 1991) attempts to minimize both kinds of biases. First, these studies are unusual in the number of variables that they are able to include as controls for background differences between central city and suburban minorities. Second, they also address the issues of the simultaneity of location and job status by focusing on youth because location is less likely to be selected for young people just starting out in the labor market.[7]

Another strategy for dealing with the issue of selective migration is to employ longitudinal data on workers. Using longitudinal data would allow us to get a better grasp of two issues. First, panel data can be used to improve controls by eliminating the influence of fixed, unmeasured characteristics. Second, longitudinal data would help us to examine the direction of causality between employment and residence. Extant empirical work on this question has shown evidence that such workplace and residential location decisions are made jointly (Quigley 1985; Waddell 1993) so that it is usually not possible to draw the arrow of causality in only one direction. However, in this, and a few other studies of rather special circumstances (see below), it is possible to use longitudinal data to determine which way causality runs. In Holzer's (1991, pp. 118–19) words, we can see "whether good jobs precede residential changes or whether such changes lead to improved employment."

To my knowledge, the only longitudinal study to have addressed the spatial mismatch hypothesis has been a study of a firm relocation from the central city to the suburbs (Zax 1989, 1990; Zax and Kain 1991). This research treats the firm's move as an exogenous bump to the labor market, and then compares data on individuals' commuting behavior and household relocation before and after the move.[8] Because it is the firm that is moving, any minority disemployment that results will not be due to selective migration.

The Zax study examined 8 years of employment records (from 1971 to 1978), including the records for new hires, for an 800-person firm in the service industry located in Detroit's central business district (Zax 1989, 1990; Zax and Kain 1991). During the fourth year, the firm moved to the suburban ring, near Detroit's border with Dearborn. The study then looked at the effects of the relocation on workers' moves, quits, and commuting adjustments. While this study is limited in some important ways (see Fernandez 1994), the results showed strong evidence that residential segregation constrained blacks' options in adjusting to the relocation of the firm. While all workers make trade-offs between income and commuting (in general, workers are willing to commute farther for better-paying jobs), African-American workers were not as free to make the trade-off as were white workers. This is shown in the much stronger relationship between commuting and incomes for whites than for blacks. African Americans were being forced to commute to jobs to which whites would not commute. In addition to commuting, changing residence, and quitting are also readjustment mechanisms for spatial mismatch, and we would also expect these to be traded off with one another. Again, blacks were much more constrained than whites in using these options for resolving the spatial disruption that the firm's relocation had imposed. Moves and quits were directly substitutable reactions to the relocation for whites, but this was not the case for African Americans.

In sum, researchers in this area have mounted a sustained and multi-faceted response to the main source of equivocation on the question of spatial mismatch — the issue of selective migration. In my judgment, this triangulated strategy has paid off. In light of these recent studies, it is very difficult to argue that spatial mismatch effects are *in general* a simple artifact of selective migration.

What Do We Still Need to Know?

Throughout the 30-year period of scholarly debate on the spatial mismatch hypothesis, researchers have not been shy about offering policy prescriptions. However, before turning to consider what the options are, I think it is important to flag what it is we do *not* know. Despite the progress that has been made in the research in this area, some important puzzles remain to be solved, and we need to keep them in mind when thinking about policy prescriptions.

As I see it, even if we accept that spatial mismatch between residences and workplaces has placed extra burdens on minorities, there is the question of what is behind the mismatch. *Why* space matters is hard to understand if we do not know what is motivating employers to move to the suburbs. If we assume that most firms move to the suburbs to avoid minorities for reasons of taste, then space would have to be seen as a tool to achieve this goal. Contrast this situation with one where we knew that firms locate in the suburbs because they want to exploit the selectivity of black migrants to the suburbs. (In fact, it is common for employers to cite "workforce quality" as a reason for moving to the suburbs.) Here, too, space is being used as a tool, but to a very different end. In this case, space would matter because it is being used as a screening device. A third scenario is that the reasons for metropolitan decentralization of employment are largely technologically driven and are not motivated by workforce considerations to any great extent. In this view, firms are simply seeking lower land prices and responding to decades of infrastructural changes (in the form of better highways and transportation networks), which makes operating out of a suburban location less costly.

While these examples do not exhaust the possibilities, they are useful to consider. If space is being used as a tool, I, for one, would be reluctant to talk about the effect of space *independent* of other factors. Obviously, the policy implications of these various scenarios are dramatically different. In the first case, policies that aim to give inner-city workers better access to suburban jobs by improving transportation (see below) would be a waste of time and money. So too are policies that try to break down residential segregation in the suburbs. Those blacks who do overcome spatial barriers will still not be hired. Under the second set of circumstances, transportation policies to make the suburbs more accessible to inner-city African Americans would also be undermined at the hiring stage. But housing-related policies would be much more likely to be effective. If the third scenario were the dominant one, then both transportation and housing solutions might be viable.

We need more information on the demand side of the labor market in order to fashion policy responses to these scenarios. If we assume conservatively that all three scenarios are operating simultaneously, then we need research that is designed to separate the likely impacts of these different motivations for metropolitan decentralization. Such research has been nonexistent. Perhaps not surprising in light of the fact that I see a need for this work, this is where I have chosen to concentrate my research efforts. I am currently engaged in a "best-case" study of a firm relocation that is designed to gauge the impact of "technological" motivations for metropolitan decentralization (Fernandez 1994).

Policies for Ameliorating the Effects of Spatial Mismatch

What, then, are the policy options in this area? By my reading, three kinds of policy suggestions have recurred over the past 30 years. The first set of policies suggests creating incentives for employers to locate jobs in the central cities. The second set focuses on the housing market and on opening up the suburbs to minorities. The third set increases minorities' access to suburban jobs by designing transportation policies to facilitate the reverse commuting of minorities, for example, by means of vanpools. All three of these options have strong proponents as well as detractors. I will close this essay by pointing to what I see as the costs and benefits of pursuing these various options in light of what we know, and do not know, about spatial mismatch.

The proposal to infuse poor central city areas with resources has gone under a number of rubrics. Downs (1968) calls this the "enrichment" strategy; Kain and Persky (1969) refer to this as "ghetto gilding." While the latest incarnation of this policy is the idea of "enterprise" zones, these ideas go back to the area redevelopment projects that emerged in the mid-1950s. During the post–Korean War recession, the federal government focused attention on areas that were characterized by abnormally high unemployment. As the recession ended and there was a general economic recovery, many of these areas remained "substantial labor surplus areas." As the numbers of these areas began to spread during the late 1950s, calls for government action increased. Several failed congressional bills during the 1950s, and the election of 1960, resulted in the Area Redevelopment Act of 1961. The act established the Area Redevelopment Administration (ARA) under the U.S. Department of Commerce. Throughout the 1960s, ARA activities were focused on public works projects in rural areas, such as Appalachia, and inner cities, such as Philadelphia and Oakland. During the 1970s, the ARA shifted attention to redevelop the downtowns of major metropolitan areas. While there were some notable successes in a few cities where federal funds were managed by state and local governments and there was active participation by private interests, conditions in the ghettos on the edges of the downtowns appeared to worsen. Few businesses located in the ghettos, despite vacant land and surplus labor, citing fear of crime, redlining by banks, and a poorly educated workforce (Hansen 1991).

While it remains politically attractive today to advocate that jobs be brought to the central cities,[9] current opponents of this strategy cite costs as the major reason for avoiding this approach. For at least 30 years, real estate and tax policies, and transportation infrastructure, have been designed to facilitate the decentralization of employment. Designing incentives for employers to buck these trends and locate in poverty areas is likely to involve a huge investment of resources (Hansen 1991). In addition to cost considerations, Kain and Persky (1969) opposed "ghetto gilding" because it would serve to increase the segregation of ghetto residents, to the further growth of ghettos, and to a worsening of other ghetto-related problems.

I think it would be swimming upstream to rely exclusively on an enrichment strategy for poverty areas. The forces arrayed to decentralize employment are simply too great to be overcome without great costs. However, I think it is important to note that if we were to muster these resources, there is less reason to be concerned that such problems would exacerbate ghetto problems today than when Kain and Persky (1969) first expressed their opposition to this strategy. Kain and Persky (1969) worried that an infusion of resources into ghetto areas might lead to increased in-migration of blacks from the South, diluting the effect of job creation efforts in poor urban areas. However, net migration of African Americans is now from the North to the South, and while new resources might slow the rate at which blacks leave the North, it is not likely that the trend will reverse. While new resources invested in ghetto areas would tend to reinforce the racial segregation of blacks, there is no reason to believe that additional resources would *worsen* the plight of segregated ghetto residents. In fact, segregation would serve to focus the impact of new jobs on precisely those who are in the segregated area, just as the effect of a secular rise in the poverty rate under segregated conditions concentrates poverty among those who are segregated (Massey and Denton 1993).[10]

A second major approach to ameliorating the impact of spatial mismatch takes the housing market as its point of departure. The "dispersal strategy" (Kain and Persky 1969; Downs 1973) suggests facilitating the movement of people out of central city poverty areas closer to jobs located in suburban areas. Advocates of this approach recommend a range of options, from simply enforcing the existing fair housing laws (Massey and Denton 1993), to Section 8 subsidies to encourage suburban residence (as in the Gautreaux housing program; see Rosenbaum and Popkin 1991), to locating scattered-site public housing in the suburbs.

The research on spatial mismatch suggests two crucial issues to consider when thinking about dispersal strategies. First, in order to lessen the spatial mismatch between people and jobs, it is not enough to simply move people to the suburbs; *which* suburb matters a lot. In the context of the Chicago metropolitan area, black suburbanization has been growing in the south and southwest suburbs, but the major area of job growth has been the northwest corridor. Because Chicago's transportation network has been designed on a hub-and-spoke pattern, residents of these areas are even more poorly placed to gain access to the new centers of job growth. Irrespective of the means of accomplishing this, in order for dispersal strategies to work, central city residents of poverty areas will need to gain access to the suburbs where jobs are growing in order to improve the situation.

This leads to a second consideration, which unfortunately spatial mismatch research has not yet resolved. Simply put, if dispersal strategies were to be implemented in such a way that minorities could gain access to the northwest corridor, there is still the question of whether employers located there would actually hire minorities. If the suburban location of jobs were largely to be due to the technological reasons cited above, then locating minorities' residences closer to the jobs will help to solve the problem. However, if suburban location is being used to avoid minorities, then moving minorities closer to these employers will not work.

My sense is that some employers located in the northwest corridor would hire minorities. I say this because some employers are participating in programs to bring workers out to the northwest, and that the chronic labor shortages reported in the area have a way of opening up employers to new possibilities. However, I do not have a sense of whether such employers would dominate the local labor market.

It is important to realize that the political barriers to implementing dispersal strategies on a large scale are formidable. Almost by definition, dispersal strategies are likely to involve the support of multiple municipalities, and local opposition to proposed scattered-site public housing has been fierce. And support for such strategies within minority communities is also limited. Whatever else dispersal might do, it dilutes the hard-won political base of support for minority politicians and elected officials and exposes their constituents to rule by distrusted outsiders.[11] Moreover, since this strategy often has a secondary goal of moving the central city poor to white suburban areas in small numbers so as not to trigger a "white-flight" response on the part of whites, a dispersal strategy often asks minorities to "fly without a net," that is, to move to the suburbs without the safety in numbers of their co-ethnics. There is poignant evidence in Rosenbaum's studies of the Gautreaux housing program of this kind of burden; using national data, Goodman and Streitwieser (1983) provide evidence that African Americans are loath to move to the suburbs.

The last set of policy proposals seeks to increase minorities' access to suburban jobs by designing transportation policies that help minorities to reverse-commute from the city to suburban jobs. The most recent proponent of this strategy is Hughes,[12] but similar transportation-related proposals were put forth by Kain and Persky (1969). In essence, this approach to solving spatial mismatch problems devises ways for minorities to absorb the spatial disruption of metropolitan decentralization by means of commuting, by subsidizing commutes, by improving public transportation, or by supporting private vanpools.

While using transportation as the means of bridging the spatial gap between minority residences and jobs avoids many of the sticky political problems inherent in the other approaches, it has a number of limitations. First, it imposes the entire burden of commuting on minorities. Second, it increases the premium for car ownership, a dimension along which minorities have always lagged behind. Third, it increases traffic congestion in the suburbs — the very areas least well prepared to deal with increased traffic loads (Downs 1992). Fourth, given the social geography of the Chicago area, black suburban residents are likely to experience extra burdens in such a strategy. While the Regional Transportation Authority is working on improving suburb-to-suburb transportation, it is unclear how high linking the south and southwest suburbs with the northwest suburbs is on their list of priorities.[13] Finally, by accepting a large spatial gap between minorities' jobs and residences, transportation policies are likely to reinforce informational gaps between minority job seekers and employers.

While I think all three approaches have their strengths and weaknesses, at least in terms of what we know about spatial mismatch, there is nothing preventing us from pursuing a careful mix of all three approaches. I will close by briefly outlining one such mix, which I think is not contraindicated by the scholarly evidence on spatial mismatch.

I agree with Kain (1992) that solutions in this area have to start with housing policy. Nothing in my reading of the scholarly literature on spatial mismatch would lead me to argue against policies that expand housing opportunities for minorities. There is even reason to think that such expanded opportunities will help chip away at the problems of extreme segregation in the suburbs. As Kain (1992, p. 442) has argued,

> There has been some improvement in the extent and severity of housing market discrimination. The most significant change is that suburban communities with *no* Afro-American residents are much less common than in the past . . . this is a very important change. . . . It is much easier to prevent or discourage a single Afro-American household from moving into a community with *no* Afro-American residents than it is to monitor and limit the number of black households that move into a community that has a small number of Afro-American residents.

Minorities who want to move to the suburbs should be supported in those efforts. Vigorous enforcement of existing fair housing statutes is certainly the place to start.

Next, my reading of the scholarly evidence on spatial mismatch suggests that transportation strategies will work — in the sense of increasing minority employment and wages — if two potentially serious problems can be overcome. First, information gaps associated with increased distance must be overcome in some way. Job banks with sophisticated information systems or the private or public employment agency can fill this void. Second, ways must be found to subsidize minorities in their commutes. There is precedent in using tax policies to have firms encourage carpooling for pollution abatement, although these policies have shown mixed results at best. Creative solutions to this problem have been forthcoming. Some private firms located in the northwest corridor do pay for at least part of the cost of vanpools, and temporary employment agencies often include transportation as part of their services. While not a panacea, mobility strategies might also serve to reinforce the dispersal strategy by providing a first exposure for minorities to suburban areas.

Finally, while I am more worried about the cost-effectiveness of place-based efforts to attract jobs to the central city (e.g., enterprise zones), I cannot argue against the infusion of resources to improve key services in the central city, if only to provide residents with their fair share. Deteriorating schools will undo whatever good might be done by increased access to suburban jobs. If we are asking minorities to cast their fate in the labor market with the greater metropolitan area by supporting mobility strategies to break down the relationship between place and jobs, so too must we be willing to break the place-based formulas for school funding. If we endorse "aspatial" employment relations, we must also endorse "aspatial" citizenship rights.

NOTES

1. See Kasarda (1989) for details of the job classification scheme used here.

2. The only other example of a metro area net gain in these job categories is Detroit. There the net growth in clerical and sales jobs in the suburbs outpaced the central city job losses in clerical and sales jobs.

3. Data for Hispanics in this context are not readily accessible due to changes in the census definitions of Hispanics.

4. To quote their policy implications: "Taken together, these findings tell a very mixed story. They provide no direct support for the hypothesis that residential segregation affects the aggregate level of demand for black workers. They provide some support for the idea that job proximity increases the supply of black workers, but the support is so mixed that no prudent policy analyst should rely on it" (Jencks and Mayer 1990, pp. 218–19).

5. Christopher Jencks, personal communication with author, 1993.

6. Jencks and Mayer (1990) only became aware of Zax's work after their review was in press. Holzer (1991) mentions an unpublished paper by Zax and Kain, but does not review the strengths and weaknesses of the design.

7. It is important to note that the problem of selective migration also manifests itself in spatial studies of wages, but in a more subtle way. As Kain (1992) has cautioned, the theoretical predictions for wages involve countervailing tendencies, which are more difficult to evaluate empirically. Urban models predict that wages (corrected for human capital characteristics) will decrease with distance from the center of the city (e.g., Mills and Hamilton 1989), but the spatial mismatch argument posits that the oversupply of minorities in the central city will lead to low wages in the central city as well. This would lead to a lack of wage differences for minorities between the suburbs and the central cities; this has prompted some observers (e.g., Danziger and Weinstein 1976) to argue that minorities are not likely to be motivated to commute by higher suburban wages. Kain's (1992) response to this is to point out that such wage comparisons are, by definition, based on people who already have a job. A high local unemployment rate in the central city might lead minorities to commute great distances to the suburbs even if the wages paid at the suburban jobs are no higher than jobs in the central city. Consequently, comparing wage or commuting alone, without considering the employment/unemployment trade-off, can be misleading. Although research on wages is more limited, Ihlanfeldt and Sjoquist (1989) explicitly address these trade-offs and show results that are supportive of spatial mismatch effects.

8. Another approach is to study household relocation as an exogenous bump to the housing market, looking for responses in commuting and on the labor market. The trick is to find cases where household relocations are truly exogenous and occur without respect to where people work. I have come across two such examples, although one does not deal with race comparisons in the United States. Kasper (1973, 1983) collected data on workers relocated by the Glasgow Housing Commission (GHC) from council (public) housing that was being torn down. The GHC did not take into account the location of workers' jobs when relocating these families. His findings showed that men responded very well to the shock of household relocation, but that because women were tied to a more local labor market, they had a much harder time adjusting their employment to the new housing market. The second case is more relevant for our purposes. Rosenbaum and Popkin (1991) use an experimental design to compare the employment and earnings of low-income black females who move to the suburbs around Chicago with a comparable group that moves within the city. They found that women who move to the suburbs are significantly more likely to be employed after the move.

9. Most recently, enterprise zones were a centerpiece of President George Bush's urban policy, but Democrats embraced versions of this plan during the War on Poverty (see, e.g., Kennedy 1968).

10. I am making two assumptions in this analysis. First, while net migration for blacks is now from the North to the South, the cities are hosts to new immigrants who tend to be disproportionately Hispanic. It is possible that inner-city job creation efforts might be swamped with additional Hispanic immigrants. However, the spatial barriers which other minorities face in the housing market are considerably less than those which African Americans face. Therefore, I am assuming that this less severe pattern of housing segregation would continue even after the infusion of new resources. A second assumption is that segregation per se does not lead

to any "additional round" or interaction effects with other variables that might affect the life chances of segregated blacks. In other words, I am assuming that there are no benefits to African Americans coming into contact with white people that could not be substituted for by the infusion of resources into the area by an enrichment strategy. To the degree that this is wrong, then the increase in segregation associated with enrichment itself might introduce additional problems I have not anticipated here.

11. I read the very real opposition to closing Cabrini Green among its residents as indicative of this.

12. Hughes (1991a, 1991b) includes other policy suggestions such as job training and job information systems, but the core of his "mobility" strategy is pithily described in the title of his op-ed piece, "Take the Poor to Where the Jobs Are" (Hughes 1992).

13. To my knowledge, the proposed suburb-to-suburb railway is designed to link the far western suburbs (e.g., Aurora) with the northwest suburbs (e.g., Hoffman Estates).

REFERENCES

Danziger, Sheldon, and Michael Weinstein. 1976. "Employment Location and Wage Rates of Poverty Area Residents." *Journal of Urban Economics* 3:127–45.

Downs, Anthony. 1968. "Alternative Futures for the American Ghetto." *Daedalus* 97(4)(Fall):1331–78.

———. 1973. *Opening Up the Suburbs*. New Haven, Conn.: Yale University Press.

———. 1992. *Stuck in Traffic: Coping with Peak-Hour Traffic Congestion*. Washington, D.C.: Brookings Institution.

Fernandez, Roberto M. 1994. "Race, Space, and Job Accessibility: Evidence from a Plant Relocation." *Economic Geography* 70:1–27.

Goodman, John L., and Mary L. Streitwieser. 1983. "Explaining Racial Differences: A Study of City-to-Suburb Residential Mobility." *Urban Affairs Quarterly* 18:301–25.

Hansen, Susan, 1991. "Comparing Enterprise Zones to Other Economic Development Techniques." In *Enterprise Zones: New Directions in Economic Development*, edited by Roy E. Green, pp. 7–26. Newbury Park, Calif.: Sage Publications.

Holzer, Harry J. 1991. "The Spatial Mismatch Hypothesis: What Has the Evidence Shown?" *Urban Studies* 28(1):105–22.

Holzer, Harry J.; Keith R. Ihlanfeldt; and David L. Sjoquist. 1994. "Work, Search, and Travel among White and Black Youth." *Journal of Urban Economics* 35:320–45.

Hughes, Mark Alan. 1991a. "Emerging Settlement Patterns: Implications for Antipoverty Strategy." Paper presented at the annual meeting of the American Association for the Advancement of Science, Washington, D.C., February.

———. 1991b. "Employment Decentralization and Accessibility: A Strategy for Stimulating Regional Mobility." *Journal of the American Planning Association* 57(3)(Summer):288–98.

———. 1992. "Take the Poor to Where the Jobs Are." *Chicago Tribune*, May 5.

Ihlanfeldt, Keith R. 1988. "Intra-Metropolitan Variation in Earnings and Labor Market Discrimination: An Econometric Analysis of the Atlanta Labor Market." *Southern Economic Journal* 55(1)(July):123–40.

———. 1992. *Job Accessibility and the Employment and School Enrollment of Teenagers.* Kalamazoo, Mich.: W. E. Upjohn Institute for Employment Research.

Ihlanfeldt, Keith R., and David L. Sjoquist. 1989. "The Impact of Job Decentralization on the Economic Welfare of Central City Blacks." *Journal of Urban Economics* 26:110–30.

———. 1990. "Job Accessibility and Racial Differences in Youth Employment Rates." *American Economic Review* 80(March):267–76.

———. 1991. "The Effect of Job Access on Black Youth Employment: A Cross-Sectional Analysis." *Urban Studies* 28:255–65.

Jencks, Christopher S., and Susan E. Mayer. 1990. "Residential Segregation: Job Proximity, and Black Job Opportunities." In *Inner-City Poverty in the United States,* edited by Laurence E. Lynn, Jr., and Michael G. H. McGeary, pp. 187–222. Washington, D.C.: National Academy Press.

Kain, John F. 1964. "The Effect of the Ghetto on the Distribution and Level of Nonwhite Employment in Urban Areas." *Proceedings of the Social Statistics Section of the American Statistical Association,* pp. 260–69.

———. 1968. "Housing Segregation, Negro Employment, and Metropolitan Decentralization." *Quarterly Journal of Economics* 82(2)(May):175–97.

———. 1992. "The Spatial Mismatch Hypothesis: Three Decades Later." *Housing Policy Debate* 2:371–460.

Kain, John F., and J. J. Persky. 1969. "Alternatives to the 'Gilded Ghetto.'" *Public Interest* 14:77–91.

Kasarda, John D. 1985. "Urban Change and Minority Opportunities." In *The New Urban Reality,* edited by Paul E. Peterson, pp. 33–67. Washington, D.C.: Brookings Institution.

———. 1988. "Jobs, Migration, and Emerging Urban Mismatches." In *Urban Change and Poverty,* edited by Laurence E. Lynn, Jr., and Michael G. H. McGeary, pp. 148–98. Washington, D.C.: National Academy Press.

———. 1989. "Urban Industrial Transition and the Underclass." *Annals of the American Academy of Political and Social Sciences* 501(January):26–47.

Kasper, Hirschel. 1973. "Measuring the Labour Market Costs of Housing Dislocation." *Scottish Journal of Political Economy* 20(2)(June):85–106.

———. 1983. "Toward Estimating the Incidence of Journey-to-Work Costs." *Urban Studies* 20:197–208.

Kennedy, Robert F. 1968. "The Urban Ghetto and Negro Job Problems: A Diagnosis and a Proposed Plan of Action." In *Negroes and Jobs,* edited by Louis A. Ferman, Joyce L. Kornbluh, and J. A. Miller, pp. 256–71. Ann Arbor: University of Michigan Press.

Massey, Douglas, and Nancy Denton. 1988. "Suburbanization and Segregation in U.S. Metropolitan Areas." *American Journal of Sociology* 94:598–600.

———. 1993. *American Apartheid: Segregation and the Making of the Underclass.* Cambridge, Mass.: Harvard University Press.

Mills, Edwin S., and Bruce W. Hamilton. 1989. *Urban Economics.* 4th ed. Glenview, Ill.: Scott, Foresman.

Quigley, John M. 1985. "Consumer Choice of Dwelling, Neighborhood and Public Services." *Regional Science and Urban Economics* 15:41–63.

Rosenbaum, James E., and Susan J. Popkin. 1991. "Employment and Earnings of Low-Income Blacks Who Move to the Suburbs." In *The Urban Underclass,* edited by Christopher Jencks and Paul E. Peterson, pp. 342–56. Washington, D.C.: Brookings Institution.

Waddell, Paul. 1993. "Exogenous Workplace Choice in Residential Location Models: Is the Assumption Valid?" *Geographical Analysis* 25:65–82.

Wilson, William Julius. 1987. *The Truly Disadvantagd: The Inner City, the Underclass, and Public Policy.* Chicago: University of Chicago Press.

Zax, Jeffrey S. 1989. "Quits and Race." *Journal of Human Resources* 24:469–93.

———. 1990. "Race and Commutes." *Journal of Urban Economics* 28:336–48.

———. 1991. "Compensation for Commutes in Labor and Housing Markets." *Journal of Urban Economics* 30:192–207.

Zax, Jeffrey S., and John F. Kain. 1991. "Commutes, Quits and Moves." *Journal of Urban Economics* 29:1–13.

James E. Rosenbaum

Schools and the World of Work

American youth have great problems entering work, they experience frequent unemployment, and their jobs rarely offer advancement opportunity. The unemployment rate among 18–19-year-olds is 2–3 times that for adults. Even during the relative prosperity of the late 1980s, the rate never fell below 15 percent, and in the last few years it has been around 20 percent (U.S. Bureau of Labor Statistics 1994). Moreover, even those who get jobs have difficulty keeping them. The average high school graduate who did not pursue further education held six different jobs, and experienced more than four spells of unemployment in the first decade after high school (Veum and Weiss 1993). Since poor early work experiences account for a large part of lower earnings in later career, these early experiences can have a lasting detrimental impact (Lynch 1989; D'Amico and Maxwell 1990).

Employers also have problems finding youth qualified for their jobs. Employers often complain about high school graduates' weak skills in math and English, their poor work habits, and their instability as employees (NAS 1984; U.S. Census Bureau 1995). Moreover, employers' problems could get a lot worse. Employers are used to selecting from a large supply of applicants, but over the past 2 decades the youth cohort has been contracting while youths' academic skills have not increased (NAEP 1990). Employers are having difficulty getting qualified workers now, and these problems will increase as the economy grows. Of course, employers often prepare for potential supply disruptions, so they can begin to take steps to prepare for a serious disruption in the supply of skilled employees.

There has been a great deal of concern about these issues. Many types

This essay is based on research conducted with Amy Binder, Stephanie Jones, Takehiko Kariya, Melinda Krei, Shazia Miller, Ginny Mills, Karen Nelson, and Kevin Roy. Some of the ideas in this essay were developed in separate papers written in collaboration with them. I am indebted to the Spencer Foundation, the Pew Charitable Trusts, the W. T. Grant Foundation, and Northwestern's Center for Urban Affairs and Policy Research for support of this research. Of course, the ideas presented here do not represent their views.

of programs have tried to help youth enter work, and a great deal of research has studied these various approaches. Unfortunately, most of these efforts have not had promising results. Vocational programs have tried to improve job training in schools, and co-op programs have tried to give students school-supervised work experience. These programs are occurring on a large scale, yet, as I shall show, the results are not encouraging.

On the other side of the labor market, large-scale job-training programs have tried to help unemployed youth, and youth apprenticeships have tried to provide training in workplaces. However, as I shall note, the former programs have had no effect or even negative effects, while the latter are extremely expensive and unlikely to serve large numbers of youth in the United States.

Since both of these approaches have been extensively reviewed elsewhere (Osterman 1980, 1988; NAS 1984; Parcel 1987; Hamilton 1989; NCEE 1990; Bailey and Merrit 1993; Ray and Mickelson 1993; Stern et al. 1994a; Rosenbaum 1996) and since the results are not very promising, I will not conduct a lengthy recap of those findings here. After conducting a brief review of some of the research on school-based and work-based approaches, I shall devote most of this esssay to a third approach, which has been largely neglected until recently.

Rather than trying to improve schools or workplaces, this third approach seeks to improve the transition itself. I find examples of this approach most clearly in Japan, where high schools have direct semiformal contacts with employers for placing students in jobs. Moreover, departing from most accounts of the German system, which have focused solely on apprenticeships, I describe the linkages between schools and apprenticeships in Germany as having a distinctive influence on improving youths' ease of work entry.

The school-work relationships in both Japan and Germany have three underlying conditions that encourage the effectiveness of the linkage: (1) Employers value students' academic skills and work habits, and they are willing to take actions to get them. (2) Work-bound students exert effort because their school performance is relevant to their future careers. (3) Teachers have authority to give students access to desirable jobs and to give employers dependable student evaluations.

I propose that these three attributes may be preconditions for effective school-employer linkages, and this essay presents studies exploring to what extent these conditions exist in the United States. It describes how Germany and Japan accomplish the same conditions by very different means, and it presents recent research findings indicating that these conditions occur in the United States, albeit in fragmentary and sporadic ways. I propose policies that could encourage fuller implementation of these conditions, and I consider what problems arise from the unsystematic character of the U.S. approach.

Research on School-Based and Work-Based Programs

There are three main approaches to improving the school-to-work transition: school-based, employer-based, and linkage approaches. School-based programs focus on school improvements to prepare students for the workforce. Vocational education is the most common way to aid work entry. Meyer and Wise (1982) found that vocational training in high school has no effect on subsequent employment or wage rates. However, research on the National Longitudinal Survey of Youth (NLSY) sample using school transcript data (as opposed to student self-reports) found that vocational education increased earnings for women, but not for men (Rumberger and Daymont 1984). One of the most careful reviews of this literature concluded that vocational education has positive effects on earnings if students are able to get "skill-relevant jobs," that is, jobs in the area they received training (Grasso and Shea 1979). Unfortunately, many youth fail to get skill-relevant jobs, and the causes for this are unstudied.

Co-op programs are another common school-based effort for aiding work entry. Co-op programs give work exposure to a wide range of students (about 8 percent of high school juniors and seniors). Studies of its effects have not found positive economic outcomes. Analyses of the NLSY found that school-supervised job (co-op) programs did not increase earning or lower unemployment in the first few years after graduation (Lewis et al. 1983). Other studies find mixed effects (Bishop, Blakemore, and Low 1985). Students express high satisfaction with co-op programs, but research indicates that co-op experiences with one employer are often not recognized by other employers (Stern et al. 1994a). This suggests that additional reforms must accompany co-op programs, such as certification or skill tests (Stern et al. 1994a).

Several recent reforms are possibly more promising. Career academies integrate academic subjects with career themes (Stern 1992). School-based enterprises (SBE) operate businesses inside schools to teach academic and vocational skills (Stern et al. 1994b). Simulated work tasks create classroom role-playing exercises to teach academic skills (Berryman 1992). Some encouraging results have been reported. However, randomization is rare in all these experiments, so true effects are hard to assess. Moreover, since these programs are relatively new, little is known about long-term outcomes.

Work-based reforms try to improve youth skills in job-training programs or in workplaces. Many federal initiatives have tried job-training programs to improve youths' skills after they have left high school. These programs have had little success (Basi and Ashenfelter 1986). As one research review concluded, "So far, there does not appear to have been any federally supported program for out-of-school youth that has been found . . . to produce significant gains in earnings" (Stern et al. 1994). The recent random assignment evaluations of the Job Training and Partnership Act are illustrative. They find no effects in some comparisons, and negative effects in others (Cave and Doolittle 1991; Bloom et al. 1992*a*). The Job Corps program, a particularly expensive residential training program, is one of the few programs to show some positive effects on employment and earnings, although it did so during the strong labor market of the late 1970s (Betsey et al. 1985). However, JOBSTART, which built upon the Job Corps approach, did not lead to earnings gains (Cave and Doolittle 1991). Similarly, the Youth Incentive Entitlement Pilot Projects did not improve school completion, and though it led to small earnings gains ($10 per week), youth unemployment remained extremely high — 60 percent among black youths (Farkas et al. 1984).

The most discouraging findings in these studies are the negative effects, that is, that youth getting training sometimes have worse employment outcomes than control group youth who got no services. Some have speculated that these training programs actually create stigmatic labels to their participants (Lerman 1994), and the general conclusion is that job-training programs have been oversold (Heckman 1994). Small-scale local programs have been initiated by community centers, local clubs, business groups, and charitable organizations, but these programs are rarely systematically evaluated. While new research may produce more hopeful results, at present, the most promising approach would be to focus on preparing youth while they are still in school.

The most impressive work-based approach is for youth apprenticeships. The German apprenticeship model, which integrates school with early job training, has been seen as a promising approach, and it has had great success in Germany. But German apprenticeships are built on a 500-year tradition, which the United States will not build in a few years. In addition, its high costs and reliance on employer-provided training have limited the number and size of programs. Currently, fewer than 5,000 youth are in such programs across the United States (GAO 1991). While youth apprenticeships offer great promise, they will not easily be scaled up to serve large numbers of youth in the near future (Witte and Kalleberg 1994).

While most proposals for improving the school-to-work transition focus on reforms in schools or in workplaces, a third approach seeks to improve the transition itself. Many problems arise in the school-to-work transition; however, since transitions occur between institutions, it is not easy to see where to make changes. We can get a much clearer view of the U.S. transition by seeing how school-to-work transition operates in a different society. Japan provides a model of a radically different approach, and it suggests ideas of how to improve the transition in the United States.

If the German apprenticeship system is the usual standard for an effective system, the Japanese system is as good or better in many respects. Indeed, concerned that their system is providing narrow training, German researchers are studying the Japanese system for directions for reform. The Japanese system also requires far less expense and less infrastructure to implement. In Japan, employers have long-term hiring relationships with certain high schools; these linkages are conditional on teachers giving employers dependable evaluations of students' academic achievement and on employers offering good jobs to the schools' better work-bound students. The threat of employers' terminating the linkage discourages teachers from inflating evaluations or departing from expected criteria. In turn, employers continue offering good jobs to a school to keep their access to the school's best students. Japan's long-term linkages between high schools and employers give employers good information about students' skills and work habits, give teachers authority over work-bound students, and give students a reason to exert effort in school.

While no one wants the United States to imitate the Japanese system exactly, the Japanese system has many desirable features that would be useful to incorporate. It provides a clear way for employers to get good workers, for students to gain good academic skills and work habits, and for teachers to have authority. It is inexpensive, easy to implement, and can be readily scaled up. It uses existing schools and does not require new bureaucracies, only new relationships between teachers and employers. It does not require extraordinary actions; it only requires a clearly organized linkage between schools and employers. Moreover, linkage reform may be a necessary prerequisite for other kinds of reforms. School-based and employer-based reforms may not be effective unless the transition between them is improved, so their benefits may depend on the effectiveness of linkages. As I shall show, linkage reform is a way that local and regional efforts can seek to remedy work-entry problems.

Do the Three Prerequisites for Linkages Apply in the United States?

The Japanese system of school-employer linkages for employing new high school graduates has three central attributes: (1) employers value students' academic skills and work habits, and they are willing to take actions to get them; (2) work-bound students exert effort because their school performance is relevant to their future careers; and (3) teachers give students access to desirable jobs and give employers dependable student evaluations (Rosenbaum and Kariya 1989, 1991). While successful transition systems do not have to duplicate the Japanese system exactly, a successful transition system will probably have these essential features. If employers do not value school information, if work-bound students do not respond to career incentives, if teachers do not give students job access or give employers dependable information, then there is little basis for an effective transition system. Indeed, the U.S. transition to *college* has the same attributes: colleges value school information, college-bound students respond to college incentives, and teachers give colleges dependable information.

Do these three conditions apply in the United States? In the following, I will describe what is known from existing research, and I will describe recent findings from recent studies conducted at Northwestern University. In particular, I will describe findings from recent studies I have been conducting with colleagues at Northwestern University: Amy Binder, Stephanie Jones, Melinda Krei, Shazia Miller, Ginny Mills, Karen Nelson, and Kevin Roy. These studies describe current practices, and they indicate some unresolved issues for further research.

1. DO AMERICAN EMPLOYERS VALUE ACADEMIC SKILLS?

American employers often complain about the academic skills of high school graduates who enter work (NCEE 1990). Since employers would seem a good source of information about the academic skill shortcomings of workers, employers' complaints have been taken seriously.

These employer complaints would appear to answer our question if it were not for some problems with these complaints. First, the blue-ribbon panels of top corporate executives may not know how the managers in their own firms actually hire workers. Indeed, many corporations have explicit policies against hiring youth under age 25, so they have no experience with recent high school graduates. Second, such complaints are sometimes dismissed as "just words." It is easy to state a need for socially desirable educational skills to which employers have little commitment.

Third, some critics have suggested that employers may complain in order to justify offering poor pay and benefits to workers (Bowles and Gintis 1976). Finally, since employers seldom use school grades as a hiring criterion for youths (Crain 1984; Rosenbaum and Kariya 1991), one must wonder if employers really care about academic skills.

These criticisms suggest that in order to discover whether employers actually value academic skills, researchers must go to the right informants. Rather than rely upon corporate executives' views, researchers must look lower down in organizations, to the actual people who hire entry-level workers — the plant, office, and human resources managers. Since worker skill problems arise in the daily operation of firms, managers are likely to have the clearest perceptions, particularly since their actions determine the outcomes our research imperfectly measures. In addition, unlike official panels, managers rarely indulge in flowery idealism about the needs of the twenty-first century; they hire people who they think can do the job today.

These criticisms also suggest that rather than relying on employers' complaints alone, researchers must also look at employers' actual behaviors: what actions do employers take in response to these stated skill deficiencies? Research must not only analyze employers' complaints, but also get details about the problems they confronted, and examine what actions they took to respond to their expressed skill deficiencies.

To examine these issues, we interviewed managers in 51 firms in Chicago and in the western suburbs. To get beyond top executives' views, we conducted lengthy interviews with plant, office, and personnel managers to explore these issues. We examined whether skill deficiencies were "just words," or whether employers were also taking actions and incurring expenses in response. Amy Binder and I analyzed the results, which I briefly summarize here. For a more extended treatment, see Rosenbaum and Binder (1994).

The sample is mostly small or medium-size firms, but includes a few large ones. We excluded industries likely to offer only "youth jobs" without advancement opportunity, jobs in restaurants, small stores, and other service industries. While the sample cannot be considered a random sample of all employers, it includes a wide representation of the kinds of adult jobs that are available in the labor market. We conducted the 1-hour interviews with managers at their office sites.

Of 51 employers interviewed, 35 report that high school graduates lack basic skills in math, English, and verbal self-expression needed for their entry-level jobs. Thirteen employers stress that math skills are important in their entry-level jobs. They report that graduates are unable to perform the simplest arithmetic functions, convert and add fractions, and understand algebra and trigonometry. The general manager of one Chicago steel manufacturing company reports that applicants for his general labor plant jobs "have no concept of adding, or reading a ruler or tape measure." The owner of a Chicago manufacturing company recounts the story of a recent hire who reported with some surprise, "You know, down in that shipping room, you've got a lot of numbers out there." He was particularly puzzled to find that there are periods between some of the numbers, and he asked, "what's that all about?" After explaining, the owner asked, "Where were you when they learned decimals in school?" He replied, "I must have been absent that day."

Seven of the 35 employers concerned about basic academic skills report problems with English skills. One office manager tells the story of an office employee "who tried to spell 'quick' with a *w*, and didn't know that words that have *q* need a *u*. Many employers report that applicants for jobs such as data entry and claims adjustment "can't understand some of the questions on the job application," can't spell simple words, and can't read manuals written at a high school level.

What about the other 16 employers, why don't they complain about the skill levels in high school graduates? This difference in opinion seems to depend on the opportunities for advancement. In general, when companies promise little upward mobility, academic skills in entry-level positions are seen as less important. Of the 16 employers who are satisfied with applicants' academic skills, 12 state that basic academic skills are unnecessary for their entry-level jobs, although the next level of jobs in their companies does require skills. (The remaining four do not complain because they have effective prescreening procedures — tests and high school contacts.)

Where employers see career ladders for their entry-level employees — and 36 of 51 companies say they do — employers are more concerned about workers' deficient academic skills. Many employers want to hire skilled high school graduates for their lowest-level jobs in the hopes that they will eventually move up into their higher-skilled jobs. Where these skills are absent at the lowest-level jobs, employees and their employers face problems later on at promotion time. The vice president of a commercial printing firm in Chicago says:

> There are some [reading and math] deficiencies, but none that would probably keep them from performing their entry-level jobs. [But] it may affect them, you know, when it comes time to move up the ladder. . . . Once they get on to a piece of equipment, once they're perform-

ing a job that requires regular reading of customer job tickets . . . or written instructions from their supervisor, then it could become more of a problem.

Complaining about the lack of skills in today's high school is commonplace, but do these complaints affect employers' actions? Do employers take actions that entail extra effort or cost to ensure the selection of better academic skills?

Although these are mostly small employers, lacking large personnel budgets, these employers nonetheless invest in a number of different activities to improve the quality of their workforce. We find that many employers invest in maintaining contacts with high schools, apprenticeships, or union programs to get the benefit of their prescreening of applicants: 45.1 percent have such contacts with high schools, and 15.7 percent invest in contacts with apprenticeships or unions. Almost two-thirds (62.7 percent) pay for training for workers. A substantial minority (39 percent) also make efforts to accommodate workers with good skills by creating jobs or by waiving hiring restrictions when capable applicants appear. Moreover, contrary to claims that employers complain to justify poor treatment of workers, we find that complaining employers are more likely than noncomplainers to invest in training, good pay, prescreening, and referral contacts.

In sum, despite concerns about distorted employer reports, the stories we heard were so specific and detailed as to be highly credible. The present research indicates that employers' complaints about academic skills are not "just words." Nor are they complaints from top corporate executives; they come from managers in small firms that hire young workers. They are accompanied by actions and investments to improve the selection and training of workers. These results suggest that American employers, like Japanese employers, care about youths' academic skills, and many American employers are investing in ways to improve the academic skills of the workers they hire.

Having shown that employers are willing to invest in improving the quality of their workers, I am now prepared to investigate key aspects of this issue. Research is needed to examine what kinds of employers are willing to invest in improving their worker pool. We must also discover how employers differ in their approach to improving their workforce: What is their relative willingness to invest in relationships with high schools versus investing in relationships with colleges, trade schools, or other employers? Do employers prefer to invest in better recruiting or to invest in in-house training? What kinds of circumstances encourage employers to trust or mistrust teacher recommendations? What kinds of school-provided information are employers willing to use in hiring decisions?

These issues are likely to differ by industry and by the specific organization of the workforce. A regional approach is necessary. Employers in some regions may take one vantage point, while those in another region may take another. In part, this may also be influenced by specific historical factors, and by attitudes toward the local schools or specific experiences that an owner or manager has had with the schools. The potential for a linkage may depend on whether the school has developed vocational training in a relevant field. While chambers of commerce and business associations can encourage their members to take certain actions, it is particularly valuable for them to survey their members before deciding which approaches to take.

2. WOULD WORK-BOUND STUDENTS RESPOND IF SCHOOL WAS RELEVANT TO THEIR FUTURE CAREERS?

Improving high school students' efforts and achievement in school is an enduring goal of educators. Students who work hard in school develop skills, knowledge, and work habits that can help them achieve in higher education, in work, and in other aspects of their lives. Previous studies focused on the ways achievement and school effort are influenced by peers and parents (Kandel and Lesser 1972), parenting practices and ethnicity (Steinberg, Dornbusch, and Brown 1992), and socioeconomic status (Heyns 1972; Sewell, Hauser, and Featherman 1976; Rosenbaum 1980). The problem with such findings is that social policy cannot do much to change parenting practices, peer influences, or socioeconomic status, so these findings do not point to practical policy actions.

While many people believe that students' poor school efforts are due to problems in their past histories, Stinchcombe (1964) hypothesized that students' school efforts are affected by their perceptions of school's relevance for their future. Stinchcombe contends that, in addition to being influenced by the past and present, adolescents are also influenced by the future — at least their perceptions of their future options. Individuals assess their future options and what future payoffs exist for present efforts. "Students who do not see themselves gaining an increment of future status from conformity in high school" are less likely to work hard in school or to conform to school rules (Stinchcombe 1964, p. 49). Stinchcombe saw articulation as a structural property of the relationship between high schools and other societal institutions (workplaces and colleges). He inferred that college-track students, college-aspiring students, and students aspiring to high-status jobs have high articulation: they know their current efforts and high grades will help them gain admission to college.

However, for non-college-bound students, incentives are ill-defined. As noted, employers seldom use school grades as a hiring criterion for youths (Crain 1984; Rosenbaum and Kariya 1991). According to Stinchcombe's hypothesis, this may explain why work-oriented students are less likely to work hard in school: they see no future payoffs for school effort. In other words, students' poor efforts in school are not necessarily due to any internal motivational deficiencies, but rather to the environment's failure to present them with incentives for their efforts.

To test Stinchcombe's ideas, we have chosen to focus on two aspects of individuals' perceptions of school's relevance to their future lives: (1) whether students believe that high school education has relevance for their future success (hereafter "future relevance") and (2) whether students believe that there is no penalty for poor school performance (hereafter "no penalty" attitude). The first variable refers to students' belief that high school can help their future careers; the second refers to beliefs that bad school performance cannot hurt their future careers. Following Stinchcombe's terminology, we shall call these "articulation variables."[1]

We administered surveys to 671 high school seniors enrolled in four high schools in a large, midwestern metropolitan area: two in the city, and two in the suburbs. Respondents represented diverse ethnic and socio-economic backgrounds. (Preliminary analyses found that race, sex, and mother's and father's education have negligible correlations with school effort, so these variables are omitted from the analyses.) Karen Nelson and I analyzed the results which I briefly summarize here. For a more extended treatment, see Rosenbaum and Nelson (1994).

As did previous research, we find that parent, peer, school, and psychological variables affect students' school efforts; together these variables explain 27 percent of the variance in school effort, a large influence. The two articulation variables also have strong influences on students' school efforts, and they each have influence separate from the other (coefficients of .251 for future relevance, −.225 for no penalty). Moreover, even after controlling for the influence of parents, peers, school, and personality, these two articulation variables still have significant influences, with no penalty having a larger influence than future relevance.

Finally, these analyses were run separately for students in vocational education programs. Previous research has noted that many graduates of vocational programs get higher wages and better jobs if they get jobs in the area of training, but vocational programs vary in their effectiveness at getting students into skill-relevant jobs (Grasso and Shea 1979). We found that future relevance was greater in vocational programs than in other programs. In addition, when we repeated the above analyses for students in vocational education programs, we found that future relevance had even greater influence on students' efforts in vocational programs than it does for students who are in other programs. In other words, while vocational programs do not always improve students' efforts, these findings indicate that vocational education programs that improve students' perceptions of future relevance have strong benefits for students' efforts.

These findings have implications for theory and practice. Theoretically, this study supports Stinchcombe's articulation hypothesis. As Stinchcombe proposed, students do vary in whether they see school as relevant to their future lives, and this variable is strongly associated with their school efforts. Moreover, beyond Stinchcombe's idea, we also identify a second measure of perceived articulation, the no-penalty attitude, and we show that both future relevance and no-penalty attitudes have significant, independent effects on school effort in the full model.[2]

It is unfortunate that many youth see no penalty to avoiding schoolwork, school learning, or school attendance. These students not only see school as unrelated to their future, but they believe they can accomplish their goals regardless of what they do in school. This attitude reveals a measure of personal confidence; but it is more than that. It suggests that adolescents who espouse this no-penalty attitude are overlooking the possibility that school could help their careers in any way, even as a "fallback" option if their career dreams do not work out. Moreover, the results indicate that these individuals are less likely to work in school, so they may be letting such attitudes undermine their preparation for other, more realistic options.

These findings also have practical applications. They point to interventions that can substantially influence students' school efforts. If these strong independent "effects" do indeed indicate causal influences (a matter that cannot be definitively inferred from the method of our study), then school programs that increase students' perceptions of school relevance will improve their school efforts. We find that school career help and teacher help can improve students' perceptions of school relevance. Our findings also suggest that vocational programs are effective at increasing students' perceptions of future relevance and in increasing the relationship between future relevance and school effort. Current school reforms that seek to integrate academic and vocational curricula may also help to improve students' perceptions of the relevance of academic courses. School efforts to connect school activities to actual employment opportunities will also contribute to students' seeing the future relevance of school.

In addition, our findings indicate that this no-penalty attitude is less common among students who have responsive parents or teachers. Therefore, parents and school staff should look out for these attitudes and inform students of the low probability of success for these strategies. Our interviews found many youth express no-penalty attitudes and rely on their hopes that their athletic or musical prowess will lead to wealth without indicating any awareness of the low probability of success in such fields. While youth should be allowed to follow their dreams, parents and school staff should inform students about the odds for success in these fields. Students should be advised that working hard in school offers more certain, albeit less glamorous, payoffs. Such information is not meant to discourage students' aspirations and efforts toward such dreams, but it can inform them that they should not make all their bets on such dreams. "Backup" plans may be less glamorous, but may offer a higher probability of attainment.

This study is very encouraging for it suggests a way for policy to motivate students. This research suggests that American students, like Japanese students, will respond if they see school as relevant to their future careers. Students who see school as having future relevance and those who see a penalty to poor school performance are more likely to work hard in school. We may infer that programs that improve future relevance and decrease no-penalty attitudes will increase students' school efforts.

Further research is needed to examine what practices can help students to see school as having relevance to their future lives, and what practices can reduce their tendency to see no penalty to poor school performance. What can schools and teachers do to enhance these perceptions? Obviously, these issues involve influences that go beyond the walls of the school, so research needs to consider the impact of employer hiring practices and college admissions practices. Are there ways that colleges can create clearer incentives for achievement? Do open admissions policies in community colleges reduce students' tendency to see a penalty to poor high school performance? While research finds "community colleges having negative effects on educational attainment," this may actually begin well before students enter these colleges when high school students realize that they can gain admission without working in high school. What can employers do to encourage students to see high school achievement as relevant to their future jobs?

Even school reforms sometimes ignore this question. For instance, the

Boston Compact of the 1980s promised jobs to all high school graduates. While this provided a clear incentive for graduation, it did not provide an explicit incentive for academic achievement. Do students see such policies as encouraging doing only the minimum necessary to graduate, rather than achieving competencies? If so, then this policy may have inadvertently encouraged students to see no penalty to poor school performance (beyond doing the minimum needed to graduate).

3. DO TEACHERS GIVE STUDENTS ACCESS TO DESIRABLE JOBS AND GIVE EMPLOYERS DEPENDABLE STUDENT EVALUATIONS?

Regardless of what reforms we implement, teachers will play a key role. How do teachers see their responsibilities about helping youth enter work, and what roles do they now play? We currently have little research on teachers' informal activities in facilitating students' transitions to work, but teachers are crucial to improving the school-to-work transition. Vocational teachers are of particular interest. They serve many of the students who will enter the workforce directly after high school and may have contacts with employers through their industry experiences or advisory connections. Moreover, while academic teachers can help meet employers' needs, vocational teachers have an even clearer relevance. Therefore, vocational teachers' views and actions can help us understand the transition process and their role in influencing students' work entry.

Given the meager state of knowledge about what teachers do to help youth enter work, we conducted a descriptive study to find out what teachers do and how they view the issue. Based on detailed interviews, this study describes teachers' conceptions of their responsibilities toward students and employers, their assessments of types of help students need, and the ways in which teachers offer aid both to students and to their prospective employers by facilitating the school-to-work transition. Furthermore, we investigate teachers' reports of the social and institutional constraints that prevent teachers from doing more. Stephanie Jones and I analyzed the results, which I briefly summarize here. For a more extended treatment, see Rosenbaum and Jones (1995).

We conducted detailed 1-hour interviews with 26 vocational teachers in a variety of vocational fields at the same four high schools where we studied students. One of the city high schools has a vocationally focused curriculum, while the other three are comprehensive schools offering vocational programs of varying depth. Although our small, qualitative sample allows us to make only tentative generalizations about the larger teacher population, our data provide rich descriptions of teachers' perceptions and behaviors and provide indications of previously neglected phenomena that are key to the high school to work transition.

We have noted that the lack of a formal work entry system in the U.S. creates serious problems and missed opportunities. Nowhere is this more evident than in the job of vocational teachers. Indeed, the lack of a formal work-entry system creates a serious conflict for American teachers. We found that virtually *all* vocational teachers say they are *not responsible* for aiding work entry. It is a responsibility neither of theirs nor of the school more generally. Indeed, even teachers and work coordinators who facilitate and evaluate students' participation in co-op jobs assert that helping students arrange their *post*-high school jobs does not fall into their professional domain. Moreover, nearly every teacher reports that there are *no incentives to encourage them to assist students in getting jobs after high school.* None of the high schools rewarded such activities, and, indeed, none provided any time or relief from other job duties for such help.

This leads to several implications. First, even with a small sample, such total consensus is a striking figure that cannot be ignored. Second, the fact that teachers are not responsible for aiding work entry is not inevitable; indeed, it is not the case in Japan. Third, the current American policy that absolves teachers of any responsibility to aid work entry has certain consequences: both costs and benefits. A potential benefit is the freeing of teachers' time for other activities, including instruction. However, some costs may also arise, as we shall note.

Despite the lack of formal expectations for teacher help toward workbound students, *all vocational teachers feel that their students need help entering the labor market.* Teachers note that students lack future orientation; they lack practical, applied knowledge; and they hold unrealistic expectations about the job world with regard to job requirements, market conditions, work environments, and pay scales. The fact that teachers are not responsible for aiding work entry means that no one is responsible for meeting these students' needs.

But, even though they are not required to attend to students' needs, vocational teachers cannot ignore students' needs. Over three-quarters (76 percent) of our respondents reported that seniors regularly approached them for help in finding a job, and another 10 percent observed that students regularly went to the co-op teachers for help. Even in higher-income suburban areas where it is commonly assumed that students have relatives, friends, or neighbors who can help them get jobs, teachers report that many students ask them for help in the school-to-work transition. As a result, *many teachers report that they feel a personal responsibility to do more than what their job requires them to do.*

Interestingly, teachers also get requests from another direction — employers. Some teachers report that employers ask them to nominate good students to apply for their jobs, and some of the employers we interviewed confirmed that they make such requests. While helping employers fill *part-time* jobs is a formal responsibility of co-op teachers, these employer requests are for filling *full-time* jobs (which are not co-op teachers' responsibility), and many of the requests are to non-co-op teachers. Even though this is not a formal responsibility, teachers report that helping employers meets students' needs also has other benefits for their programs and for the school.

Thus teachers are confronted with a conflict. While teachers believe that helping students get jobs after high school lies outside their formal responsibilities, they also see that many students need help to enter the labor force. These teachers face a choice between simply doing their jobs and extending their duties to include helping students gain entry to the work world. Since neither their jobs nor their personal training specify *what* they should do for aiding students' work entry, teachers must figure out for themselves what to do.

Moreover, since teachers' actions are improvised, policy makers do not know what informal actions teachers are taking to help students' work entry. While policy analysts urge the building of new programs and systems, we know virtually nothing about the range of activities that teachers are now doing informally in response to students' needs and students' and employers' requests.

If teachers are to be an important part of any school-to-work system, it is important to know what range of activities teachers are already doing, what more they could do, what factors influence which practices are being done and not done, what activities are effective, and what factors influence their effectiveness. Effective program reforms must be based on such information.

Our study has begun a first effort to describe the range of teacher practices. We find that *virtually all our vocational teachers provide some kind of help in making contact with the work world.* While their relationships to the work world vary from weak to strong, all teachers express interest in helping young people, and they engage in activities to help their students make the transition to the job world.

Teachers offer various kinds of help in preparing students for the world of work. Most teachers offer general information about work and most also provide practical work exposure in field trips, guest speakers, co-op jobs, and simulations. But we also find that some teachers go further to match students with relevant desirable jobs.

We find that just over half ($n = 15$) of our 26 vocational teachers give students access to desirable jobs in the area of students' preparation. These teachers have contacts with specific employers in relevant fields, and they try to match students' interests and abilities with employers' needs. Many teachers report, "I match students with employers." These teachers stress that they are putting students in jobs that use their skills. In turn, this leads teachers to structure their programs to prepare students for employers' needs. Since research indicates that vocational education only improves students' earnings if they get skill-relevant jobs (Grasso and Shea 1979), these efforts are likely to enhance students' careers.

In addition, we find that about half of these 15 teachers go even further; they provide a "quasi-warranty" to employers about student quality. In essence, these teachers know specific employers' needs, and they select students of suitable quality to meet these needs. These teachers report that they develop enduring contacts with employers and they use standards that satisfy these employers. They say that they recommend the best students for the best jobs, and if they do not have any students of adequate quality for an employer in a given year, they will say this to the employer. If they are mostly positive, but they have reservations, they will "tell employers exactly what they're getting." Given the long-term nature of many of these contacts, they become trustworthy relationships. Interestingly, some of the employers we interviewed also noted their reliance on such dependable teacher linkages.

Though not numerous, these linkages are important and are highly valued by employers and teachers. Employers report that these linkages provide a valuable source of workers. One employer notes that when he hires from a particular teacher, "I know I have the top of the class." Another reports that he cannot judge the quality of the average students in a school because he knows that he gets "the better ones." Another reports that when he gets a student highly recommended by a trusted teacher, he is confident the student can handle the job. In turn, teachers report that their linkages permit them to help students get jobs, and teachers with contacts are confident they could get a good job for their better students. Linkages are also a way to motivate students to work in class. Students know that if they do well in classes, the teacher will recommend them to good local employers, and that can have a big impact.

While the potential benefits of such linkages are evident, critics have raised concerns about vocational education being too specialized, teaching only job-specific skills, and potentially restricting students' career options. These concerns would be particularly relevant to career linkage help, which has the potential of being even narrower. In particular, we may wonder whether career linkage help is solely oriented to job-specific skills and whether it discourages academic skills and higher education.

In fact, our study found the opposite: career linkages are usually used to encourage students to work harder in academic areas. We find that nearly all of the teachers who do linkage activities also stress the importance of doing well in academic subjects. Moreover, although students usually choose vocational programs because they do not want further education, linkage teachers encourage students to get postsecondary education in order to get better jobs. However, we do not know whether students follow either suggestion.

Indeed, teachers report that their contacts with employers help them to show students the importance of academic skills. Here, the teachers' linkages give students better information about reality than they would otherwise get. The job world actually presents the "wrong message" to students. Students see that *entry* jobs do not require academic skills, but they do not see that later advancements require academic skills (Rosenbaum and Binder 1994). Teachers with linkages help their students see that academic skills ultimately have a payoff in better career advancements.

Further research is needed to understand why certain teachers initiate linkages and others do not. Are there some types of individuals or personal backgrounds that encourage such behaviors? We hypothesize that teachers with previous industry experience may have more contacts and be more willing to make such initiatives. We also hypothesize that teachers who were asked by employers to help them identify good workers would be more willing to extend these activities, and that teachers' initiatives that are well-received by employers would lead to more such initiatives. We might expect that some kinds of school policies might encourage these practices, particularly policies that offer incentives and release time.

Given the regional concerns of this conference, it is important to note that regional programs may influence whether employers encourage teachers' initiatives. Some employers told us that they view an isolated call from a teacher as a distraction, and we suspect that this may be a common reaction. However, we also suspect that a regional program may alert employers to the potential benefits to the company and to the entire region. Some local chambers of commerce and business associations have encouraged school-employer contacts, and research is needed to see which employers respond to which kinds of efforts. Since these groups are often unsure what kinds of contacts are most helpful, research is needed to help these groups choose what approaches to encourage. Their efforts should also be evaluated to guide their efforts in future years and to provide guidance to other organizations seeking to provide similar programs.

Further research is now needed to examine the effectiveness of various approaches to linkages. Are linkages effective in increasing students' academic course taking, academic performance, and perhaps even their postsecondary education, as linked teachers urge them to do? Various other kinds of desirable outcomes may be considered: do students identify appropriate job options, make timely job applications, obtain jobs easily, and get good jobs appropriate to their training? As noted, research finds that vocational education only benefits students if they obtain skill-relevant jobs (jobs that use the skills they have learned in school), yet researchers have not examined what determines whether students obtain skill-relevant jobs. A plausible hypothesis is that vocational teachers' help may be an important determinant of students' obtaining skill-relevant jobs. This is an important issue to study.

Research must examine the costs and benefits of various approaches. Teacher linkages raise a number of potential risks. It is possible that teachers use inappropriate criteria to influence jobs, yet if employers really care about academic skills and work habits, teacher evaluations may be the most appropriate available information about these attributes. Teacher job help also runs the risk of teacher biases hurting some students' chances for good jobs. Yet while bias is a risk in any human endeavor, "objective" tests may not be free of bias, so it is not clear which procedure contains less bias. Furthermore, currently, very few youth get good jobs, so if reforms substantially increase youths' opportunities, minority youth have more to gain than to lose from linkage reforms. Research must consider whether teacher influence may increase youths' chances of getting good jobs, despite its potential risks.

Our study has discovered considerable variation in practices, but it is too small to analyze the correlates of such practices systematically — either antecedents or consequences. Larger surveys are needed.

Conclusions

These findings indicate that the United States possesses some of the prerequisites for school-to-work linkages: (1) some employers value school information about academic skills and work habits; (2) work-bound students exert effort because school is relevant to their future careers; and (3) teachers give students access to desirable jobs and give employers dependable student evaluations for hiring decisions. These are the same attributes we noted in the Japanese system. Unlike Japan, these features are not explicit or formal in the United States. Yet since these attributes operate informally, they create linkages that provide some employers with valued information, provide some work-bound students with incentives for school effort, and provide some teachers with the ability to help students get good jobs and help employers get dependable information about job applicants. Of course, the fact that this system is informal and not explicit may mean that fewer people benefit than would do so if it were more formal, and many employers, students, and teachers may not be aware of such linkages and get no benefits from such relationships.

Because the process is informal, policy discussions of the school-to-work transition have not considered the actual and potential functions of teachers as "mediating actors." Our analysis of the types of teacher help and their likely effects is meant to encourage such discussion. Teachers with strong linkages provide employers with dependable information about job applicants and provide students with information about job requirements and ways to prepare themselves for good jobs.

These teacher activities have not previously been noted in the academic literature nor in the literature on school reform. Most reforms envision a school-to-work system as a set of institutions and rules. In the more extensive visions, systems are composed of bureaucracies regulating what curricula students study, when students gain work experiences, and what training employers must provide to youth. But while the Japanese system has a government bureau to oversee and set guidelines for its work-entry system, the bureaucracy only sets minor rules for ensuring fairness, and the main elements of the Japanese system are in the widely shared expectations of schools and employers about how they should interact.

Employers fear that an improved work-entry system requires a new bureaucracy, but such a bureaucracy is not necessary. Indeed, the college application process in the United States is a model. Without bureaucratic control, the college application process has very clear rules, schedules, and criteria. The process is well specified. Applicants must take the SAT/ACT exams, compose application essays, and submit applications, and the timetables are specified.[3] College selection criteria are also specified: grades, test scores, and activities. The college application procedure is very clear, so college-bound students know exactly what to do and when.

The work-entry process lacks this clarity, and, given the diversity of employers, perhaps it can never be as clear as the college application system. Yet teachers with linkages are able to create a clarity for their students, and like the college application system, this constructed work-entry system mobilizes students' efforts and satisfies employers' needs. Obviously, one cannot make policy based on extraordinary individuals, and the most active teachers may be just that. However, other teachers can be encouraged to do such activities by new policies, role expectations, and incentives.

Our findings suggest that most vocational teachers we interviewed would be responsive to school practices that encourage them to offer more help to work-bound students. Teachers already see the need, they are asked by students anyway, and they already assist students or employers on their own time and initiative, though often in a piecemeal way. Yet currently students do not expect or encourage teachers to create linkages or to help students get jobs. To encourage teachers to create linkages, certain kinds of policy directions are needed. Since this is an entirely new process in the United States, research will be needed to identify the best ways to proceed on each of them.

The following propositions are my judgments about the measures that would improve the linkages between schooling and the labor market. They constitute a set of hypotheses that need to be tested if society is to strengthen the incentives for administrators, teachers, employers, and young people to treat school as an economically productive mechanism.

1. *High schools should make employment assistance part of a teacher's job.* They should give teachers the message that it is important to spend time helping students get jobs, just as they spend time writing college recommendations and advising students about college choices. However, research needs to examine how these additional duties can be added to the job, and how they can be integrated with other obligations.

2. *High schools should provide time in the teacher's paid workday to do this.* Obviously, this adds new costs, which are difficult given limited school budgets. Yet the incremental costs are vastly smaller than the costs required to create entirely new training and apprenticeship programs, and the bureaucracies needed to administer them. However, it is not clear how much time linkages should take or when they should be done. Research must examine whether efficiencies can be gained by having a single teacher do this for a whole school, a particular vocational area, or a certain set of employers. This is not just a matter of efficiency; there are some trade-offs. The more the teacher knows a student, the more individualistic information the teacher can provide to the student and to the employer. Yet if more teachers contact an employer, this takes more time from the employer.

3. *High schools should provide some incentives for teachers to do this.* Most colleges hire job placement staff to cultivate contacts with

employers and place students in jobs (Kariya and Rosenbaum 1995). High school teaching and counseling staffs could be structured to serve both college placement and job placement needs equally. However, research will be needed to discover what incentives teachers respond best to and whether other incentives in the system must be altered to make the new system effective.

4. *Teachers should build personal relationships of trust with employers, ascertain their needs, and design curricula and student evaluations that reflect those needs.* Research is needed to discover what kinds of teachers can do this, and how to help more teachers do such activities. We have hypothesized that teachers with industry experience may be more effective at this. However, other teachers can gain industry experience in summer programs, and research will need to examine whether that provides sufficient basis for building the necessary relationships.

5. *Linkages should convey useful information to employers, to teachers, and to students.* One of the primary ways that linkages have benefits is in passing useful information to employers, to teachers, and to students. Research needs to examine what information each party needs. What information do employers need to know about students to make hiring decisions? Some kinds of information are difficult to convey, like information about students' work habits. What do teachers say about work habits that is most helpful to employers? What information do teachers need to know about employers' needs to make useful recommendations to them and to provide relevant instruction to students? Contrary to critics' concerns that employers' influence will lead to narrow skill training, research indicates that employers do not want narrow skill training from schools, they would want to do it themselves (Osterman 1980). Rather, as we have noted, employers are interested in academic and thinking skills, but they may not know how to specify which such skills they need. Teachers with experience in industry may be able to help employers articulate their needs and to help academic teachers design useful academic curricula. On the other hand, research also should examine what information students need to know about the work world that will help them make plans and invest effort in achieving their plans. Despite decades of research on students' aspirations, little is known about how students formulate their plans and particularly about how they infer what efforts are required to actualize their plans. The no-penalty attitude is clearly one indication of a faulty inference that may hurt students' career futures.

6. *Linkages should create dependable relationships among employers and teachers.* We have said very little about the nature of relationships that are needed to make these linkages work. We have provided some general descriptions of these relationships, but much more needs to be done. Certainly, expectations are crucial. If teachers expect employers to hire all of their "strongly recommended" students, then they will put much more into this process than if employers rarely hire them. Moreover, a responsive employer is likely to get more help from teachers than less responsive employers. These relationships are likely to operate by a delicate balance of reciprocity expectations, just as any other kind of exchange relationship does. While a company's sales department understands reciprocity factors, it is not clear whether human resources departments are accustomed to dealing with them, especially in recruiting workers. Teachers may have even less experience with these matters. Research needs to investigate how these various actors understand their relationships, and how they go about learning how to develop new relationships.

In sum, these findings suggest that American employers might benefit from receiving dependable information from schools (as Japanese employers do); that American teachers can, and sometimes do, give employers dependable information that affects hiring for adult jobs; and that that American work-bound students may increase their school efforts if schoolwork appears relevant to their future careers. These findings suggest that something like the "Japanese model" of school-employer linkages may be workable in the United States.

NOTES

1. To represent a concept that we call "future relevance," we devised several items (answered on a 5-point agree-disagree scale): "My courses give me useful preparation I'll need in life. Nothing I learn in school is relevant to my future. School teaches me valuable skills." Summing these items, we called the scale "future relevance." We believe that this scale measures students' perceptions that school prepares them for the future. Second, to represent a scale that we call "no-penalty" attitudes, we devised four items. "Even if I don't work hard in school, I can still make my future plans come true. What I don't learn in school, I can always pick up later. People can do OK even if they drop out of high school. Students with bad grades in high school often get good jobs after high school."

2. We do not have a very good understanding of adolescents' no-penalty attitudes. One possibility is that adolescents' no-penalty attitudes can be viewed in psychological terms as a defensive reaction to poor current academic performance. Simply put, students may deny the importance of school performance just because

they are doing poorly. However, it is likely to be more than this. In pilot interviews at city and suburban high schools, we asked high school seniors about their occupational plans. Many students mentioned plans to be discovered as a famous athlete or music star. Some seemed to use such dreams to rationalize their lack of effort in school. Therefore, the no-penalty attitude may arise from peculiar perceptions of reality, and it may be a cause, rather than a result, of poor effort. It is possible that such no-penalty attitudes have their origins in American culture and media. American literature and films often portray nonschool routes to success. Since educational routes to success make dull plots, movies often show ways that the hero gains wealth and fame through charm, conniving, inheritances, and myriad other contrived circumstances emerging from screenwriters' imaginations. If life does not imitate art enough to make these nonschool strategies a practical plan of action for most people, newspapers still find (or reconstruct) enough stories from time to time to make glamorous long shots seem plausible routes to success. While our aim is not to study the origins of these attitudes, these pervasive one-in-a-million success stories in the media may have some influence on youths' beliefs about future success without school performance. Indeed, this nonschool strategy is not a total fiction. Some individuals *do* strike it rich in ventures that do not depend on schooling. Adolescents are particularly aware of the salaries and lifestyles of rock stars and sports stars. Since some people do strike it rich without working hard in school, there is nothing wrong with youth having dreams of achieving similar success. The problem, of course, is a matter of probabilities. While "strike it rich" outcomes are possible, they are not very probable, so they do not make a good basis for one's entire career plan.

3. Many students do not learn about this system, especially when high schools have poor guidance departments. This reinforces the importance of having adequate staff in the high schools, as we recommend below.

REFERENCES

Arnouw, S. 1968. *The Transition from School to Work*. Princeton, N.J.: Woodrow Wilson School. (Background reference)

Attewell, P. 1992. "Skill and Occupational Changes in U.S. Manufacturing." In *Technology and the Future of Work*, edited by P. S. Adler, pp. 46–88. New York: Oxford University Press. (Background reference)

Bailey, T. 1989. "Changes in the Nature and Structure of Work." Technical Paper no. 9. New York: Columbia University, Teachers College. (Background reference)

———. 1994. "Barriers to Employer Participation in School-to-Work Transition Programs." Presented to a seminar on Employer Participant in School-to-Work Transition Programs, Brookings Institution, Washington, D.C., May 4. (Background reference)

Bailey, T., and D. Merrit. 1993. *The School-to-Work Transition and Youth Apprenticeship*. New York: Manpower Demonstration Research Corporation.

Basi, L., and O. Ashenfelter. 1986. "The Effect of Direct Job Creation and

Training Programs on Low-Skilled Workers." In *Fighting Poverty: What Works and What Doesn't*, edited by S. Danziger and D. Weinberg, pp. 133–51. Cambridge, Mass.: Harvard University Press.

Berryman, Sue E. 1992. "Apprenticeship as a Paradigm for Learning." In *Youth Apprenticeship in America*, edited by J. Rosenbaum, pp. 25–40; New York: W. T. Grant Foundation Commission on Youth and America's Future.

Betsey, C. L., et al. 1985. *Youth Employment and Training Programs: The YEDPA Years*. Washington, D.C.: National Academy Press.

Bills, David. 1988a. "Educational Credentials and Hiring Decisions: What Employers Look for in Entry-Level Employees." *Research in Social Stratification and Mobility* 7:71–97. (Background reference)

———. 1988b. "Employers and Overeducation." Paper presented at the annual meeting of the American Sociological Association, Atlanta. August 24. (Background reference)

Bishop, J.; A. Blakemore; and S. Low. 1985. *High School Graduates in the Labor Market*. Columbus: Ohio State University, National Center for Research in Vocational Education.

Bloom, H. S.; L. L. Orr; G. Cave; S. H. Bell; and F. Doolittle. 1992a. "A Survey of Employer Surveys." *Research in Social Stratification and Mobility* 11:3–31.

———. 1992b. *The National JTPA Study*. Bethesda, Md.: Abt Associates. (Background references)

Boesel, D.; L. Hudson, S. Deich; and C. Masten. 1994. *Participation in and Quality of Vocational Education*. Vol. 2, National Assessment of Vocational Education. Washington, D.C.: U.S. Department of Education. (Background reference)

Borman, K. M. 1991. *The First Real Job*. Albany: State University of New York Press. (Background reference)

Bowles, S., and H. Gintis. 1976. *Schooling in Capitalist America*. New York: Basic Books.

Cappelli, P., and N. Rogowsky. 1993. "Skill Demands, Changing Work Organization, and Performance." Philadelphia: University of Pennsylvania, National Center on the Educational Quality of the Workforce. (Background reference)

Cave, G., and F. Doolittle. 1991. *Assessing Jobstart*. New York: Manpower Demonstration Research Corporation.

Committee for Economic Development (CED). 1985. *Investing in Our Children: Business and the Public Schools*. New York: CED.

Crain, R. 1984. "The Quality of American High School Graduates: What Personnel Officers Say and Do." Unpublished manuscript. Baltimore: Johns Hopkins University.

D'Amico, R., and N. Maxwell. 1990. *Black-White Employment Differences during the School-to-Work Transition*. Palo Alto, Calif.: SRI International.

Daymont, T. N., and R. W. Rumberger. 1982. "Job Training in the Schools." In *Job Training for Youth*, edited by R. Taylor, H. Rosen, and F. Pratzner. Columbus: Ohio State University, National Center for Research in Vocational Education. (Background reference)

Diamond, D. E. 1970. *Industry Hiring Requirements and the Employment of Disadvantaged Groups.* New York: New York University School of Commerce. (Background reference)

Ellwood, D. 1982. "Teenage Unemployment: Permanent Scars or Temporary Blemishes?" In *The Youth Labor Market Problem,* edited by R. B. Freeman and D. A. Wise. Chicago: University of Chicago Press. (Background reference)

Faist, Thomas. 1994. "States, Markets, and Immigrant Minorities." *Comparative Politics* (July):439–60. (Background reference)

Farkas, George; G. R. Olsen; E. Stromsdorfer; L. Sharpe; F. Skidmore; D. A. Smith; and S. Merrill. 1984. *Post-program Impacts of the Youth Incentive Entitlement Pilot Projects.* New York: Manpower Demonstration Research Corporation.

Gamoran, Adam. 1994. "The Impact of Academic Course Work on Labor Market Outcomes for Youth Who Do Not Attend College: A Research Review." Unpublished draft, National Assessment of Vocational Education. Washington, D.C.: U.S. Department of Education. (Background reference)

General Accounting Office (GAO). 1991. "Transition from School to Work." Washington, D.C.: GAO.

Granovetter, M. 1995. *Getting a Job.* 2d ed. Chicago: University of Chicago Press.

Grasso, J. T., and J. R. Shea. 1979. *Vocational Education and Training: Impact on Youth.* Berkeley: Carnegie Council on Policy Studies in Higher Education.

Griffin, J. L., et al. 1981. "Determinants of Early Labor Market Entry and Attainment: A Study of Labor Market Segmentation." *Sociology of Education* 54:206–21. (Background reference)

Hamilton, S. F. 1989. *Apprenticeship for Adulthood.* New York: Free Press.

Harhoff, D., and T. J. Kane. 1994. "Financing Apprenticeship Training: Evidence from Germany." National Bureau of Economic Research Working Paper no. 3557. Cambridge, Mass.: National Bureau of Economic Research. (Background reference)

Heckman, James. 1994. "Is Job Training Oversold?" *The Public Interest* no. 115 (Spring):91–115.

Heyns, B. 1974. "Social Selection and Stratification within Schools." *American Journal of Sociology* 79(6):1434–51.

Kandel, D., and G. Lesser. 1972. *Youth in Two Worlds: United States and Denmark.* New York: Jossey-Bass Behavioral Science Books.

Kariya, T., and J. E. Rosenbaum. 1987. "Self-Selection in Japanese Junior High Schools." *Sociology of Education* 60(3):168–80. (Background reference)

———. 1995. "Institutional Linkages between Education and Work as Quasi-Internal Labor Markets." *Research in Social Stratification and Mobility* 14:99–134.

Lerman, R. 1994. "Building Hope, Skills and Careers." Unpublished manuscript. Washington, D.C.: American University, Department of Economics.

Lewis, M. V., et al. 1983. *School-Supervised Work Experience Programs.* University Park: Pennsylvania State University, Institute for Research on Human Resources.

Lynch, L. 1989. "The Youth Labor Market in the 80's." *Review of Economics and Statistics* 71(1)(February):37–54.

Lynn, I., and J. Wills. 1994. "School-Work Transition Lessons on Recruiting and Sustaining Employer Involvement." Washington, D.C.: Institute for Educational Leadership. (Background reference)

Meyer, R., and D. Wise. 1982. "High School Preparation and Early Labor Force Experience." In *The Youth Labor Market Problem*, edited by R. B. Freeman and D. A. Wise. Chicago: University of Chicago Press.

Michelson, R. A. 1990. "The Attitude/Achievement Paradox among Black Adolescents." *Sociology of Education* 63:44–61. (Background reference)

National Academy of Sciences (NAS). 1984. *High Schools and the Changing Workplace: The Employers' View.* Washington, D.C.: National Academy Press.

National Assessment of Educational Progress (NAEP). 1990. *Learning to Read in Our Nation's Schools.* Princeton, N.J.: Educational Testing Service.

National Center on Education and the Economy (NCEE). 1990. *America's Choice: High Skills or Low Wages!* Rochester, N.Y.: NCEE.

National Research Council. 1989. *Fairness in Employment Testing.* Washington, D.C.: National Research Council. (Background reference)

Neckerman, Kathryn M., and Joleen Kirschenman. 1990. "Hiring Strategies, Racial Bias, and Inner-City Workers." Paper presented to the annual meeting of the American Sociological Association, Washington, D.C., August 11. (Background reference)

Olneck, M. R., and D. Bills. 1980. "What Makes Sammy Run?" *American Journal of Education* 89:27–61. (Background reference)

Osterman, P. 1980. *Getting Started: The Youth Labor Market.* Cambridge, Mass.: MIT Press.

———. 1988. *Employment Futures.* New York: Oxford University Press.

———. 1994. "Strategies for Involving Employers in School to Work Programs." Paper presented at a conference at the Brookings Institution, Washington, D.C., May. (Background reference)

Parcel, T. 1987. "Theories of the Labor Market and the Employment of Youth." In *Research in the Sociology of Education and Socialization*, vol. 7, edited by A. Kerckhoff, pp. 29–55. Greenwood, Conn.: JAI Press.

Ray, Carol A., and Roslyn A. Mickelson. 1993. "Restructuring Students for Restructured Work." *Sociology of Education* 66:1–20.

Rosenbaum, James E. 1976. *Making Inequality.* New York: Wiley. (Background reference)

———. 1978. "The Structure of Opportunity in Schools." *Social Forces* 57:236–56. (Background reference)

———. 1980. "Track Misperceptions and Frustrated College Plans: An Analysis of the Effects of Tracks and Track Perceptions in the National Longitudinal Survey." *Sociology of Education* 53:74–88.

———. 1996. "Policy Uses of Research on the High-School-to-Work Transition." *Sociology of Education* 69(2)(May):102–22.

Rosenbaum, J. E., and A. Binder. 1994. "Do Employers Really Need More

Educated Youth?" Paper presented at the annual meeting of the American Sociological Association, Los Angeles, August.

Rosenbaum, J. E., and S. A. Jones. 1995. "Creating Linkages in the High School-to-Work Transition: Vocational Teachers' Networks." In *Making Schools Work*, edited by M. Hallinan. New York: Plenum.

Rosenbaum, J. E., and T. Kariya. 1989. "From High School to Work: Market and Institutional Mechanisms in Japan." *American Journal of Sociology* 94(6)(May):1334–65.

———. 1991. "Do School Achievements Affect the Early Jobs of High School Graduates in the U.S. and Japan?" *Sociology of Education* 64(April):78–95.

Rosenbaum, J. E.; T. Kariya; R. Settersten; and T. Maier. 1990. "Market and Network Theories of the Transition from High School to Work." *Annual Review of Sociology* 16:263–99. (Background reference)

Rosenbaum, J. E., and K. A. Nelson. 1994. "The Influence of Perceived Articulation on Students' School Effort." Paper presented at the annual meeting of the American Educational Research Association, New Orleans, April.

Rumberger, R. W., and T. N. Daymont. 1984. "The Economic Value of Academic and Vocational Training Acquired in High School." In *Youth and the Labor Market*, edited by M. E. Borus. Kalamazoo, Mich.: Upjohn Institute.

Sedlack, M. W.; C. W. Wheeler; D. C. Pullin; and P. A. Cusick. 1986. *Selling Students Short*. New York: Teachers College Press. (Background reference)

Sewell, W.; R. A. Hauser; and D. L. Featherman. 1976. *Schooling and Achievement in American Society*. New York: Academic Press.

Squires, G. D. 1979. *Education and Jobs*. New Brunswick, N.J.: Transaction Books. (Background reference)

Steinberg, L.; S. M. Dornbusch; and B. Bradford Brown. 1992. "Ethnic Differences in Adolescent Achievement: An Ecological Perspective." *American Psychologist* 47(6):723–29.

Stern, David. 1992. "School-to-Work Programs and Services in Secondary Schools and Two-Year Public Postsecondary Institutions." Berkeley: University of California, Berkeley, School of Education.

Stern, David; N. Finkelstein; J. R. Stone; J. Latting; and C. Dornsife. 1994a. *Research on School-to-Work Transition Programs in the United States*. Berkeley: National Center for Research in Vocational Education.

Stern, David; M. Rahn; and Y. Chung. 1994. *High School to Career*. Berkeley: University of California, Berkeley, California Policy Seminar. (Background reference)

Stern, David; J. Stone III; C. Hopkins; M. McMillion; and R. Crain. 1994b. *School-Based Enterprise*. San Francisco: Jossey-Bass.

Stinchcombe, A. 1964. *Rebellion in the High School*. Chicago: Quadrangle Books.

U.S. Bureau of Labor Statistics. 1994. *Employment Projections for 1995*. Washington, D.C.: U.S. Department of Labor.

U.S. Census Bureau. 1995. *Survey of Employers*. Washington, D.C.: U.S. Bureau of the Census.

Veum, J. R., and A. B. Weiss. 1993. "Education and the Work Histories of Young Adults." *Monthly Labor Review* 116(4)(April):11–20.

White, H. 1970. *Chains of Opportunity.* Cambridge, Mass.: Harvard University Press. (Background reference)

Witte, James, and Arne L. Kalleberg. 1994. "Determinants and Consequences of Fit between Vocational Education and Employment in Germany." In *School-to-Work: What Does Research Say about It?* edited by Nevser Stacey, pp. 3–32. Washington, D.C.: U.S. Office of Education.

Zemsky, R. 1994. "What Employers Want." Philadelphia: University of Pennsylvania, National Center on the Educational Quality of the Workforce. (Background reference)

Organizational Coordination

Howard Chernick & Andrew Reschovsky

Urban Fiscal Problems
Coordinating Actions among Governments

Introduction

In 1979, William Oakland wrote a paper on the "fiscal plight" of central cities. Over the past 15 years, the fiscal condition of most of the nation's central cities has grown worse. Employment in central cities, especially in manufacturing, has continued to decline. Residents, especially those in the middle class, have continued to leave the cities for the suburbs, while cities' minority and low-income populations have grown rapidly.

In addition, city governments have had to cope with a wide range of societal ills, including drugs, crime, AIDS, homelessness, and welfare dependency, problems that have for the most part worsened over the past decade. A central premise of Oakland's paper was that the key to understanding the fiscal condition of cities is the realization that they are severely constrained by being only one among many local governments within a metropolitan area.

The primary purpose of this essay is to explore what we know and, more important, what we do not know, about the fiscal condition of the nation's central cities. We try to define exactly what is meant by the "fiscal plight" of cities, and then to explore a set of policies that might improve the fiscal conditions under which most city governments operate.

When most people think about the fiscal crisis of the cities, they often remember the near bankruptcy of New York City in the mid-1970s and the threat of bankruptcy that Philadelphia faced in the early 1990s.[1] Although these situations served as lightning rods for public attention to city fiscal problems, restricting one's definition of fiscal distress to cities on the verge of bankruptcy ignores the plight of many cities. Most states require that cities follow strict budgetary accounting procedures that make it exceedingly difficult for local governments to run current-account deficits. Consequently, they are rarely in danger of financial bankruptcy.

We would like to thank John Pepper for his superlative research assistance and Alice Honeywell for her very careful editing of the manuscript.

The real fiscal problem facing many central cities is much more structural than budgetary. The loss of jobs and middle-income residents experienced by many cities diminishes the size of their tax bases. At the same time, federal and state governments mandate city governments to perform a growing number of functions. The continuing concentration of poor persons in cities is also raising the costs of providing a wide range of public services. In addition, city residents are usually responsible for financing services that provide benefits to nonresidents — both commuters and those enjoying the cultural and recreational facilities of the city. Responding to these demands results in higher city spending, which in most cases must be financed by higher taxes.

These structural problems may induce out-migration by the city's most mobile residents and businesses. Their departure further reduces the fiscal capacity of city governments leading to a new round of out-migration. These malignant cycles of city decline have been referred to as cumulative deterioration (Oates, Howry, and Baumol 1971).

The critical element in this story is that individual behavior involving the departure of either individuals or businesses from the city generally has associated with it *fiscal externalities*. That is, a purely private decision to move from the city to a suburb, whether fiscally motivated or not, affects the fiscal health of the city. First, the out-migration of middle-income city residents, especially when they are replaced by in-migrants with lower incomes or not replaced at all, tends to reduce the capacity of the city government to raise revenue, thereby requiring the city to increase tax rates or reduce spending.[2] Second, by changing the mix of consumers of public services, the out-migrant may raise the per capita cost of providing public services to the remaining city residents.[3] Finally, these changes in fiscal capacity or in costs may, through their impacts on tax rates or service delivery, lead other city residents to migrate.

It may appear that once urban deterioration has started, a continuing spiral of decline is inevitable. The inevitability, however, of this outcome depends on a number of behavioral assumptions, most notably that out-migration is fiscally induced. It also assumes that there is no intervention in the process by outside forces that might alter the outcome. Finally, it assumes that city governments respond to structural problems by reducing services or increasing taxes. If, however, these governments can reduce spending without reducing services (i.e., increase efficiency), then out-migration may be reversed.

A major goal of this essay is to explore the issue of the fiscal plight of our central cities. We first attempt to determine the extent to which we can be confident that the story outlined above provides a true picture of the current fiscal position of our major cities. We then turn to a discussion of policy interventions that may have some promise for improving the fiscal condition of American cities. Throughout, our focus will be on clarifying what we know and what we need to know in order both to understand the fiscal plight of cities and to move forward in developing solutions to the urban fiscal problems. We will try to distinguish between obstacles to progress on both these fronts that come from a lack of knowledge and obstacles that are more political in nature and tend to take the form of conflicting incentives preventing cooperative solutions to a range of urban problems.

Focusing on Cities with Fixed Boundaries

Which cities shall we study? Since our focus in this essay is the fundamental metropolitan nature of urban fiscal problems, we restrict our attention primarily to large cities that serve as the central city of major metropolitan areas. As David Rusk (1993) has emphasized, fiscal problems are most severe in cities with fixed boundaries. We now limit our discussion to cities that are unable or unlikely to grow by annexing neighboring communities. We thus exclude from consideration a number of rapidly growing cities in the South and Southwest, such as Jacksonville and Houston, which are able to annex their surrounding territory as their populations grow.

Measuring Cities' Fiscal Health

To explore solutions to urban fiscal problems, we must clearly identify the nature of the problem. The first step is to determine which cities are in the poorest fiscal health. We begin by drawing a distinction between *structural* fiscal problems and *budgetary* problems. To get a good sense of a city's structural fiscal health requires knowledge of the effectiveness of the city government in providing residents a set of basic public services *relative* to the tax burden placed on its residents. By this definition, a city will be in poor fiscal health if it provides inadequate levels of public services — for example, if police are not generally available, trash is infrequently collected, and there are large class sizes in its public schools, despite the fact that its residents face average city tax burdens. A city will also be considered weak fiscally if its residents must pay extremely high local taxes in order to achieve only minimally adequate levels of public services.

This perspective on urban fiscal problems can be found in the work of Bradbury et al. (1984) and Ladd and Yinger (1991). We define the fiscal condition of city governments as the gap between cities' expenditure need and their revenue-raising capacity. A city's expenditure need indicates the amount that it must spend per resident to provide an average level of public services given its service responsibilities and the harshness of the environment for providing services. A city's revenue-raising capacity indicates the amount of revenue per resident it has available if its residents face an average tax burden. Revenue-raising capacities are enhanced by cities' receipt of intergovernmental grants.

The most important element of a need-capacity gap as a measure of a city's fiscal health is that it is a structural measure, one that (at least in principle) measures only those characteristics of the fiscal environment in which a city operates that are *beyond the control of local public officials.* On the spending side, this includes factors such as the concentration of low-income or otherwise high-need populations within the city, the age of a city's infrastructure, and the number of nonresidents using city streets. On the revenue side, the size and composition of a city's tax base, and state-government-imposed constraints on revenue sources, are examples of structural factors over which local public officials have no control.

On the basis of a measure of *standardized fiscal health* that "reflects only the economic, social, and demographic factors that constrain a city's finances, not its political or institutional setting," Ladd and Yinger (1989) calculate that in 1982 in 19 of the nation's 71 major central cities, city revenues (presumably from outside sources) would have to increase by at least 25 percent in order to enable the city government to provide an average quality of public services while placing an average tax burden on its residents. In an update of their analysis, Ladd and Yinger (1991) find that despite the growth of the economy during the mid-1980s, a number of large cities remained in very weak fiscal health. For example, in 1988, Chicago's revenues would have had to grow by over 50 percent in order to allow the city to provide an average quality of public services while placing an average tax burden on its residents.

This focus on structural factors is not meant to imply that actions of local public officials cannot seriously exacerbate the fiscal problems faced by cities. It is certainly not difficult to find examples where city government spending is inflated due to ineffective management, inefficient and outdated union-negotiated work rules, and needless and wasteful administrative structures. For example, in Philadelphia until recently, entry-level city employees received 52 days off each year and secretaries were paid

50–70 percent more than their private-sector counterparts (Eggers 1993). Until recently, many New York City trash collectors worked about 4 hours, yet got paid for a full day's work. The initiation of recycling reduced the volume of trash and allowed some trash collectors to finish their routes early, but union work rules prevented the Sanitation Department from reassigning those workers to new routes.

The point we want to emphasize is that even if cities can save millions of dollars through better management and changes in work rules, many will continue to be plagued by serious structural fiscal problems.

Fiscal Disparities—The Key to Fiscal Problems

Evidence suggests that the differences between the fiscal condition of cities and their suburbs are probably even greater than the differences between cities.[4] The fiscal health of cities is substantially worse than that of the average suburb. Rafuse and Marks (1991), for example, find substantial fiscal disparities within the Chicago area. Even after accounting for the receipt of state and federal aid, the fiscal condition of the City of Chicago is 13 percent below the average of the 40 communities in their sample.[5] These fiscal differences, generally referred to as *fiscal disparities*, exacerbate big-city problems. The larger need-capacity gaps of central cities relative to their suburbs provide an incentive for individuals and businesses to leave the city, thereby worsening the relative fiscal condition of the city, and leading to an inefficient pattern of economic development within a metropolitan area. These fiscal disparities are also generally considered inequitable because citizens of communities in the weakest fiscal positions must face higher tax burdens in order to benefit from identical public services as citizens of communities in stronger fiscal positions.

As a first step in developing policies to improve the fiscal condition of central cities, we must look more closely at the reasons why so many metropolitan areas within the United States are characterized by substantial intrametropolitan fiscal disparities. There are four major reasons why the fiscal conditions of many central cities are poor relative to their suburbs: (1) relatively low fiscal capacity in many cities, (2) higher uncontrollable costs in cities relative to their suburbs, (3) declining intergovernmental assistance, and (4) a prosuburban bias in federal housing, transportation, and tax policies. In the following paragraphs, we discuss each of the reasons for the decline of the fiscal health of cities relative to their suburbs.

LOW FISCAL CAPACITY

The fiscal capacity of a government refers to its ability to raise revenues. Because the property tax is the dominant form of local government revenue in the United States, much of the discussion of fiscal capacity has focused on the property tax base of local governments. A broader measure of fiscal capacity, one that has served as a foundation for the work of Ladd and Yinger, measures capacity as the amount of revenue that could be raised if residents face a standard burden (measured relative to income) and account is taken of the ability of local governments to "export" taxes to nonresidents. Exporting can occur in a number of ways, including purchases of goods and services by visitors, property ownership by nonresidents, and the ability of itemizers to deduct local property and income taxes in calculating their federal income tax liabilities.

Unfortunately, no comprehensive data on the fiscal capacity of cities and their suburbs exist. A number of indicators suggest, however, that in most metropolitan areas, the fiscal capacity of central cities is declining relative to the capacity of their suburbs. The decline in employment, especially manufacturing employment, in many of the nation's largest central cities has been well documented. Even in central cities that have experienced employment growth, the growth has been slow relative to the growth of employment in the suburbs. Bahl, Martinez-Vazquez, and Sjoquist (1992) present data for 35 of the largest metropolitan areas that show that in 1970 the average employment-to-population ratio in the central cities was twice as high as the employment-to-population ratio in the average suburb. By 1987 the city ratio was only 63 percent higher than the suburb ratio, indicating the suburbanization of employment.

Another indicator of the decline in the relative fiscal capacity of central cities is their loss of middle- and high-income population. Of the 10 most populous cities in the Northeast and the Midwest, only one, Columbus, Ohio, experienced a population increase between 1970 and 1990. In the remaining nine cities, population fell on average by 17 percent over this period. An indication that the population loss experienced by these nine cities was dominated by the out-migration of high- and middle-income families and individuals is that in all nine cities the ratio of per capita income inside the central city to per capita income in the suburban ring has fallen between 1960 and 1989. For example, in Chicago in 1960 the ratio of per capita income in the city relative to the income in Chicago's suburbs was 0.86. By 1989 this ratio declined to 0.66. Similarly, in New York, the ratio fell from 0.84 to 0.68. The declining average income of city residents has adverse effects on central city fiscal capacity. As cities' population becomes increasingly poor, cities' tax bases usually shrink.

The structure of employment in cities has also changed. Losses in manufacturing jobs have been at least partially replaced by increases in white-collar employment in business services and in finance, insurance, and real estate. To the extent that a smaller number of high-paying central city jobs are replacing a larger number of more modestly paying manufacturing jobs, the central city, not as a residential location, but as an employment center, is replicating, or perhaps even exaggerating, the increased dispersion of wages that has occurred throughout the economy in recent years (Danziger and Gottschalk 1993). This trend in the wage structure could have significant fiscal implications for central cities. If the holders of high-paying central city jobs prefer to live in the suburbs and commute to work, then the shift in the employment structure of central cities may mean greater suburbanization of high-income residents.

Thus the increasing income differential between central city and suburban residents may reflect three separate trends — suburbanization of jobs, suburbanization of high-income people working in the central city, and an increase in the relative wages of highly skilled people.

The decline both in the number of central city jobs and in the income of central city residents leads directly to a reduction in central city fiscal capacity. The fiscal implications of changes in the type of central city employment, however, as opposed to changes in the level of employment, depend on the features of the local tax system, particularly the property and income taxes. For the property tax, which is the most important local revenue source, the impact of the changing composition of cities' employment bases on their fiscal capacities is not clear. On the one hand, as the value of machinery is generally exempt from property taxation, manufacturing property may be taxed at a lower effective rate than commercial property, due to the higher ratio of machinery value to structure value in manufacturing. On the other hand, in a number of cities that have experienced rapid growth in white-collar employment over the past decade, developers of new office towers have been able to negotiate substantial long-term property tax abatements from city governments.[6] Thus for the foreseeable future the property tax yield from new office employment may be substantially reduced.

The city's ability to capture a share of the higher wages from the centrally located high productivity industries depends on whether the city has in place a local income or wage tax, and whether it is able to tax the income of nonresidents who work in the central city. For example, New York City has a progressive local income tax that is sensitive to changes in wages and is effective at capturing revenue from the relatively high wages generated by the securities industry. However, income earned by nonresidents is taxed at a very low rate. We return to the issue of local wage taxes in the section of the essay on policy options.

Another possible explanation for the relatively weak fiscal position of cities is the large amount of property that is exempt from taxation. In New York City, nearly a third of property value and 20 percent of parcels are exempt from taxation (New York State Board of Equalization and Assessment 1994). The proportion of property value that is exempt in the suburban counties surrounding New York is far lower.[7] For the most part this property is owned by churches, nonprofit organizations, and governments. By virtue of their "centrality," central cities are an efficient location for many tax-exempt entities such as zoos, museums, libraries, hospitals, and other cultural institutions. Rosett (1991) finds that although 29 percent of the nation's population lives in the largest 10 metropolitan areas, museums in these 10 areas account for 70 percent of museum attendance, total spending, and revenue.

As tax-exempt status is usually determined by state government statute, most city governments have little discretion over the amount of their property value that is tax exempt. In New York, for example, 46 percent of all property tax exemptions and 87 percent of the total exempt value were attributable to state mandates. The remaining exemptions were granted at the option of local governments (New York State Board of Equalization and Assessment 1994).

The tax-exempt status of most cultural institutions means that cities are helping to finance such institutions both directly, through contributions to their operating budgets, and indirectly, through forgone property tax revenues. Nonprofits frequently argue that their contribution to the local economy more than compensates for the costs imposed on cities. Since admission charges cover only a fraction of the total expenses of nonprofit institutions, however, and the benefits are enjoyed by the entire metropolitan area, a case can be made for state or regional subventions. State grants to cultural institutions may be an alternative way of getting at this problem. State-level subsidies are generally small, however, and are a declining share of total expenditures of these institutions (Rosett 1991).[8]

HIGH COST OF PUBLIC-SERVICE PROVISION

The second reason many cities face structural fiscal problems is that for a set of reasons largely beyond the control of local officials, the costs of providing public services tend to be higher in cities than in their surrounding suburbs. There are a large number of reasons why costs may be higher in central cities than in suburbs. These can be divided into three broad categories: costs associated with the poor, costs associated with the age of the infrastructure and housing stock, and costs of providing services to nonresidents.

In 1978, 15.4 percent of the population of central cities had income below the poverty line; by 1992 this figure had increased to 20.5 percent (U.S. House of Representatives Committee on Ways and Means 1994). This concentration of the poor in the nation's central cities is exacerbated by zoning and land-use regulations enforced by most suburban communities. Evidence suggests that labor market and housing discrimination against the poor, and especially against minorities, enforces the concentration of these groups within the central cities (Galster 1991).

Studies by Bradbury et al. (1984), Ladd and Yinger (1991), Ladd, Reschovsky, and Yinger (1992), and Green and Reschovsky (1994) suggest that the growing concentration of low-income households within central cities is increasing the costs to city governments of providing public services. Problems that hardly existed 10 or 15 years ago, such as the crack cocaine epidemic and the related rise in violent crimes, the spread of homelessness, and the AIDS epidemic, all place substantial fiscal burdens on cities In many cases, city governments are the service provider of last resort, required by state governments to provide shelter to the homeless and medical care to the indigent. Mandates requiring such services are therefore likely to have a greater impact on cities than on suburbs.

The increased concentration of low-income households results in additional service requirements being placed upon the cities. And the cost of providing standard services such as education and public safety may also rise. There is some evidence that the demographic composition of neighborhoods affects the cost of providing any given level of public services (Summers and Wolfe 1977; Crane 1991). For example, Crane finds strong evidence of neighborhood effects in ghettos, but little evidence in other communities. Despite these findings, the body of evidence on neighborhood effects is inconclusive. Many studies find ambiguous results (Jencks and Meyer 1990) and, due in part to data limitations, few studies have quantified the fiscal impacts of concentrations of poverty. One such attempt is by Pack (1995), who reports that cities with large populations (500,000–1,000,000) spent $199 per capita on direct poverty functions — including public welfare, health care, and hospitals — compared with $67 per capita in cities with populations between 300,000 and 500,000. Pack also finds that even after controlling for differences across cities in fiscal structure, in city size, and in per capita income, cities with high concentrations of poor persons spend substantially more on non-poverty-related municipal functions than cities with relatively few poor persons.

The second set of reasons for higher costs in cities is associated with the fact that cities, at least those in the Northeast and Midwest, are considerably older than their suburbs. This implies that the cost of maintaining existing infrastructure and replacing obsolete infrastructure (such as streetlights) is likely to be higher than in the suburbs. Furthermore, an older housing stock, with its older wiring and absence of modern fire-retardant building material, is likely to increase the costs of guaranteeing any given level of fire safety. The higher density of central city development also contributes to the higher costs of fire fighting in central cities.

Although old city infrastructure is more expensive to maintain than newer suburban infrastructure, from a societal standpoint it may still be considerably cheaper to maintain or even expand existing infrastructure in the central city than to build new infrastructure in the suburbs. For example, the average cost of building sewer lines in the suburbs is likely to be higher than the cost of new hookups or maintenance in the central city because of the lower density of suburban development (thus necessitating more miles of pipe) and the longer distances to existing (often centrally located) sewage treatment facilities.[9]

The final reason cities have higher public service costs than their suburbs is that cities generally provide public services to a substantial number of nonresidents, whether they be suburbanites commuting to central city jobs or taking advantage of the city's cultural and entertainment facilities or tourists drawn to the cities' cultural, entertainment, and commercial attractions. Nonresidents benefit especially from public safety, sanitation, and recreation spending by city governments.

In the 1970s there was considerable academic interest in what came to be called the "suburban exploitation" thesis (Neenan 1970; Bradford and Oates 1974; Greene, Neenan, and Scott 1974). The argument was that suburbs exploit their central cities because there is a net flow of fiscal benefits from city to suburban residents. This benefit flow occurs because the benefits suburbanites receive from city facilities such as zoos, museums, and libraries exceed the costs suburbanites face in the form of taxes or user fees paid to city governments. These taxes and fees might take the form of a city-imposed sales tax or a fee for entrance into city facilities. Tests of the suburban exploitation hypothesis were conducted for a number of metropolitan areas. The results were mixed, both because there was no general agreement on a methodology for measuring the benefits suburban residents derive from cities and because the ability of city governments to tax nonresidents varies tremendously across metropolitan areas (more on this last point later).

There are some reasons why we might want to reopen this line of research. For central cities that do not tax suburbanites, quantifying a flow of net benefits out of the city might provide a political justification for broadening the scope of taxing power available to the city government, or it might help convince state legislators to provide additional state aid to compensate city government for the benefits provided to nonresidents.

Despite the evidence of higher costs of providing public services in cities, a great deal of uncertainty concerning the magnitude of these costs remains. The studies cited above are all based on indirect estimates of costs. Despite the shortcoming of this type of analysis,[10] direct measures of the costs of providing public services require that we have good measures of the *output* of public services — for example, the amount of police protection received by the average citizen, or the amount of education provided to a typical student. Unfortunately, public-sector output is notoriously difficult to measure. The importance of conducting more research on municipal costs is more than academic. Higher costs are an important element in determining the fiscal condition of municipal governments. As we will discuss in more detail below, in most states, one of the purposes of state aid is to assist local governments and school districts in weak fiscal positions. Unfortunately, with a few exceptions, most states completely ignore cost differences among local governments in distributing state aid. Ignoring cost differences almost certainly results in a pattern of aid distribution, for both school and general government purposes, that is detrimental to central cities. This is so because most aid formulas depend primarily on population, adjusted for property tax wealth. Given the decline in central city populations and the increase in costs, such formulas will not provide enough aid to offset the weak fiscal position of central cities.

DECLINING INTERGOVERNMENTAL ASSISTANCE
TO CITIES

The third reason the fiscal condition of central cities has deteriorated in recent years is that intergovernmental assistance from the federal government, and to a lesser extent from state governments, has declined as a percentage of city government spending. Table 1 provides data for the nation's 24 largest cities (all with populations over 500,000 in 1988) and for all cities. For the largest cities, federal aid declined from 13.6 percent of spending in fiscal year 1977 to 4.3 percent of spending in fiscal year 1992. The data for all cities show a similar decline in federal aid. While some state governments made up federal aid cuts (Nathan et al. 1983), the aggregate data show that, relative to city spending, state aid actually declined between 1977 and 1992, from 25.4 percent to 21.2 percent for all cities.[11] These figures represent averages. In some states, aid to large central cities actually grew between 1977 and 1992. For example, state aid as a share of

TABLE 1. *Intergovernmental Revenues as a Percentage of Total City Expenditures*

Intergovernmental Revenue Sources	24 Largest Cities		All U.S. Cities	
	$ Million	Percentage of City Expenditures	$ Million	Percentage of City Expenditures
1976–77:				
State	7,837	34.8	14,236	25.4
Federal	3,060	13.6	8,917	15.9
Local	267	1.2	1,023	1.8
Total	11,164	49.6	24,176	43.1
City expenditures	22,516		56,145	
1979–80:				
State	8,144	30.5	15,393	21.2
Federal	4,103	15.4	10,872	15.0
Local	327	1.2	2,005	2.8
Total	12,574	47.1	28,270	39.0
City expenditures	26,682		72,445	
1984–86:				
State	11,543	29.8	23,082	21.8
Federal	3,599	9.3	10,292	9.7
Local	606	1.6	2,464	2.4
Total	15,748	40.7	35,838	33.9
City expenditures	38,695		105,697	
1991–92:				
State	19,036	29.7	36,317	21.2
Federal	2,779	4.3	8,003	4.7
Local	827	1.3	3,898	2.3
Total	22,642	35.3	48,218	28.2
City expenditures	64,029		171,377	

Source: United States Bureau of the Census (various years).

Note: Represented are U.S. cities with 1988 populations greater than 500,000 except for Washington, D.C.

total expenditures grew from 22 percent to 41 percent in Boston, reflecting in large part the state's response to Proposition 2½, the voter-approved property tax limitation. Over the same period, state aid's share of expenditures grew from 11.9 percent to 17.2 percent in Chicago. The dominant trend, however, is one of reduced state assistance to large cities. In a few cases, the reduction in state aid reflects, at least in part, state assumption of responsibilities for the financing of services previously funded by city governments. This would appear to be the case in New York City, where, in response to the fiscal crisis of the mid-1970s, the state assumed responsibility for most of the operating costs of higher education and the courts.

Ongoing efforts by the Congress to achieve a balanced budget by the year 2002 will undoubtedly result in further cuts in direct federal aid to central cities. For example, substantial cuts in mass transit operating subsidies, in federal education programs, and in Community Development Block Grants will probably occur over the next few years. In addition, as we shall discuss in more detail below, proposed reductions in federal spending on the poor are likely to have quite detrimental fiscal impacts for many of the nation's central cities.

ANTIURBAN SPATIAL BIAS IN THE FEDERAL POLICIES

While the demographics of urban centers are primarily determined by private incentives as well as legal and institutional regulations, some federal government programs have unintended spatial biases. The most salient examples are found in transportation, housing, and tax policies used by the federal government. These policies tend to reinforce both the market incentives that cause middle- and upper-income residents to migrate to the suburbs and the growing concentration of the poor in the central cities (McGeary 1990). For example, while the primarily federally funded interstate highway system appears to have stimulated central city employment, it has also facilitated the suburbanization of high-income households.

Federal housing policies can directly affect the composition of neighborhoods. There is no question that low-income public housing projects have fostered urban segregation. Not only are these projects concentrated in urban areas — over 70 percent of them are located in central cities — but they also tend to foster immobility among project residents. For example, in the Cabrini Green public housing project in Chicago, 59 percent of the residents lived in the same housing unit between 1975 and 1980, while in the surrounding low-income neighborhood, only 40 percent of the residents lived in the same units during this 5-year period (McGeary 1990).

Current housing policies, which rely heavily on rent subsidies to low-income households, are intended to make it feasible for low-income residents to find housing in the suburbs. These policies, however, appear to have had limited impact on the mobility of the low-income households (McGeary 1990). This failure is due to a combination of factors, including the low level of subsidy compared with the cost of housing and transportation in the suburbs, discrimination in suburban housing markets, and the reluctance of many low-income households to search for housing in neighborhoods far from their current residence.

To eliminate the practice of redlining and to encourage financial institutions to make more loans to inner-city residents, and in particular to minorities, Congress in 1977 passed the Community Reinvestment Act (CRA). The effectiveness of CRA in increasing homeownership rates in minority communities and in stabilizing declining city neighborhoods is the subject of considerable debate. Schill and Wachter (1994, p. 14) suggest that an unintended consequence of CRA may be to "intensify the spatial concentration of poverty." They argue that in order to meet lending requirements of CRA, banks may pursue policies that make it easier for low-income applicants to receive a loan in a poor than in a middle-income neighborhood.

A number of features of the federal tax code also may have an implicit prosuburban bias. The most important of these are the tax treatment of owner- versus renter-occupied housing, and the incentives for new construction versus rehabilitation and maintenance of the existing stock of housing. Renters are more concentrated in the city than in the suburbs, for both demand and supply reasons. On the demand side, income levels in the central city are lower than in the suburbs, and rates of home ownership are strongly correlated with family income levels. On the supply side, density limits and other zoning practices frequently preclude the construction of multifamily rental housing in the suburbs. In part for the same reasons, new housing is more likely to consist of detached, single family homes constructed in the suburbs. Therefore, if the tax code favors owners, or encourages new construction and the early retirement of existing housing, it encourages demand for suburban locations.

The tax code lowers the cost of owning compared to renting because the imputed income from housing — the income that owners in effect pay to themselves for the use of a house — is not observed in the market, and is therefore excluded from taxation. The favorable treatment of capital gains from the sale of houses also benefits owners. If the home-owning taxpayer is an itemizer, the major housing expenses — mortgage interest payments and property taxes — are deductible expenses. For the owner of rental housing, all expenses of providing the housing are deductible, but net income is fully taxable. It should be stressed that it is this difference in the treatment of income, not the fact that renters cannot deduct rental payments from their income tax, that provides an advantage to owning. Until 1986, the advantage to owning was at least partially offset by favorable depreciation provisions for rental housing.

Researchers differ on the net effect of these subsidies. Peterson (1980) estimated that the tax subsidy for homeownership was directly responsible for raising the rate of ownership by about 15 percentage points between 1940 and 1970. Gordon, Hines, and Summers (1986) argued that prior to 1986, on balance, federal tax policy was favorable to renters. The Tax Reform Act of 1986 (TRA86) reduced the incentives for housing consumption for both owners and renters, but shifted the balance towards ownership (Poterba 1990). The most recent federal tax changes, by raising marginal rates for the highest income taxpayers, have increased the housing subsidy mainly for wealthy homeowners.

The major tax incentive for new construction was the difference in depreciation rates for new versus rehabilitated housing (Peterson 1980). Accelerated depreciation for rental properties was eliminated by TRA86, so this implicitly prosuburban incentive no longer exists. At the same time, the major tax provision explicitly favoring older areas, the federal Historic Rehabilitation Tax Credit, was also eliminated by TRA86.

The other major feature of the federal tax code, which has the implicit effect of deconcentrating the metropolitan area, is the use of tax-exempt financing for housing, infrastructure, and industrial development. State housing finance agencies, through their expanded use of tax-exempt financing for middle-class housing, have contributed to the exodus of middle-class people from the central city (Peterson 1980). Tax-exempt financing of new infrastructure in effect shifts the cost of suburban development from local residents to the federal government. Since manufacturing facilities have been relocating to the suburban fringe, tax-exempt financing of industrial parks may also favor the suburbs. Restrictions on the tax-exempt financing for so-called private purpose bonds under TRA86 have curbed the very rapid growth in tax subsidies to facilities such as suburban industrial parks.

Most of the spatial effects of federal tax policy are implicit — that is, they are the by-product of other more dominant goals of the tax system. As such, it is unlikely that the tax code will be specifically altered to favor central cities. The one exception is federal tax subsidies to enterprise (or empowerment) zones.

In accordance with provisions in the Omnibus Budget Reconciliation

Act of 1993 (OBRA), the Clinton administration in late 1994 authorized the creation of 104 empowerment zones and enterprise communities, many of them in the nation's largest central cities.[12] The OBRA legislation provides cities with designated zones a number of economic and fiscal incentives designed to create jobs and spur both economic and community development. Special efforts will be made to coordinate federal programs within the zones and, where possible, to waive federal regulations. In addition, businesses located in empowerment zones will be entitled to receive wage and job training credits of up to $3,000 per employee for employees who both work and live in the zone. Businesses in the zone will also be eligible for special investment credits. Finally, 1 billion dollars of funding was authorized to finance special social service block grants that designated cities may use to promote economic self-sufficiency.

Economists have generally been skeptical about the ability of enterprise zones to successfully encourage economic development. In most cases, the economic and fiscal incentives established in enterprise zones are likely to be outweighed by other factors, such as crime and the quality of the labor force, in determining the location and expansion of business firms within central cities. In a study of enterprise zones in Indiana, Papke (1994) does find some response to capital subsidies and a significant decrease in unemployment claims. However, she does not attempt to compare the benefits to the costs in forgone tax revenue, although she does find a decline in zone property tax bases because of the decline in value of machinery and equipment. In a survey piece, Papke (1993) points out that on the basis of limited evidence from a few state programs, capital incentives do increase zone investment, but that only about 10 percent of the investment represents new businesses. If the rest are relocations from already marginal areas, then the benefits to the central city fisc may be limited. She also concludes that state zone programs "do not seem to have improved the economic status of zone residents." Although the legislation establishing Empowerment Zones mandates an evaluation of their effectiveness, it is too early to tell whether the federal administration will in fact carry out the kind of carefully designed evaluation studies necessary to assess the effectiveness of enterprise zones.

The major changes in the federal tax code in the 1980s — the reduction in marginal tax rates, the decrease in the percentage itemizers, the broadening of the tax base, and the restrictions on tax exempt financing — have on balance reduced, though not completely eliminated, the prosuburban bias of the federal tax code. Though this change is encouraging for cities, in some sense the damage has already been done. It is not clear, however, that changes in tax policies are either feasible or efficacious as a means of reversing central city decline.

Do Fiscal Disparities Lead to Worsening Fiscal Distress?

We have argued that not only are many of the nation's central cities in weaker fiscal health than their suburbs, but that most of them are continuing to lose both economic activity and middle-income residents. An important question to be answered before policies can be designed to reverse these trends is the extent to which this out-migration of both businesses and residents is directly attributable to the existence of disparities in both tax rates and public service provision between cities and their suburbs.

Reviewing the large literature on firm mobility, Bartik (1991) concludes that the effects of local fiscal factors are substantial. In particular, he suggests that a 10 percent increase in local taxes will lead to a long-run reduction in business activity of between 10 percent and 30 percent. Furthermore, he finds that fiscal factors are more important in *intra*metropolitan business location decisions than in *inter*metropolitan or inter*state* business location decisions. Most of the studies reviewed by Bartik are not restricted to central city firms. Thus it is not surprising that there appears to be no consensus among researchers concerning the role of fiscal factors in locational decisions by business firms.

Several studies have also examined the impact of fiscal factors on individual mobility. While the evidence is sparse, individuals' residential location decisions appear to be affected by the fiscal conditions of state and local governments. Reschovsky (1979) finds that local fiscal conditions affect intrametropolitan location decisions. Reviewing some of the more recent empirical studies, Charney (1993) also finds that in general local tax and expenditure policies appear to affect individual migration decisions. None of these studies, however, directly addresses the reasons people choose to move out of central cities. In general, research on residential mobility suggests that many people's decisions are based on a combination of "push" and "pull" factors. City residents may decide to leave because of a fear of crime or because of high property tax rates in the city. Alternatively, their move to the suburbs may be motivated by a desire for high-quality suburban public education or the possibility of a larger garden. In the end it is difficult to disentangle the role of any particular factor in influencing decisions to move out of a central city. Within many metropolitan areas, the central city may have higher-than-average tax rates, higher crime rates, worse schools, dirtier streets, and larger concentrations of minorities. Given this correlation of factors, it is very difficult to separate out the specific role of fiscal factors in individuals' decisions to move. But it is important to try to do so. Perhaps the best way to do so is through longitudinal research, that is, surveys and statistical studies that follow people and cities over time, to determine changes in the importance of various factors.

One reason that it may be difficult to observe the out-migration of middle-class residents in response to fiscal disparities is that cities adjust their tax and expenditure policies according to the degree of competition from suburbs. In a study of taxation in big cities, Inman (1989) finds that the more the suburbs offer a potential substitute for central city locations, the more likely that cities will lower taxes that affect the middle class. Inman uses as a measure of suburban competition the ratio of city income to suburban income. He argues that when the suburbs are either very poor or very rich, as compared to the city, suburbs are not a good substitute for the city. The statistical evidence shows that while poorer cities spend less across the board, property taxes and fees are also lower when cities are more constrained by their suburbs.

Despite statements such as Kenneth Jackson's (1985, p. 289) that "no discussion of the settlement patterns of the American people can ignore the overriding significance of race," very little is known about the role of race in influencing locational decisions. The phenomenon of "white flight" has been much discussed, but we have little concrete knowledge about how important racial attitudes are in motivating people to move from central cities. Social mores against racial statements suggest that most people will not provide explicit racial reasons in answering surveys seeking to elicit the reasons why people move.

Furthermore, the few empirical studies that examine white flight draw ambiguous conclusions. Frey (1977), for example, suggests that impact of race on white flight has been "minimal," whereas Galster (1990) suggests that race is the most important influence on the migration of middle- and upper-class whites. One reason for the mixed result may be that these studies, and for that matter most studies of individual migration patterns, utilize aggregate census tract data. Drawing inferences about individual behavior from aggregate data may lead to inappropriate conclusions and ambiguous results. Furthermore, these studies do not account for the fiscal factors. Thus, to the extent that poor, minority communities have high taxes and low services, these studies may overstate the importance of race in migration patterns. While it seems unlikely that we can get precise answers regarding the role of race, it is still important that researchers try to separate this factor from other factors that are perhaps more susceptible to change through public policy.

Although conducting research on residential mobility is difficult, additional knowledge about the factors that motivate both residential and business location decisions is important in assessing the likely success of city fiscal policies. For example, to what extent do the creation of magnet schools stem the out-migration of middle-income families from cities? Which policy, cutting property tax rates or increasing spending on police protection, is most likely to influence residents and businesses to remain in the central city? Finding answers to these questions has the potential for creating more effective urban policies.

Assessing the Effectiveness of Policies Designed to Address City Fiscal Problems

What policy options are available that may ameliorate the fiscal problems faced by central cities? It is useful to divide the set of all potential policies into two groups, those that can be initiated unilaterally by public officials within central cities, and those that require explicit cooperation between cities and other units of government — federal, state, or regional.

While public officials can take some actions addressed at the underlying structural problems that contribute to their fiscal well-being, many of the actions open to local officials involve guaranteeing that the city government operates as effectively and efficiently as possible, and maximizing the quality and quantity of public services delivered to its residents given the available revenue.

One motivation for mayors to make politically difficult decisions is that unless cities "get their house in order," they will have little chance of convincing either state or regional officials to provide them with more resources. In other words, aggressive pursuit of "city-only" policies is probably a precondition, although not a guarantee, of metropolitan area cooperation.

CITY-ONLY POLICIES
The mayors of several large cities have recently been pursuing policies designed primarily to reduce spending on public services without cutting the delivery of public services. Here we outline a set of general policies that

cities can pursue. We provide examples from recent experiences in a number of cities where mayors have aggressively pursued homegrown "solutions" to urban fiscal problems. These homegrown policies fall into several categories.

The Implementation of Managerial Efficiencies
and Productivity Gains through the Use of Total
Quality Management, the Abandonment of Outmoded
Labor Practices, or the Adoption of New Technologies.

For example, Philadelphia mayor Edward Rendell has established a new Risk Management Division that is saving millions of dollars by reducing workplace injuries. In addition, Philadelphia has expanded the use of computerized systems to coordinate the use of the city's 5,800 vehicles, to develop Geographic Information Systems throughout city government, and to integrate tax collection efforts.

Chicago has employed computer technology to improve efficiency in its public health department. Field nurses now utilize hand-held computers, a move that has substantially reduced the proportion of each day spent doing paperwork. In Milwaukee, Mayor John Norquist has adopted a performance-based management system in which managers submit strategic plans and objectives. Future budgets for each agency are then determined by how well each manager meets these objectives.

The Increasing Use of the Private Sector
for a Wide Range of Public Services.

Although a number of authors have argued that substantial cost savings can be achieved through privatization (Savas 1987; Donahue 1989), much more research is necessary to determine whether the use of the private sector for the provision of core services can be achieved while maintaining broad access to the services and simultaneously providing substantial cost reductions. If the primary savings from privatization come from using private-sector labor that is cheaper because it is nonunionized, this source of savings needs to be distinguished from more productive or efficient use of personnel.

Privatization is unlikely to reduce costs if it merely replaces a single public-sector provider with a single private-sector provider. Cost savings are more likely to result if a competitive situation, with multiple providers, can be established. This approach has recently been adopted in Indianapolis, where Mayor Steve Goldsmith's competition program lets private-sector companies bid against government workers for contracts to provide services and manage assets. The goal of the program is not privatization per se, but rather, competition. In fact, some of the competitive contracts, including street repairs, have been awarded to government agencies.[13]

Personnel Compensation Reforms.

In some cases, this means cuts in "out-of-line" benefit and wage compensation packages, or the implementation of cost-saving work rule changes. For example, faced with a very real threat of bankruptcy, Philadelphia mayor Edward Rendell "saved" approximately $450 million over a 2-year period by initiating management changes and restructuring personnel compensation.

Expansion of Local Revenue Sources.

The increased use of user fees and charges provides some cities a potentially important way to expand revenues. The advantage of user fees is that they can often be structured so that a large proportion of the fees are exported to nonresidents. For example, increased fees for parking tend to generate substantial revenue from suburban commuters. Another possibility is the use of "fire fees." These fees, with the level of charge linked to the diameter of the water pipe serving each property, can be structured so that tax-exempt property (e.g., nonprofit institutions) will be subject to the fees. Though charges have grown in overall importance in the last 20 years, Downing (1992) shows that there is substantial variation among cities, even for the same service.

Tax or Spending Policies Designed to Favor Middle-Class Neighborhoods.

To the extent that the fiscal health of central cities depends on their ability to retain middle- and high-income residents, policies designed explicitly to provide extra public services, or in some cases to lower taxes, to middle-class neighborhoods may make both economic and political sense. For example, there is evidence that in New York City effective property tax rates are lower in middle- and upper-class neighborhoods than in others (New York University Graduate School of Public Administration 1980). If the implication, however, is very high effective tax rates in poor or declining neighborhoods, then such tax discrimination may not be desirable. Janet Pack (1992) reports that in the last few years there has been a rapid growth of Business Improvement Districts (BIDs). These districts operate like private governments. They levy taxes and use the proceeds to provide services within their boundaries. As Pack points out, much more must be known about whether BIDs will provide effective mechanisms for targeting services to specify needs, thereby encouraging businesses to remain in central cities. She also suggests that to the extent that BIDs can be established in a wide range of neighborhoods, BIDs will be less likely to result in inequities in service provision within cities. However, the widespread use of BIDs may be feasible only if the state or federal government is willing to assist firms in poor neighborhoods in paying the additional taxes levied by BIDs.

The Stimulation of Economic Development.

There has been a long history of city and state government efforts to stimulate economic development in central cities. Often these efforts have been in the form of property tax abatements or in some cases capital subsidies. Philadelphia, for example, has recently established "public-private partnerships" to spur downtown development. As Dick Netzer (1991, p. 234) suggests, however, "the empirical evidence on what works in economic development is thin or unpersuasive." The key and very difficult question is whether the abatements and subsidies stimulate new economic activity, or simply subsidize activities that would have taken place anyway. Presumably there is a trade-off between tax abatements for specific firms and lower rates of taxation for all firms. It is important that we do more to analyze the relative efficacy of these two policies, in terms of their ultimate effect on city employment and revenues.

Cuts in Services Directed at the City's Least Mobile Populations (Such as the Poor, the Homeless, or the Uninsured).

Although these service cuts may make life increasingly miserable for city residents who are perhaps most in need of public services, the fact remains that there are limited fiscal externalities associated with such cuts. Not only are these individuals unlikely to move, but they are also unlikely to vote or to be otherwise politically active.

INTERGOVERNMENTAL POLICIES

In the first section of this essay, we have argued that the poor fiscal health of many of the nation's large central cities is in part a function of their position as one of many governments within metropolitan areas. Because large cities' fiscal health is largely attributable to factors beyond the control of city officials, the solutions to their fiscal problems must involve other governments. In this section, we briefly discuss several of these "metropolitan solutions."

Taxing Nonresidents.

"Tax exporting" is the ability to shift tax burdens to people who live outside the city. All of the major revenue sources used by cities — property taxes, sales taxes, earnings or income taxes, and fees — are at least partly exportable. For the property tax, exporting frequently occurs when commercial and industry property is taxed, since a substantial proportion of such property is owned by nonresidents. The sales tax is exported when purchases of taxable items are made by nonresidents (e.g., a restaurant meal purchased by a commuter, or a hotel tax paid by a visitor). The earnings tax is exported when the tax base includes the city earnings of nonresidents. Property and earnings taxes can also be exported through their deductibility from federal and (sometimes state) income taxes. By contrast, local sales taxes and fees are not deductible.

From the point of view of city residents, tax exporting is desirable in that it increases the city's ability to raise revenue without burdening city residents. There is substantial evidence that cities do structure their tax systems so as to take advantage of tax exporting. Other objectives, however, such as the distribution of tax burdens by income class, also matter to local politicians, and there may be conflicts between the various objectives. The policy question is how to design the tax system so as to export as much of the burden as possible, while minimizing the economic harm to the central city.

The various taxes and fees differ in the degree to which the burden is borne by nonresidents. The most heavily exportable taxes are the property tax on commercial and industrial property, and the earnings tax. Almost all cities, Chicago included, tax nonresidential property at higher rates than owner-occupied property, in some cities through a formal classification scheme, and in other cities through de facto differences in assessment ratios. In the 1970s the effective property tax rate on nonresidential property was typically about 25 percent higher than the rate on housing (Ladd and Yinger 1991). The rate differential between the two types of property, however, differs substantially across cities. At one extreme, in New York City in 1991, the effective property tax rate on commercial property was over four times the rate on homeowners (Chernick 1992). While there is some evidence that the property tax base as a whole is sensitive to the property tax rate (i.e., goes down somewhat when rates go up), there is little evidence on the economic effects of taxing different types of property at different rates. Further research would be highly useful to determine whether the long-run economic consequences of taxing nonresidential property at a higher rate than residential property are positive or negative.

Currently six of the nation's 24 largest cities use earnings or income taxes.[14] These taxes have been growing in importance, and in 1989 accounted for about 8 percent of total expenditures in these cities. By contrast, the property tax comprises about 17 percent of total expenditures in these cities. As discussed above, an earnings tax can be an effective revenue instrument for reaping fiscal benefits from high-paying central city jobs. To do so, however, the earnings of nonresidents should be included in the tax base. At present, all six of the cities with earnings or income taxes impose a full or partial tax on the earnings of nonresidents.

As with the property tax, the problem with a local earnings or income tax is that, while it may be effective at exporting tax burdens and raising revenue in the short run, in the longer run, it may hurt the competitive position of the city. In Philadelphia, nonresident earnings are taxed at amost the same rate as resident earnings, while there is no local income tax in the suburbs. Research by Grieson (1980), Inman (1987), and Luce (1994) suggests that the employment impacts of this tax have been quite negative, but Gruenstein (1980) disputes these results. In Detroit, which taxes nonresidents at half the rate for resident earners, Dearborn (1992) reports that wage tax revenues in 1991 were less than the amount received in 1987, as past rate increases have been offset by a decline in the number of filers. In contrast to Philadelphia and Detroit, Baltimore commuters pay income tax to the county rather than to the city. While this reduces the competitive disadvantage problem, it also limits Baltimore's ability to capture revenue from high-wage earners.[15]

An important topic for further research is the long-term relationship between local tax structure and local economic performance. Since the tax structure may itself be affected by economic performance, studies must deal explicitly with the simultaneous nature of the relationship. For the income tax, the question to be addressed is whether cities with broad-based income or earnings taxes are in stronger fiscal positions than cities that do not utilize income taxes. Do such taxes enhance the performance of the entire metropolitan economy, or do they accelerate the economic decline of the central city relative to the suburbs?

Cities are dependent on the states for the authority to enact income taxes, and state legislators have been reluctant to allow additional local taxes, particularly if they impose costs on suburbanites. In the last sections of this essay, we discuss the political obstacles to expanding the earnings tax, and offer some possible solutions.

Federal Assistance to Cities.
Despite the unlikelihood of increases in federal aid to central cities, it is worth asking whether such increases, if they occurred, would improve the

fiscal health of cities. One way to answer this question is to look at how city governments used the large increases in federal aid that occurred during the 1970s and how they coped with the rapid cuts in aid in the early 1980s. (Federal aid as a share of local spending peaked in 1978.)

Uncertainty concerning the permanence of federal aid led many cities to minimize the risk of aid cutbacks by segregating federal aid into separate funds. Peterson (1986) and Nathan et al. (1987) found that these funds were generally used to finance special noncore services, often targeted for the needy, that could be adjusted in accordance with federal assistance levels.

Nathan et al. (1987) concluded that the stronger the redistributive purpose of these federally funded programs, the less likely they were to be protected by the state or local government. For example, in Chicago the federal aid cuts primarily affected social and training programs and these programs were not replaced by the city. In particular, 4,800 persons were phased out of job-training programs, over 25 percent of the staff of the Department of Human Services was laid off, and four community and five youth centers were closed. This evidence thus suggests that unless city governments perceive federal aid to be permanent, they will not use it to help finance core services and thus it will do little to improve their fundamental fiscal position.

The 104th Congress elected in November 1994 has committed itself to achieve a balanced federal budget by the year 2002. In its Budget Resolution passed in the summer of 1995, Congress called for large cuts in a wide range of federal programs, plus radical changes in the structure of programs providing assistance to low-income Americans. Although at this time (August 1995) none of the proposed budget cuts and program changes has been enacted, it appears highly likely that the budget and policy changes that Congress ultimately enacts will prove largely detrimental to the fiscal health of central cities.

Federal budgetary changes with an impact on central cities are likely to take several distinct forms. First, direct federal aid to city governments will probably be substantially reduced. Second, federal aid to other governmental units that serve city residents, such as school districts, transit authorities, and county governments, will be reduced. Third, federal funds to nonprofit organizations that provide services to city residents will probably also be cut. Fourth, reductions in federal programs that provide a wide range of services to low-income families will probably be sharply curtailed. Fifth, a likely decrease in federal outlays for means-tested entitlement programs such as Food Stamps and AFDC, and a shift from open-ended matching grants to block grants for welfare funding, will almost certainly lead to a reduction in state-government financed assistance to low-income populations.[16] Finally, added fiscal pressures on state governments resulting from their assumption of responsibilities for a wide range of services now provided by the federal government may well result in cuts in state assistance to local governments.

Although the final list of budget cuts has yet to be determined, the legislation approved by the House of Representatives includes a number of cuts in programs that currently send substantial amounts of federal funding to central cities. For example, the legislation calls for cuts of nearly 30 percent in funding for Community Development Block Grants, 25 percent in public housing operating subsidies, 40 percent in funding for the homeless, and 18 percent in compensatory education aid.

As mentioned above, evidence from responses to previous fluctuations in federal aid to cities suggests that increases in aid serve largely as a supplement to local outlays, while decreases in aid tend not to be replaced by local resources. However, Nathan et al. (1983) also found that the fiscal response was not uniform across governments. In addition, a number of factors which mitigated service reductions in the early 1980s are unlikely to play the same role today.

In some cities strong overlapping governments helped to mitigate service cuts in the early 1980s. The broader geographical scope of the current round of proposed cuts means that offsetting support from overlapping governments such as counties or special districts will not be very strong. Political ideology also had some effect on the degree of replacement, with more liberal governments replacing a higher fraction of reduced federal aid. The conservative political shift at all levels of government that began in the 1980s and has accelerated in the 1990s will tend to reinforce the service-cutting fiscal response of cities.

Another potential source of replacement funds for reduced federal aid is increased state aid. Ladd (1990) found that states replaced federal aid to cities almost dollar for dollar between 1982 and 1987, with the important exception of federal aid for education and welfare. In the latter two categories there was almost no replacement. Since the 1995 Budget Resolution calls for large cuts in both federal education and welfare spending, the experience of the 1980s suggests that state governments will do relatively little to replace these federal funding cuts. In general, the replacement of federal grant moneys by state governments is unlikely to be as great as it was in the 1990s. First, the magnitude of the currently proposed cuts is much larger than the budget reductions of the 1980s, and second, the states themselves are likely to face substantial cuts in federal funds and changes in incentives to provide aid to poor citizens.

In the early 1980s, a number of categorical grants targeted to cities were converted into block grants to state governments with pass-through provisions to local governments. Limited econometric evidence, however, suggests that these pass-through requirements were not very successful in directing resources to cities, with much of the federal aid diverted to general state government spending (Craig and Inman 1986).[17] This research suggests that more extensive reliance on block grants will only increase these fiscal leakages, to the detriment of aid to local governments.

Likely cuts in city services in health, housing, community development, and education will be reinforced by the proposed cuts in federal entitlement programs, the elimination of federal matching requirements (for AFDC and Medicaid), and the relaxation of federal mandates. Proposed reductions in the federal funding of entitlement programs, which are substantially larger than the likely cuts in direct aid to city governments, are likely to have substantial impacts on the disposable income of poor city residents. A recent estimate indicated that proposed cuts in entitlement spending would translate into cuts of at least 14 percent in the long-run disposable income of the poorest 10 percent of the population (Chernick 1995). The Census Bureau reports that in 1993, 41.5 percent of people with incomes below 125 percent of the poverty line lived in central cities. Given this concentration of the poor in cities, the proposed entitlement cuts represent a significant decline in the resources available to central city residents.

Though the proposed federal cuts are unlikely to induce immediate budgetary crises, we expect that the longer-run consequence will be to reduce the structural fiscal health of central cities, increase fiscal disparities between cities and their more prosperous suburbs, and worsen the competitive position of cities. The reduction in fiscal health will occur because cuts in services and entitlements will cause an increase in central city poverty. As we have stressed above, the cost of city services is closely linked to the extent of poverty.

City governments may be forced, either by court order or by public outcry, to provide basic services to residents who have been particularly hard hit by cuts in funding for welfare, Medicaid, and subsidized housing. Despite efforts by city governments to ratify the cuts in federal programs, there is likely to be some cost shifting to cities, which will continue to serve as the service providers of last resort. The reduction in entitlement income will also affect city fiscal health, in that the existing tax structure will now result in higher fiscal burdens on low-income city residents.

Even if the current vigorous assault on domestic spending turns out to be only temporary, is it likely that Congress would establish an aid program designed to provide the nation's most fiscally stressed central cities with substantial amounts of general purpose aid? History suggests that even if the fiscal health of some of our major cities deteriorated dramatically, Congress would be incapable of targeting aid to cities in distress. Past efforts to target aid explicitly have all failed. The political pressures to spread federal funds around to a broad set of jurisdictions are too strong. For example, although efforts were made to target General Revenue Sharing funds to needy communities, in the end, the distribution closely approximated per capita grants to all of the nation's general purpose local governments.

It will be important to conduct further research on the equity and efficiency of the current allocations of federal aid to city governments, and to monitor closely the impact of any future cuts in federal aid. For example, has there been, as some people suggest, a prosuburban bias in the distribution of federal transportation aid?[18] If so, will that bias be exacerbated under proposals that call for larger proportional reductions in federal mass transit operating subsidies than in federal highway aid? Do categorical aid programs lead to inefficient decisions by city governments? Does their replacement by block grants lead to greater efficiency in service delivery, or to less targeting of assistance to the poorest people and neighborhoods in cities?

State Government Assistance.
State assistance to central cities takes several forms. Over time, state governments have assumed from cities a number of governmental functions. The major candidates for state takeover are directly redistributive services, such as the provision of shelters for the homeless, and other services, such as prisons, whose costs are often closely linked to the greater rates of poverty in central cities. If state assumption requires higher state taxes, presumably a greater share of these taxes would come from suburban areas. Thus there would be a net fiscal gain to the central cities. Many of the potential candidates for state assumption, however, particularly welfare programs, have already been taken over by the state, so opportunities are limited.[19] Still it would be helpful to identify those public services with higher central city costs per unit of public service delivered. These would be good candidates for state assumption.

State mandates are policies that, in a sense, work in the opposite way. Local governments complain bitterly about the cost of unfunded mandates from higher levels of government. It has proved difficult, however, to document the extent and the fiscal cost of such mandates. Some mandates may be socially optimal, in that they are an efficient way to force all communities to provide some minimal level of service. From the metropolitan perspective, special attention must be paid to mandates that impose higher costs on central cities than they do on suburban jurisdictions. For example, requirements that the homeless be guaranteed shelter, or that the mentally ill be provided an appropriate level of care at the community level, are likely to impose greater costs on the central city. Research would be useful to document the extent of such differential costs. Policies to compensate cities for any cost differentials that result from state mandates should be considered.

The most direct form of state assistance is through the distribution of state grants to local governments. As we reported earlier, between fiscal years 1977 and 1992, aggregate state grants have declined relative to city government spending. In fact, Gold (1994) reports that in 1992 local government aid accounted for the lowest proportion of state spending in 35 years. Despite these reductions in the role of state aid, state assistance to large central cities has played a very important role in improving their fiscal health (Ladd and Yinger 1991).

Although no comprehensive data exist, it appears that the share of most states' intergovernmental aid budget being allocated to large cities is declining over time. This decline reflects both the reduced political influence of central cities relative to their suburbs, and also the fact that nearly all states distribute aid using allocation formulas that take little or no account of the higher costs faced by cities relative to their suburbs. It is thus not surprising that in a study of state aid to city governments in Minnesota, Ladd, Reschovsky, and Yinger (1992) found almost no correlation between local governments' per capita state aid allocations and their fiscal health.

The prospect for major new infusions of state aid to central cities is not good. The politics of aid distribution in most states makes it nearly impossible to reduce any local government's aid allocation. Thus the only way to increase state fiscal assistance to cities is to increase the state's total aid budget, an unlikely prospect in most states in light of the rising costs of corrections and Medicaid, and the prospect of increased fiscal pressures on state governments arising from federal government retrenchment.

The final way in which states can provide financial assistance to city governments is by authorizing them to utilize new revenue sources. This is potentially important in states such as Massachusetts and Wisconsin, where local governments are constrained (with minor exceptions) from utilizing anything other than the property tax. Revenue diversification may increase a city's revenue-raising capacity.[20] But if state governments authorize cities to use new revenue sources, some of the city's revenue gain will be offset if the state reduces their aid allocations. Ladd and Yinger (1991) suggest that such a trade-off does in fact occur. Additional research would be useful in assessing the appropriate mixture of state assistance and local taxing authority.

Metropolitan Area Tax Base Sharing.

One proposed solution to metropolitan area fiscal disparities that has spurred considerable interest across the country is metropolitan area tax base sharing. The one example of tax base sharing is in the Twin Cities metropolitan area in Minnesota. Under the Minnesota plan, 40 percent of all increases from a 1971 base in the market value of commercial-industrial property is shared among municipalities within the metropolitan area. The formula that distributes the shared base favors jurisdictions with low per capita property values. Proponents of the plan argue that having to share the fiscal benefit of any commercial development will reduce the incentives of local governments to compete for new development. Overall efficiency of economic development within the metropolitan area then will be enhanced. By equalizing the fiscal capacity of local governments in this way, the tax base sharing plan also reduces fiscal disparities among local governments in the metropolitan area.

After nearly 20 years of operation, tax base sharing has substantially reduced fiscal disparities within the metropolitan area.[21] In the early years of the plan and since 1994, both cities received more base than they contributed. Between 1984 and 1994, however, Minneapolis was a net contributor of shared base, reflecting primarily a boom in commercial real estate, and the fact that the distribution formula does not at all reflect the higher costs of providing public services in central cities. The Minneapolis experience illustrates the value of tax base sharing as a kind of insurance against changing fiscal fortunes.

By all reports, the Twin Cities area has avoided many of the problems of urban sprawl and inefficient land use decisions that plague most politically fragmented metropolitan areas. Although tax base sharing by itself has probably had little direct impact on the efficiency of metropolitan development (Reschovsky 1980), it appears that the very existence of tax base sharing has been an essential precondition for the enactment of other policies, such as strict land use planning regulations, that have directly influenced the pattern of economic development in the Twin Cities area.

Despite its success in Minnesota, the prospects for the establishment of tax base sharing plans in other metropolitan areas is poor. The political representatives of those communities that would be net "losers" under a tax base sharing plan, or that believe they will be net losers at some point in the near future, will oppose tax base sharing. In addition, existing regional governments are in many cases fragmented and weak. The six-county Chicago metropolitan area, for example, includes 262 separate municipal governments. If we count school districts and special districts, there are 1,200 different governmental bodies. The only general purpose regional organization serving the entire six-county area is the Northeastern Illinois Planning Commission. Although the commission can encourage metro-politan area cooperation, it lacks taxing authority and its powers are quite limited (Regional Partnership 1991).[22] In a later section, we discuss some actions that could be taken to increase cooperation and improve the pros-pect for the wider adoption of metropolitan tax base sharing.

Metropolitan Area Governments.

The United States includes a few examples of metropolitan area govern-ments, most notably Nashville and Jacksonville. Although we know of no systematic assessment of the impact of the formation of a metropolitan government on the fiscal position of either city, both cities are in relatively strong fiscal health (Ladd and Yinger 1991). This fact, however, does not answer the question of whether the residents of central cities would be helped if their city governments were replaced by general purpose metro-politan area governments. On the one hand, city residents would share in the growing suburban tax base, and the burden of providing services for the poor would be spread among all metropolitan area taxpayers. While the short-run tax burden on city residents would almost certainly be re-duced, there would probably be rising political pressure to equalize public service provision everywhere within the boundaries of the new metropolis. To the extent this occurs, total spending would probably increase, perhaps wiping out any short-run tax savings enjoyed by city residents. Because the city spends more on directly redistributive services, the equalization pres-sure may actually reduce service provision for some city residents. There is little research on the impact of the formation of metropolitan governments on the residents of central cities. In a 1974 simulation, however, Bradford and Oates (1974) suggest that forming metropolitan governments would actually lead to a decline in public spending in central cities.

Rusk (1993) suggests that cities that have annexed their suburbs have fared much better, both fiscally and economically, than cities with fixed boundaries. Nearly all the examples of active annexation, however, have occurred in rapidly growing metropolitan areas dominated by their cen-tral cities. We have no examples of the creation of a metropolitan govern-ment in a metropolitan area with a fiscally stressed central city and strong, well-developed suburbs. In fact, in many of the nation's largest central cities, such as New York, Philadelphia, Pittsburgh, Cleveland, and San Francisco, the last annexation occurred more than half a century ago. It seems clear that the only way a metropolitan government can be created is if such a creation is perceived to be beneficial to both the central city and its suburbs.

Overcoming Obstacles to Metropolitan Cooperation

No dramatic improvements in the fiscal health of central cities are possible without the cooperation of the suburbs. While this cooperation could take the form of the establishment of some type of metropolitan governance, at minimum it might involve legislative support by suburban governments of cities' efforts to diversify their tax bases.[23] We believe that an attitude held by many suburban residents is that cities' fiscal problems are primarily of their own making, and that suburban governments have neither the responsibility nor the obligation to cooperate with central cities or to assist them in any way. To the extent that this attitude dominates political discourse in the suburbs, the obstacles to metropolitan area cooperation are daunting.

The following questions must be answered before suburban residents can be convinced that it is in their self-interest to help solve the fiscal (and economic) problems of central cities:

- Is the economic vitality of a metropolitan area, including its suburbs, dependent on the economic health of its central city?
- What are the real benefits to suburbs of greater metropolitan cooperation?
- Would such cooperation simply imply redistribution from rich suburbs to poor central cities (a zero-sum game), or can the metropolitan area as a whole benefit?
- Can a case be made that suburban attempts to ignore the needs of cities are shortsighted, and that fiscal actions by suburbs (or state legislatures acting as the agent of the suburban coalition) that provide short-run fiscal benefits to suburbs, at the expense of cities, will be self-defeating in the long run?

Although researchers have begun to address these questions, definitive answers have not yet emerged. A growing recent literature on central city–suburban links suggests a mainly positive correlation between changes in central city and suburban economic performance (Ledebur and Barnes

1992, 1993; Voith 1992; Savitch et al. 1993; Blair and Zhang 1994; Inlanfeldt 1994).[24] This literature, however, is nowhere near conclusive on the fiscal policy implications of such a correlation.

One of the fiscal links between central cities and suburbs comes through the state budget. Suppose that city fiscal problems lead to deteriorating public services, which in turn increase the costs to the state. Crime might be an example: if poorer city services, say for education and youth services, lead to an increase in crime, and the state pays a substantial fraction of the cost of the criminal justice system, then there is a potential cost to suburban residents in terms of higher state taxes or forgone state aid or other state-provided services. But this is not the end of the story. If suburban legislators dominate the state legislature, and state budgetary decision making is driven primarily by local self-interest, then suburban legislators may well demand, and receive, some compensation for the increased state spending on prisons, especially if most of the criminals come from the biggest cities. This compensation may come in the form of a reshuffling of state aid to benefit suburban communities. Although there is some evidence to suggest that state budgetary decisions are dominated by this kind of self-interest, more work needs to be done on the circumstances under which local interests dominate statewide interests in state budgeting decisions.

Another rationale for metropolitan area fiscal cooperation might be the realization by suburban residents that both central city amenities and central city problems are likely to have a direct impact on suburban residents. A classic example of these *spillovers* is communicable disease. Unless cities are completely sealed off from their suburbs, inadequate public health services in the city can easily affect suburban residents. The recent reemergence of some old diseases (e.g., virulent strains of tuberculosis) suggests that this rationale for metropolitan cooperation is still powerful. Another candidate for spillovers is crime, particularly crime associated with drug dealing. In both the New York and Boston metropolitan areas, crime rates in the suburbs grew at a much faster rate than in the central cities between the early 1980s and early 1990s (Winsberg 1994). These data at least suggest that criminal activity may be "spilling out" of the central cities. Strengthening the ability of city governments to fight crime, then, may in the end reduce both the incidence of crime in the suburbs and the expenses of having to fight suburban crime.

In fact, very little is known about the magnitude of these spillovers. We need, for example, to conduct research on the relationship between the incidence and the cost of crime and other social problems in central cities and the incidence and cost of crime and other social problems in their suburbs. The direct public cost to suburban residents in terms of increased taxes for health and public safety, and the private cost of increased security, including more self-imposed restrictions on mobility, as well as the private cost of increased use of illegal drugs (because of their availability in the city), should all be considered.

There is also a longer-run fiscal *externality* of policies that allow central cities to deteriorate. As the fiscal health of central cities worsens, the incentives for current city residents and businesses to move to the suburbs are strengthened. An influx of additional city residents into the suburbs may have substantial fiscal and nonfiscal consequences for suburban communities. For instance, there is the considerable cost of replicating the public infrastructure, such as roads, schools, and sewer systems, that already exists in cities. New residents also bring with them extra congestion and often preferences for higher levels of public services than desired by current suburban residents.

One of the difficulties in convincing suburban communities that there are adverse fiscal externalities from policies that ignore the central cities is that the impact of the fiscal externalities may be outweighed by unrelated changes in the distribution of income. While fiscal competition and beggar-thy-neighbor policies may ultimately reduce economic well-being in higher-income suburbs, this negative impact on the suburbs may well be overwhelmed by increases in the incomes of suburban residents. If this occurs, it will be harder to convince these residents to join in regional cooperative schemes.

It is again worth emphasizing that a precondition for achieving any metropolitan cooperation will be convincing suburban residents that providing additional fiscal resources to central cities, either directly or indirectly, is not "pouring money down a rat hole." Concerted efforts by city governments to reduce inefficiencies in the provision of public goods may improve the willingness of suburbs to help alleviate central city fiscal problems. Here research that evaluates both managerial and technological innovations in the provision of public services will facilitate the adaptation of effective policies by city governments. Research is also needed to determine whether additional spending in central cities (e.g., for police protection) actually leads to a reduction in crime. Can resources be effectively allocated to improve services, or will they just lead to higher salaries for police and others in the criminal justice system? Efforts to publicize particularly successful efforts by city governments to improve the quality of public service provision would also be useful in reducing suburban resistance to metropolitan cooperation.

Frequently unspoken, but possibly the greatest obstacle to metropolitan cooperation, is the difference in the racial composition of cities and suburbs. To our knowledge, there has been very little research addressing the question of whether racial animosities hinder metropolitan cooperation. If racial attitudes influence fiscal policies, then collective action will be most difficult in metropolitan areas with greater racial disparity between the central city and its suburbs. Futhermore, these attitudes may lead to lower grants, reduced state support for city institutions, and more stringent fiscal zoning in the suburbs of central cities with high proportions of minorities. As Eisinger (1980) points out, however, animosity towards blacks on the parts of whites can also act to encourage metropolitan cooperation. Eisinger reports that in Nashville, curbing black political power in the central city was an explicit argument used by white supporters of efforts to annex surrounding suburban territory. Opposition to formation of metropolitan governments can also come from minorities. In particular, blacks in most cases have opposed the creation of metropolitan governments because they feared that their political power would be diluted. This argument led to a provision in the federal Voting Rights bill that allows for objections to annexation on the grounds that it will destroy racial political balance (Rusk 1993).

A Tax-Sharing Scheme for Metropolitan Areas

If efforts were successful in reducing resistance to helping the central city, how might we structure the metropolitan fiscal system to achieve such a goal? One way is to expand reliance on payroll or income taxes that are payable in the jurisdiction where income is earned. From the point of view of the central city, the least harmful structure for a local income tax would be one in which all jurisdictions in the metropolitan area levy an income tax, but the tax is paid where people work rather than where they live. Thus if a person lives in suburban Chicago, but works in downtown Chicago, the tax would be paid to the city of Chicago. Taxpayers would receive a full or partial credit on their residential income tax. This is the rule that often prevails between states, and in at least one city.[25] The problem with this approach is that it offers suburbs little incentive to surrender fiscal resources to the central city.

Since few suburbs actually have local income taxes, taxation on an origin basis, with full credit offsets from the jurisdiction of residence, might seem rather remote as a policy solution. By contrast, all jurisdictions use the property tax. Hence an alternative income tax sharing scheme would be to allow commuters to take a credit against their residential property tax bill for wage tax payments to the place where they are employed. If the credit were dollar for dollar, it is unlikely that suburbs would go along with the plan. Therefore, the state might provide an incentive by compensating localities for a portion of the forgone property tax revenues. Suppose, for example, that the locality allowed a 50 percent property tax credit against income taxes paid to another local jurisdiction. If the taxpayer works in a downtown law firm, earning $100,000 per year, a percentage point increase in the central city wage tax would cost the suburb $500 in revenue. The state, though, could further reduce the cost to both the individual and the suburban jurisdiction by making the local income tax deductible against the state income tax. If the top state marginal rate were 5 percent, then the additional $500 in local income tax would reduce state taxable income by $500, lowering state income taxes by $25. Since less than a third of all taxpayers itemize their deductions, the state could instead offer a credit for local income taxes, which would reduce the net cost by a greater amount. Federal assistance, perhaps through a partial income tax credit, could also be used to increase the incentive for this form of fiscal cooperation.

In considering such schemes, we must bear in mind one of the principal lessons learned from previous attempts to alter local fiscal arrangements. Local governments are extremely wary of higher-level policies that promise short-term benefits but may be withdrawn in the future, leaving them worse off than before. To have any hope of inducing cooperative behavior, state or federal tax incentives for cooperative behavior, however designed, must be strongly grounded politically, and firmly rooted in the state or federal tax code.

Conclusion

The fiscal health of city governments depends on their ability to provide adequate public services without placing unreasonable tax burdens on their residents. Although fiscal health is by definition a relative concept, evidence exists that a number of the nation's largest central cities, especially those in the Northeast and Midwest, are in weak fiscal health. Their fundamental problems are structural in nature, and ultimate solutions to their fiscal problems will require a combination of homegrown and intergovernmental approaches.

The fiscal position of cities is exacerbated by the fact that they are surrounded by independent suburban governments, many of which are in substantially better fiscal health. Although there are many things we do not know about cities' fiscal behavior, the major obstacle to increased metropolitan area cooperation in dealing with cities' fiscal problems is the general unwillingness of suburban residents to accept any responsibility for dealing with central city fiscal problems. There is little chance for cooperative behavior unless it can be shown to be in the self-interest of suburban residents to play an active role in the solution of central city fiscal problems. Though not stressed in this essay, fiscal disparities among suburbs have also been growing. This trend expands the potential coalition of fiscal have-nots, and may increase the possibilities for collective metropolitan actions. The task for research is twofold: (1) to make this self-interest clearer by documenting as carefully as possible the fiscal linkages between the central city and its suburbs, and (2) to suggest the best mix of solutions — including changes in local tax and expenditure policies, and changes in intergovernmental assistance — to improve the functioning of the metropolitan area.

As we see it, permanent progress towards solving the fiscal problems of central cities requires research on the following topics:

- Investigation of the differences in the costs of providing public services in center cities and suburbs, in light of differences in city and suburban populations and their problems.
- Detailed studies of central city production functions, to determine the benefits of additional expenditures.
- Studies of the optimal tax structures for central cities, including the taxation of commercial property and the level and form of earnings taxes — weighing revenue-raising capacity against loss of fiscal base.
- Studies of the appropriate mix of intergovernmental financing and local taxation and fees, and how such a mix might vary by metropolitan area.
- Studies of the factors causing middle-class people to leave the central city, using carefully designed longitudinal methods. Evaluation of the possibility of using targeted subsidies to get the middle class to stay in cities.
- Evaluation of the new wave of homegrown attempts to solve cities' fiscal problems. To what extent do these policies increase production efficiencies rather than result in cuts in public services? What are the longer-run implications of reductions in redistributional outlays?
- Studies of the spillovers from central cities to suburbs. For example, what does an increase in central city crime cost the suburbs?
- Evaluation of the metropolitan area economic effects of fiscal cooperation in those cities that share a tax base or cooperate in terms of service provision.

- Studies of the effects of federal pass-through aid on cities. Analysis of the behavior of state legislatures in allocating intergovernmental aid and other forms of assistance to cities.
- Evaluation of the costs and benefits of state and federal mandates, as they affect cities.
- In order to better understand the fiscal linkages between central cities and their suburbs, further studies of the economic linkages between cities and suburbs.

A central goal of the new Republican majority in Congress is to fundamentally change the relationship between the federal government and state and local governments. Under the Republican vision, articulated, at least in part, in their "Contract with America," the role of the federal government in a wide range of areas would be substantially reduced, with state governments gaining much more power to set their own priorities.

The exact form of any legislation to achieve these goals has not been finalized. However, we believe that, if enacted, the sharp cuts in federal grants to city governments, dramatic reductions in funding for programs addressing the needs of low-income populations, and the conversion of matching grants for welfare and other social services into block grants will prove very detrimental to the fiscal health of the nation's central cities. In the long run these changes will almost certainly worsen the competitive position of cities relative to their suburbs, and will make it all the more difficult to craft cooperative solutions to urban fiscal problems.

Although not part of the "Contract with America," the replacement of individual and corporate income taxes with a consumption tax has won the support of many congressional Republicans. Many of the major proposals now being considered by Congress would eliminate the current deduction for state and local income taxes. This will have the direct effect of raising the tax cost of local government services for many moderate- and high-income taxpayers who currently itemize deductions. As we have argued elsewhere (Reschovsky and Chernick 1989), rising tax costs will reduce the willingness of these taxpayers to support current levels of pubic spending, especially when the spending is primarily for programs that provide benefits to other (presumably lower-income) residents. In cases where city fiscal decisions largely represent the views of nonitemizers, the elimination of deductibility may not result in lower spending, but will strengthen the economic incentive of high-income residents to leave the central city. Both these outcomes are likely to further weaken the fiscal position of central cities.

1. A recent report completed for the National League of Cities concludes that "cities' fiscal conditions in 1995 are continuing along a generally favorable path begun nearly two years ago" (Pagano 1995). This assessment, however, is based entirely on short-run budgetary considerations, and ignores longer-run structural factors affecting cities' fiscal health. The distinction between budgetary and structural fiscal distress was carefully developed in three papers by Katharine Bradbury (1982, 1983, 1984).

2. Implicit in the discussion of mobility is that the out-migration of individuals and firms from the central city is not offset by in-migration. In most city neighborhoods, mobility rates are very high (Downs 1981). The typical pattern of migration for cities is that young and single people move into cities, and families with children move out. Fiscal externalities occur if in-migrants have lower incomes than out-migrants. If a family sells a house in the city, a fiscal externality will occur only if the purchasing family has lower income, or if the sale price represents a decline in property value. It is not the act of selling a property that lowers the value; a reduced sale price is merely the validation by the market of the declining value of property in the city. From a tax standpoint, however, if property is reassessed upon sale, then the act of selling may lead to a reduction in the city's tax base. In general, fiscal externalities are likely to occur if the population of a city is shrinking, so there is no net replacement of those who leave.

3. The impact of out-migration on per capita costs depends on the relationship between the average cost of services and the number of users. For many city services, such as highway maintenance, public transit, sewage disposal, and water treatment, average costs may rise sharply as the number of users declines, because these services have high fixed costs, relative to variable costs. In addition, labor costs may not decline even if the population does. For example, reduced population in a neighborhood may actually increase the incidence of crime. Also, the literature on "peer group effects" suggests that the departure of middle-class children may actually raise the cost of educating low-income students.

4. There have been very few attempts to measure intrametropolitan fiscal disparities. While recognizing that fiscal disparities are appropriately measured by comparing need-capacity gaps of central cities and suburbs, Bahl, Martinez-Vazquez, and Sjoquist (1992) employ central city–suburban differences in per capita expenditures as a measure of fiscal disparities. Using this measure with data for 35 large metropolitan areas, they find that disparities have grown between 1957 and 1987. Ladd, Reschovsky, and Yinger (1991) and Green and Reschovsky (1994) have calculated the fiscal conditions of municipal governments in Minnesota and Wisconsin, respectively, using need-capacity gap measures. In both studies, suburban governments are generally found to be in considerably stronger fiscal condition than central cities.

5. Rafuse and Marks (1991) compare an index of the revenue-raising ability of each community to an index of "representative" direct expenditures. This latter index attempts to measure the "workload" for each community in 35 different functional categories.

6. Frequently, new manufacturing facilities also receive substantial tax abatements. However, there are relatively few new manufacturing developments in central cities.

7. Approximately 13 percent of property value is exempt in Nassau County, 24 percent in Suffolk County, and 22 percent in Westchester County.

8. The information that state governments' contributions to cultural institutions have declined in recent years comes from a conversation with Dick Netzer.

9. An opposing view on this issue is provided by Oakland (1994), who argues that providing aid to places with higher costs due to, for example, higher maintenance cost for infrastructure leads to inefficient locational signals.

10. See Downs and Pogue (1994) for an excellent discussion of the strengths and weaknesses of efforts to measure the costs of local government public services through the analysis of local government spending.

11. The data on state aid to the 24 largest cities also indicate a decline in aid, from 34.8 percent to 29.7 percent. However, this large decline is driven primarily by the data for New York City, which experienced a large reduction in aid as a share of total spending between 1977 and 1992. Excluding New York City, state aid as a share of spending rose slightly from 19.4 to 19.5 percent in this 15-year period.

12. Empowerment Zones were designated in Atlanta, Baltimore, Chicago, Cleveland, Detroit, Los Angeles, New York, and Philadelphia. The list of cities chosen as enterprise communities included Boston, Dallas, Denver, Houston, Memphis, Miami, Milwaukee, Minneapolis, Nashville, New Orleans, Newark, Oklahoma City, San Francisco, Seattle, and Washington, D.C.

13. As of January 1994, the 2-year-old program has generated an estimated savings of over $100 million with more than 40 services moved to the private sector. The most notable successes are the private management of the water treatment facilities and the trash collection. Complementing this program is the "Hot Ideas" program that rewards public employees for suggesting successful cost-saving measures. In addition, the mayor reduced the number of non–public safety employees from a high of 2,752 in 1992 to 2,086 in 1994. This reduction is from management positions; no union employees have been laid off.

14. In addition, Los Angeles and San Francisco impose taxes on the total payroll of employers, and Baltimore has a county income tax paid by both city and suburban residents.

15. New York City has a broad-based personal income tax. Nonresidents are taxed on their earnings, but the rate is minimal. However, a tax on unincorporated businesses manages indirectly to capture a substantial portion of the forgone revenues on income earned by nonresidents. Replacing this tax by a higher direct tax on nonresident earnings would improve the efficiency of the local tax structure.

16. Based on a survey of the existing econometric evidence, Chernick (1996) concludes that a budget-neutral conversion of the federal program of Aid to Families with Dependent Children (AFDC) from an open-ended matching grant to a block grant would result in substantial reductions in welfare benefit levels.

17. There is also some limited evidence that attempts by the federal government to provide aid to poor persons can be effectively negated by actions of city govern-

ments. Thus, Inman (1989) argues that each city government determines, through the political process, the proportion of local resources it wants to devote to programs benefiting the poor. He then argues that a change in federal policy, such as a reduction in the federal matching rate for welfare expenditures, would lead to a decline in total welfare spending and a substitution of local funds for federal welfare spending. However, Inman finds that this pro-poor change on the expenditure side is offset by a tax response that substitutes the regressive property tax for more progressive fees and selective sales taxes. This result is suggestive of the difficulty higher levels of government have in changing the behavior of local governments.

18. See Hirschman (1991) for a discussion of this issue.

19. New York City is a major exception in this regard, as it still pays one-half of the nonfederal share of the AFDC and Medicaid, and 50 percent of the total cost of home relief.

20. If revenue diversification is restricted to central cities, there is a danger that the expansion of city tax bases will further spur out-migration of residents and businesses.

21. Based on a measure of inequality known as a Gini coefficient, by 1992 tax base sharing had reduced intrametropolitan inequalities in tax base by 28 percent (Baker, Hinze, and Manzi 1991).

22. Within the Chicago metropolitan area, one example of metropolitan cooperation is the Chicago Regional Transportation Authority, which serves the entire metropolitan area and does have the power to levy a 1 percent sales tax in Cook County and a 0.25 percent sales tax in the other five counties.

23. Although he argues that metropolitan solutions are necessary to solve many of the problems besetting our central cities, Anthony Downs (1994) concludes that there exists almost no political support for the establishment of metropolitan area governments.

24. A thoughtful critical review of this literature is provided by Hill, Wolman, and Ford (1994).

25. A local example of such a reciprocal relationship is in Toledo. The city retains only 50 percent of the tax collected from nonresidents who live in jurisdictions with a local income tax and that grant the same credit to their nonresidents. This sharing of the income base is the opposite of what has occurred in Pittsburgh: there, the residential jurisdiction has first claim on the local income tax. Suburban communities in Pittsburgh have an overwhelming incentive to enact a local income tax, because if they fail to do so, commuters would pay the entire wage tax to the central city.

REFERENCES

Bahl, Roy; Jorge Martinez-Vazquez; and David L. Sjoquist. 1992. "Central City — Suburban Fiscal Disparities." *Public Finance Quarterly* 20(October):420–32.

Baker, Karen; Steven Hinze; and Nina Manzi. 1991. "Minnesota's Fiscal Disparities Program." Presentation to the Fiscal Disparities Taskforce of the House Tax Committee, Minnesota House of Representatives Research Department, St. Paul, July 23.

Bartik, Timothy J. 1991. *Who Benefits from State and Local Economic Development Policies?* Kalamazoo, Mich.: W. E. Upjohn Institute.

Blair, John P., and Zhongcai Zhang. 1994. " 'Ties That Bind' Revisited." *Economic Development Quarterly* 8(November):373–77.

Bradbury, Katharine L. 1982. "Fiscal Distress in Large U.S. Cities." *New England Economic Review* (January–February):33–44.

———. 1983. "Structural Fiscal Distress in Cities — Causes and Consequences." *New England Economic Review* (January–February):32–43.

———. 1984. "Urban Decline and Distress: An Update." *New England Economic Review* (July–August):39–57.

Bradbury, Katharine L.; Helen F. Ladd; Mark Perrault; Andrew Reschovsky; and John Yinger. 1984. "State Aid to Offset Fiscal Disparities across Communities." *National Tax Journal* 37(June):151–70.

Bradford, David F., and Wallace E. Oates. 1974. "Suburban Exploitation of Central Cities and Government Structure." In *Redistribution through Public Choice*, edited by Harold M. Hochman and George Peterson. New York: Columbia University Press.

Charney, Alberta H. 1993. "Migration and the Public Sector: A Survey." *Regional Studies* 27(December):313–26.

Chernick, Howard. 1982. "Block Grants for the Needy: The Case of ADFC." *Journal of Policy Analysis and Management* 1(Winter):209–22.

———. 1992. "Real Property Taxation in New York City: The Need for Immediate Reform." Report prepared for the City Project, New York, February.

———. 1995. "The Intermediate Income Distributional Impact of Cuts in Entitlement Programs." Paper prepared for the Economic Policy Institute, Washington, D.C., September.

———. 1996. "Fiscal Effects of Block Grants for the Needy: A Review of the Evidence." *Proceedings of the 88th Annual Conference on Taxation of the National Tax Association, 1995*, Columbus, Ohio: National Tax Association.

Craig, Steven G., and Robert P. Inman. 1986. "Education, Welfare, and the 'New' Federalism: State Budgeting in a Federalist Public Economy." In *Studies in State and Local Public Finance*, edited by Harvey Rosen. Chicago: University of Chicago Press.

Crane, Jonathan. 1991. "The Epidemic Theory of Ghettos and Neighborhood Effects on Dropping Out and Teenage Childbearing." *American Journal of Sociology* 96(March):1226–59.

Danziger, Sheldon, and Peter Gottschalk. 1993. "Introduction." In *Uneven Tides: Rising Inequality in America*, edited by Sheldon Danziger and Peter Gottschalk. New York: Russell Sage Foundation.

Dearborn, Phillip. 1992. "City Finances in the 1990s." Paper prepared for the Urban Institute, Washington, D.C.

Donahue, John D. 1989. *The Privatizational Decision: Public Ends, Private Means.* New York: Basic Books.

Downing, Paul B. 1992. "The Revenue Potential of User Charges in Municipal Finance." *Public Finance Quarterly* 20(October):512–27.

Downs, Anthony. 1981. *Neighborhoods and Urban Development*. Washington, D.C.: Brookings Institution.

——. 1994. *New Visions for Metropolitan America*. Washington, D.C.: Brookings Institution and the Lincoln Institute of Land Policy.

Downs, Thomas A., and Thomas F. Pogue. 1994. "Adjusting School Aid Formulas for the Higher Cost of Educating Disadvantaged Students." *National Tax Journal* 47(March):89–110.

Eggers, William D. 1993. "City Lights: America's Boldest Mayors." *Policy Review* 65(summer):67–74.

Eisinger, Peter K. 1980. *The Politics of Displacement: Racial and Ethnic Transition in Three American Cities*. New York: Academic Press.

Frey, William H. 1977. "White Flight and Central-City Loss: Application of an Analytic Migration Framework." Institute for Research on Poverty Discussion Papers no. 453-77. Madison: University of Wisconsin.

Galster, George C. 1990. "White Flight from Racially Integrated Neighborhoods in the 1970s: The Cleveland Experience." *Urban Studies* 27(June):385–99.

——. 1991. "Housing Discrimination and the Urban Poverty of African-Americans." *Journal of Housing Research* 2(2):87–122.

Gold, Steven D. 1994. *State Fiscal Brief*. Albany, N.Y.: Rockefeller Institute of Government, Center for the Study of the States, June.

Gordon, Roger H.; James R. Hines, Jr.; and Lawrence H. Summers. 1986. "Notes on the Tax Treatment of Structures." National Bureau of Economic Research Working Paper no. 1896. Cambridge, Mass.: National Bureau of Economic Research, April.

Green, Richard K., and Andrew Reschovsky. 1994. "Fiscal Assistance to Municipal Governments." In *Dollars and Sense*, vol. 3, edited by Donald A. Nichols. Madison: University of Wisconsin, Robert M. La Follette Institute of Public Affairs.

Greene, Kenneth V.; William B. Neenan; and Claudia D. Scott. 1974. *Fiscal Interactions in a Metropolitan Area*. Lexington, Mass.: D. C. Heath.

Grieson, Ronald E. 1980. "Theoretical Analysis and Empirical Measurements of the Effects of the Philadelphia Income Tax." *Journal of Urban Economics* 8(July):123–37.

Gruenstein, John M. L. 1980. "Jobs in the City: Can Philadelphia Afford to Raise Taxes?" *Business Review*, Philadelphia Federal Reserve Bank (May–June):3–11.

Hill, Edward W.; Harold Wolman; and Coit Ford III. 1994. "Can Suburbs Survive without Their Central Cities? Examining the Suburban Dependence Hypothesis." Report no. 94-99. Cleveland: Cleveland State University, Urban Center, Levin College of Urban Affairs, June.

Hirschman, Ira. 1991. "Spatial Equity and Transportation Finance: A Case Study of the New York Metropolitan Region." Ph.D. dissertation submitted to Rutgers University, Department of Urban Planning and Policy Development, October.

Ihlanfeldt, Keith R. 1994. "The Importance of the Central City to the Regional and National Economy: A Review of the Arguments and Empirical Evidence." Paper prepared for the National Urban Policy Report, February.

Inman, Robert P. 1987. "Philadelphia's Fiscal Management of Economic Transition." In *Local Fiscal Issues in the Philadelphia Metropolitan Area*, edited by Thomas F. Luce and Anita Summers. Philadelphia: University of Pennsylvania Press.

———. 1989. "The Local Decision to Tax: Evidence from Large U.S. Cities." *Regional Science and Urban Economics* 19(August):455–92.

Jackson, Kenneth T. 1985. *Crabgrass Frontier: The Suburbanization of the United States.* New York: Oxford University Press.

Jencks, Christopher, and Susan E. Meyer. 1990. "The Social Consequences of Growing Up in a Poor Neighborhood." In *Inner-City Poverty in the United States*, edited by Laurence E. Lynn, Jr., and Michael McGeary. Washington, D.C.: National Academy Press.

Ladd, Helen F. 1990. "State Assistance to Local Governments: Changes during the 1980s." *American Economic Review* 80(May):171–75.

Ladd, Helen F.; Andrew Reschovsky; and John Yinger. 1992. "City Fiscal Condition and State Equalizing Aid: The Case of Minnesota." *Proceedings of the 84th Conference on Taxation of the National Tax Association, 1991.* Columbus, Ohio: National Tax Association.

Ladd, Helen F., and John Yinger. [1989] 1991. *America's Ailing Cities: Fiscal Health and the Design of Urban Policy.* Baltimore: Johns Hopkins University Press.

Ledebur, Larry C., and William R. Barnes. 1992. *Metropolitan Disparities and Economic Growth.* Washington, D.C.: National League of Cities.

———. 1993. *All in It Together.* Washington, D.C.: National League of Cities.

Luce, Thomas F., Jr. 1994. "Local Taxes, Public Services, and the Intrametropolitan Location of Firms and Households." *Public Finance Quarterly* 22(April):139–67.

McGeary, Michael. 1990. "Ghetto Poverty and Federal Policies and Programs." In *Inner-City Poverty in the United States*, edited by Laurence E. Lynn, Jr., and Michael McGeary. Washington, D.C.: National Academy Press.

Nathan, Richard P., et al. 1983. *The Consequences of Cuts.* Princeton, N.J.: Princeton Urban and Regional Research Center.

———. 1987. *Reagan and the States.* Princeton, N.J.: Princeton University Press.

Neenan, William B. 1970. "Suburban–Central City Exploitation Thesis: One City's Tale." *National Tax Journal* 23(June):117–39.

Netzer, Dick. 1991. "An Evaluation of Interjurisdictional Competition through Economic Development Incentives." In *Competition among States and Local Governments: Efficiency and Equity in American Federalism*, edited by Daphne A. Kenyon and John Kincaid. Washington, D.C.: Urban Institute Press.

New York State Board of Equalization and Assessment. 1994. *Exemptions from Real Property Taxation in New York State: 1992 County, City and Town Assessment Rolls.* Albany, N.Y.: Office of Policy Analysis and Development.

New York State Comptroller, Office of the State Deputy Comptroller for the City of New York. 1994. "Review of the Financial Plan of the City of New York, Fiscal Years 1995 through 1998." Report no. 3-95. New York: New York

State Comptroller, Office of the State Deputy Comptroller for the City of New York, July 27.

New York University, Graduate School of Public Administration. 1980. *Real Property Tax Policy for New York City.* Study conducted under contract with the City of New York, Department of Finance, December.

Oakland, William H. 1979. "Central Cities: Fiscal Plight and Prospects for Reform." In *Current Issues in Urban Economics*, edited by Peter Mieszkowski and Mahlon Straszheim. Baltimore: Johns Hopkins University Press.

———. 1994. "Fiscal Equalization: An Empty Box?" *National Tax Journal* 46(March):199–210.

Oates, W.; E. Howry; and W. Baumol. 1971. "The Analysis of Public Policy in Dynamic Urban Models." *Journal of Political Economy* 79(January–February):142–53.

Pack, Janet Rothenberg. 1992. "BIDs, DIDs, SADs: Private Governments in Urban America." *Brookings Review* 10(fall):18–21.

———. 1995. "Poverty and Urban Public Expenditures." Working Paper no. 197. Philadelphia: Wharton School of the University of Pennsylvania, Wharton Real Estate Center, May.

Pagano, Michael A. 1995. "City Fiscal Conditions in 1995." Research report of the National League of Cities. Washington, D.C.: National League of Cities.

Papke, Leslie E. 1993. "What Do We Know about Enterprise Zones?" In *Tax Policy and the Economy*, vol. 7, edited by James Poterba. Cambridge, Mass.: MIT Press.

———. 1994. "Tax Policy and Urban Development: Evidence from the Indiana Enterprise Zone Program." *Journal of Public Economics* 54(May):37–49.

Peterson, George E. 1980. "Federal Tax Policy and the Shaping of Urban Development." In *The Prospective City*, edited by Arthur P. Solomon. Cambridge, Mass.: MIT Press.

———. 1986. "Urban Policy and the Cyclical Behavior of Cities." In *Reagan and the Cities*, edited by George E. Peterson and Carol W. Lewis. Washington, D.C.: Urban Institute Press.

Poterba, James M. 1990. "Taxation and Housing Markets: Preliminary Evidence on the Effects of Recent Tax Reforms." In *Do Taxes Matter? The Impact of the Tax Reform Act of 1986*, edited by Joel Slemrod. Cambridge, Mass.: MIT Press.

Rafuse, Robert W., and Laurence R. Marks. 1991. *A Comparative Analysis of Fiscal Capacity, Tax Effort and Public Spending among Localities in the Chicago Metropolitan Region.* Chicago: Regional Partnership.

Regional Partnership. 1991. *Seeking a New Balance: Paying for Government in Metropolitan Chicago: An Analysis of Revenues and Spending Patterns by Chicago-Area Units of Government.* Executive summary based on papers produced for the Regional Revenue and Spending Project. Chicago: Regional Partnership.

Reschovsky, Andrew. 1979. "Residential Choice and the Local Public Sector: An Alternative Test of the 'Tiebout Hypothesis.'" *Journal of Urban Economics* 6(October):501–20.

———. 1980. "An Evaluation of Metropolitan Area Tax Base Sharing." *National Tax Journal* 33(March):5–66.

Reschovsky, Andrew, and Howard Chernick. 1989. "Federal Tax Reform and the Taxation of Urban Residents." *Public Finance Quarterly* 17(April):123–57.

Rosett, Richard N. 1991. "Art Museums in the United States: A Financial Portrait." In *The Economics of Art Museums*, edited by Martin Feldstein. Chicago: University of Chicago Press.

Rusk, David. 1993. *Cities without Suburbs*. Washington, D.C.: Woodrow Wilson Center Press.

Savas, E. S. 1987. *Privatization: The Key to Better Government*. Chatham, N.J.: Chatham House.

Savitch, H. V.; David Collins; Daniel Sanders; and John P. Markham. 1993. "Ties That Bind: Central Cities, Suburbs, and the New Metropolitan Region." *Economic Development Quarterly* 7(November):341–57.

Schill, Michael H., and Susan M. Wachter. 1994. "The Spatial Bias of Federal Housing Programs." Working paper no. 191. Philadelphia: Wharton School of the University of Pennsylvania, Wharton Real Estate Center, October.

Summers, Anita, and Barbara Wolfe. 1977. "Do Schools Make a Difference?" *American Economic Review* 67(September):639–52.

U.S. Bureau of the Census. Various years. *City Government Finances*. Tables 1 and 7. Washington, D.C.: U.S. Government Printing Office.

U.S. House of Representatives, Committee on Ways and Means. 1994. *1994 Green Book: Background Material and Data on Programs within the Jurisdiction of the Committee on Ways and Means*. Table H-8, p. 1165. Washington, D.C.: U.S. Government Printing Office.

Voith, Richard. 1992. "City and Suburban Growth: Substitutes or Complements?" *Business Review*, Federal Reserve Bank of Philadelphia (September–October):21–33.

Winsberg, Morton. 1994. "Crime in the Suburbs: Fact and Fiction." *American Demographics* 16(April):11–12.

Jerome Rothenberg

Public-Private Partnerships and the "Crisis" of Local Government

Introduction

The purpose of the Metropolitan Assembly on Urban Problems was to examine what we know and what more we need to know in order to deal with the extremely difficult and highly complex problems of urban areas. Public-private partnerships are a particular class of instruments for such policy intervention. The variety of such partnerships that will be summarized in this essay indicates that we know some things about many particular partnerships. We do not, however, have much systematic understanding about them in general. With such variety in goals, participants, and structures, it is difficult to know the meaning of success, the sources of success, and the relative strengths and weaknesses of each mode of attacking urban problems. What follows is a framework for directing attention to what needs to be known to evaluate particular partnership modes.

Urban areas in the United States are plagued by what seems like an ocean of interconnected social, economic, and political problems, familiar but swelling uncontrollably before our eyes. Many people have looked with growing disillusionment at the performance of local government in meeting these problems, and criticisms are going increasingly beyond deploring error, inaction, and inefficiency. More and more, local urban governments are coming to be seen as having inherent deficiencies that make it vain to expect solutions from them. At the same time, partly influenced by this pessimistic conclusion but more directly out of pragmatic desperation, a variety of innovative kinds of government action characterized as public-private partnerships has arisen. In this approach, the weaknesses and strengths of conventional governments are linked with the strengths and weaknesses of private organizations to achieve results that neither public nor private entities can achieve on their own.

Many forms of "partnership" have been tried and judged, but there has been little systematic evaluation of their successes and failures. What do we know about the effectiveness and limitations of public-private partnerships, and what more do we need to know in order to utilize such partnerships more effectively in dealing with pressing urban problems? I have chosen to interpret "what is known" as a brief description of the types of partnerships that have been tried and their relevance to the solution of some of the elements of the "urban crisis." The major portion of this chapter consists of my interpretation of "what more we need to know" as *how to evaluate* the various kinds of partnership with respect to their contribution to leading us out of the crisis. The "success" of a particular partnership, however, may not indicate what has been gained by its existence that could not have been achieved in other ways. Since so many partnerships have goals that are mixtures of public and private concern, the *public* contribution is not always self-evident. Accordingly, I focus on the distinctive kinds of public goals to which partnerships lend themselves, and the mechanisms through which the partnerships influence the achievement of these public goals. What we need to know is what specific types of characteristics and structural features of partnerships lead to greater or lesser success in achieving their stated aims.

Kernaghan defines a public-private partnership as "a relationship involving the *sharing* of power, work, support and/or information with others for the achievement of joint goals and/or mutual benefits." He describes four basic kinds of partnership, in decreasing order of "sharing": collaborative, operational, contributory, and consultative. *Collaborative* involves the sharing of power in decision making, and the pooling of money, information, and labor resources. *Operational* involves the sharing of work but not decision making. *Contributory* involves the sponsorship or support, usually financial, of one organization by another. *Consultative* involves a public organization seeking advice from others outside government (Kernaghan 1993, pp. 61–64). While contributory and consultative are often not considered true partnerships because of the decisive asymmetry of power among participants, I include them here to display the wide variety of partnership forms — and the different social goals sought through each. Considerably more research is necessary, however, before we are able to make confident predictions about the effects of partnership form on social effectiveness.

The Crisis of the Cities and the Plight of Urban Local Government

The failure of local governments to resolve critical problems is laid to the following factors:[1]

- Public bureaucracy is too cumbersome and inefficient, resulting in outright waste, poor quality of services, procedural paralysis (i.e., limited adaptive ability and internal opposition to change), and opposition to new technology.
- There is an inability to meet the differentiated needs of a heterogeneous population, due to bureaucratic emphasis on uniformity and nondiscrimination.[2]
- There is widespread public perception that public agencies are wasteful, indecisive, corrupt, and not imaginative enough to handle difficult problems — all of which induce a lack of support by the public for government initiatives and a lack of budget with which to carry out normal functions.

These features form a larger pattern of elements that result in a serious mismatch between what local government is called on to do and its ability to do it. The resulting "plight of local government" can be sketched briefly.

The public wants and expects local government to contribute strongly to solving the critical problems plaguing the city — but does not trust it to do so. Despite these expectations, we are still traveling in a tax revolt context. The public will not accept higher tax rates or new taxes, even to pay for something they want from government. Because they believe there is large-scale waste in government, they perceive it as capable of increasing its efficiency substantially and thus able to undertake new initiatives without additional tax revenues. Indeed, some believe that if taxes are cut, the austerity will elicit internal reform and improved incentives to the point that government will actually be able to *improve* services on a lower overall budget!

In large urban areas, urban governance is fragmented into many political jurisdictions. There is no pooling of functional responsibility or fiscal capacity to meet problems of the metropolitan area as a whole. Better-favored suburbs, in fact, typically try to increase their separation from their central cities and less fortunate sister suburbs to avoid being damaged by the problems faced by these neighboring jurisdictions.

And, finally, there is a public perception that however poor central city government performance may have been in the past, it has worsened appreciably with respect to quality of service, waste, corruption, and responsiveness.

In summary, the "plight" of local government is that it is expected to do much more, much better, with fewer resources, and in an atmosphere of increasing public disfavor.

Relevance of Public-Private Partnerships
to the Plight of Local Government

Public-private partnerships increasingly are being promoted to over-come these governmental shortcomings.[3] Many problems of local govern-ment allegedly stem from lack of governmental imagination and initiative. In contrast, the private sector is stereotyped as a source of high entrepre-neurial initiative, freeing talents to generate novel solutions and try them out. Unlike the public sector, risk taking is characteristic of the private sector where substantial profits may be earned by bearing risk. The pri-vate sector includes both a profit-oriented and a nonprofit wing. While the profit-making wing is willing to assume new risks for the prospect of profits, the nonprofit wing is claimed to have the advantages of small size, flexibility, and dedication to finding solutions to new and changing social challenges.

Private market-oriented groups must be responsive to clients in order to make profits; they must pay attention to changing wants and circum-stances, as well as find new, less costly, or improved ways of meeting client demands. In consequence, updating and change are habitual in successful private operations. Nonprofit groups have the aforementioned advan-tages of size, informality, flexibility, and dedication to the clients' welfare, carrying with them at least the potential for high responsiveness to clients, and readiness to make changes.

Many of the areas in which government operates have been the scene of substantial nonprofit activities for long periods of time. These groups are repositories of expertise and operational experience, usually in the form of small enterprises specializing in particular categories of need. Together, they are capable of satisfying a variety of specialized client de-mands with customized targeting. Governments do not have this ability. Accordingly, an alliance between government and nonprofits can cover the diversity and breadth of needs better than either type of organization alone.

Private organizations have access to additional financial sources not generally available to governments. Thus, a partnership can enable gov-ernment to leverage its scarce financial resources.

The last three advantages of partnerships conjoin notably in the wel-fare and human services area. Diversity of targeting, a variety of estab-lished skills and experience, and an experimental outlook, along with a high degree of dedication to client needs, offer broad coverage, skilled operation, and flexibility for meeting changing circumstances. In addi-tion, many nonprofits receive partially or wholly donated labor and other inputs. Charitable nonprofits, receiving donations in money and time, can augment the overall reach of government redistributional programs.

When reform of large, complex systems seems needed, government agencies are likely to be defensive and receptive only to incremental change. Fresh examination of the overall system and its problems by relative outsiders (i.e., partners) encourages a wider variety of bold analysis and policy reform. Constructive partnership between government and outsiders permits a merging of the professional experience of public officials with the greater readiness of outsiders to examine boldly the larger aspects of the system. This perspective is not firmly rooted in social science research, but it reflects commonly held views that are, at least, plausible.

The Variety of Public-Private Partnerships

I am interpreting "public-private partnership" broadly to include such examples of quasi-privatization as cities contracting with private firms to clear streets or collect garbage. In this kind of case, the city in initiating association with nongovernmental organizations and individuals demonstrates a willingness to use governmental powers to combine, coordinate, and integrate the mobilization of resources from a variety of public and private sources. The goal is, or at least should be, the flexibility and the situational opportunism typically absent in conventional government roles. This is close in spirit but not identical to what has been called "entrepreneurial government" (Osborne and Gaebler 1992).

Public-private partnerships are not new. They existed before the 1970s and experienced significant expansion and diversification in the 1980s as local governments sought to find means for dealing more effectively with the mounting difficulties confronting them. These efforts were not always successful, although careful assessments of their value have not been made. Nevertheless, partnerships have proliferated in great variety. Listed below are some of the fields in which these have appeared, together with an indication of types of participants involved and kinds of mechanisms employed.

REAL ESTATE DEVELOPMENT

- *Indianapolis.* Partnerships of private for-profit and nonprofit organizations are formed with local governments to develop a nation-class sports capability, as part of a program to revitalize the city (Osborne and Gaebler 1992, p. 27).

- *San Francisco and Boston.* Real estate development is linked with other social goals by trading permission to private developers to build downtown in exchange for private child care and low-income housing projects elsewhere (Osborne and Gaebler 1992, p. 28).

INDUSTRIAL-BUSINESS GROWTH

- *Lowell, Massachusetts.* A variety of public subsidies is established to encourage new firms to locate there and existing firms to expand there (Osborne and Gaebler 1992, p. 17).
- *Massachusetts.* (*a*) Capital Resource Company, a private investment company, is fueled by public quid pro quos in the form of loans, tax cuts, and regulatory changes. (*b*) Community Development Finance Corp. and Government Land Bank are both public-private partnerships to leverage private investments to teach private investors how to invest in particular areas; where no private-sector activity presently exists, government initiates development activity (Osborne 1988*a*, p. 280).
- *Pennsylvania.* The Ben Franklin Partnership ("probably the most comprehensive economic development institution in the country"; Osborne 1988*b*, p. 56) is a state technology program that makes "challenge grants" to university-based projects, with business applications funded by business (Osborne 1988*b*, pp. 48–49).

EDUCATION

- *East Harlem, New York City.* Programs include radical decentralization of school formation and operation, together with parent-student school choice. Echoed in six other states (Osborne and Gaebler 1992, pp. 5–8).
- *South Carolina.* Performance incentives are provided for teachers and schools, with competition for funding of new ideas and prizes for success (Osborne and Gaebler 1992, p. 17).

WASTE REMOVAL, STREET CLEANING,
SOLID WASTE DISPOSAL

- More than 500 cities have public contracts for private refuse collection. These arrangements are significantly less costly than direct government operation, with equal or better-quality performance (Savas 1979, pp. 1–13).

- *Phoenix*. Department of Public Works competes with private companies for contracts in waste removal, street repair, and other works services (Osborne and Gaebler 1992, p. 16).

HEALTH CARE

- *Ohio*. Local boards manage outpatient mental health and mental retardation services via contracts with 400 nonprofit organizations, including drug abuse clinics, day treatment centers, and family programs (Osborne and Gaebler 1992, p. 40).
- *Arizona*. Department of Social Services contracts with nine nonprofit organizations and local governments for both steering functions and field operations for adult mental health services (Osborne and Gaebler 1992, p. 41).

POVERTY, WELFARE, HOMELESSNESS

- *Newark, New Jersey*. Numerous partnerships exist between the public sector and community organizations dealing with AIDS, homelessness, and housing for the poor (Osborne and Gaebler 1992, p. 27).
- *Pittsburgh*. Advisory Committee on Homelessness, composed of representatives from government, university, community, and religious organizations, coordinates policy on homelessness, using federal, state, and corporate funds. Services include food banks, soup kitchens, counseling, job training, and housing (Osborne and Gaebler 1992, p. 40).

EMPLOYMENT, LABOR MARKETS

- *Federal Job Training Partnership Act*. Many Private Industry Councils have been generated, whereby local government and private leaders together manage job training activities; the councils use performance contracts with other organizations to do the actual training (Osborne and Gaebler 1992, p. 40).

HOUSING

- *Visalia, California*. The city created a private nonprofit organization to encourage increased production of affordable housing. By loaning money and/or selling its own excess land to private clients, the plan increased the supply of such housing.

- *Newark, New Jersey.* The city's government-community organization partnership dealt with increasing the supply of affordable housing (Osborne and Gaebler 1992, p. 27).
- *Boston.* The Boston Housing Partnership, Inc., is a nonprofit corporation formed to push the development and operation of low-income housing through financing and access to technical assistance. Scale economies are achieved by bundling individual projects into "programs." Members include state and local governments, major banks, utilities, and insurance companies, local universities, local businesses, community housing development organizations, and the Massachusetts Housing Finance Agency. The partnership mobilizes federal and state rental assistance subsidies, and promotes neighborhood revitalization and economic opportunity. An important showpiece (Boston Housing Partnership, Inc., 1990)

The Variety of Alternatives to Standard Public Service Delivery

The appendix indicates the variety of ways public-type services can be provided other than directly by the government. Most of these are incorporated into the various specific partnerships listed above.

Types of public-private partnerships may be classified according to the major kinds of benefits they may be expected to generate, the sources of such benefits, and the factors that influence their magnitude. The analysis that follows is a mixture of theory and informal observations of "stylized facts" about actual partnerships. I do not pretend to do more than clarify the structure of questions that must be addressed by further research in order to understand why a particular partnership mode is attractive and how it may be improved.

Partial Privatization: Private Delivery of Services

Private delivery of services seems the most straightforward extension of governmental opportunity. Large, complex public bureaucracies characterized by ingrained, outdated technology and techniques, weak motivation, and the near-paralysis of enormous procedural thickets are far more costly means for supplying services than competitive, lean, scale- and technology-efficient private enterprises. The key to taking advantage of this disparity is for local government to contract with private firms simply to *deliver* the required services, while government continues to set the specifications for both the nature and quality of such services, and the terms on which the services are distributed to the population. In Osborne's and Gaebler's terms, government would be "steering but not rowing" (Osborne and Gaebler 1992, repeated motto).

The shifting away from direct governmental service delivery does, of course, imply loss of employment for released civil service employees; this may be legally prohibited or fraught with difficulties for government labor relations. Some communities have tried to smooth this difficulty by contracting with private firms to employ civil service workers. Even where acceptable to the firms (by no means frequently the case), this approach has not been highly successful because the affected workers may be forced to shift from protected employment conditions with seniority pay and benefits to what is often a much less attractive employment situation (Savas 1987, p. 283).

The crux of this type of partnership is that a product or service produced and supplied independently can fulfill the government's responsibility for deciding what is to be "produced," with what specifications and at what quality, and on exactly what terms the product or service is to be distributed to the public. There are not many governmental functions, however, that can be dealt with in this manner (Savas 1987, p. 279). Among the most popular are sanitation services, electric power, solid waste disposal, and some forms of health care and education. Most notably, trash collection services have been privatized in many cities (Savas 1979).

The potential for cost savings depends on the existing level of waste and inefficiency in the government's own service delivery. But probably of greater quantitative significance is the potential for superior performance by private contractors. This depends on the availability of technology newer than that employed by the city, and on either economies or diseconomies of scale not available to the government's history-determined workforce (Savas 1987, chap. 6). In some cases a smaller, more flexible decentralized operation is superior (e.g., in special education); and sometimes a larger scale is necessary to take advantage of new capital-intensive technology (e.g., in solid waste disposal).

Such cost-saving opportunities certainly exist, and can be substantial. Still, private contracting does not guarantee success without the presence of a number of conditions. First, the service must be appropriate for a separation between "steering" and "rowing." Second, the contracting must be the result of genuine competition among the potential private bidders. Third, the government must carefully specify the exact terms of production and distribution of the service. Fourth, the private firm must be closely monitored to ensure that it is carrying out its contractual obligations.

None of these conditions can be taken for granted. The first, to which I have already referred, may be in principle the most important; the others are probably more practical concerns. The condition of competition among candidates for a contract is especially likely to be violated.[4] In cases where the efficient scale of operations greatly exceeds that of a particular local government, private firms may have a market area much larger than the individual city. The market power of a private firm, however, may greatly exceed that of the city, so the contract agreed upon may well shortchange the city. In another pattern, unfortunately not rare, the private contractor may gain noncompetitive market power not "naturally" but by coercion. There are examples (e.g., New York City) where contracted-out services are dominated by organized crime or where competitive entry is blockaded illegally and the contractor subsequently controls the terms of the contract to its own advantage. Even monopolistic civil service bureaucracy is better in these cases than criminal monopolization by the private sector.

The third condition, specification of service terms, is an issue because city governments may assume that circumstances existing when the contract is agreed to will continue. But service provisions must be carefully spelled out, and modifications needed or desirable under changing circumstances must be anticipated and explicitly expressed. Poorly drawn contracts can lead to substantial shortfalls to the city's expected, and warranted, real cost savings.

Finally, monitoring is important. A city government needs information on whether the service is being provided with the intended quality characteristics and distributed in the intended fashion. Governments are often lax in monitoring their own performance; thus, it is reasonable to assume that they may have difficulty carrying out the more demanding task of monitoring the performance of outside organizations, whether for-profit or nonprofit.

In sum, real cost economies and quality improvement are sometimes possible through privatization. However, the conditions under which decoupling of government responsibility from government production and distribution will be successful call for observant and resolute behavior by city governments, which are often not aware of the serious issues involved.

Service Quality and Differentiation

Government provision of public services is often hampered by bureaucratic rigidities that allow service quality to decline over time. Moreover, when technological and organizational improvements would disturb established procedures if implemented, they are less likely to be adopted by government because of the difficult organizational adaptation that would be required. Finally, a hallmark of governmental action is universality (i.e., nondiscrimination in application).[5] This promotes homogeneity of service character across classes of public recipients, and discourages adapting to changing conditions and tailoring the character of service to meet differentiated needs and preferences on the part of a heterogeneous public.[6]

A considerable number of services for which universality is less appropriate than differentiation because of client heterogeneity are personal services such as welfare, health, education, recreation, drugs, vocational training, and work skill enhancement. Many of these issues are part of the government's overall program for real income redistribution among the population, such as special compensatory and enhancing services for the disabled and disadvantaged. The circumstances, needs, and personality characteristics of these groups are often unconventional, and they need services and distribution of services that fit their special situation. Such differentiation is extremely expensive and a procedural nightmare for a complex bureaucratic organization, and thus extraordinarily difficult to specify in a contract with a private organization.

Such services, however, are particularly appropriate for partnerships between government and voluntary nonprofit organizations. Many nonprofits come into being because of perceived inadequacies of both government and private for-profit suppliers. Government services are often too uniform or unbending to meet both various and varying needs, and private for-profit services may be perceived as taking advantage of consumer ignorance about a complex commodity solely in the interest of profit.[7] The nonprofit's mission may be seen as fulfilling a service niche that resolves both problems. A problem-solving challenge is often a central motivating reason for creating the nonprofit organization itself. The large numbers, small size, and flexible procedures of nonprofits, combined with their likelihood of specializing to master specific implementation problems, make them likely to be at the frontier of knowledge and implementation. Alliance with these organizations unites the local government's standardized mode of delivery, overview experience, and fiscal muscle with the more discriminating articulation of nonprofits' know-how.

While the dedication exists in these nonprofit groups to provide services, they typically need some form of government financial support to make them viable. Partnership here generally involves the government's extending money or other aid to nonprofits.[8] Nonmonetary aid may consist of waiving regulatory controls or zoning restrictions. In effect, the government is using its fiscal resources or regulatory power to leverage a considerably larger overall effort — the readiness of these groups to volunteer personnel and other resources or to organize private resources into effective instruments for the generation and/or delivery of services. Moreover, the result of such joint efforts is not simply an increase in the amount of services, but an increase in the quality and variety of services, and an improvement in responsiveness to the differential needs of the public. These, at least, are the hope.

Thus, in a period when city dwellers increasingly complain that their government is unresponsive to the needs of an increasingly heterogeneous mix of citizens, partnerships of this sort are likely to be seen more frequently. The number of nongovernmental organizations in these various areas of service has been broad and diversified, with various forms of partial support by government waxing and waning over time. There are, however, important new areas where considerable expansion of effort is needed (e.g., drug abuse and control, crime control, and health and custodial services such as those for AIDS). In sum, explicit and implicit partnerships in this area seem like useful techniques for augmenting direct government provision of services, by employing both governmental and nongovernmental modes.

The challenge for research concerns the factors that make for success and failure in diversified fields of service. Are there clear indicators of useful and wasteful operation? Are there policies that a government can adapt to help generate appropriate forms of variation without undue duplication? Can the government specify criteria for allocating scarce fiscal and other resources among the various, and presumably too-numerous, candidates for aid? Can policies be framed to determine what technical and informational capabilities government should have to enable it to perform its part of a partnership effort? Can the government engage in the right amount and kind of monitoring of the partners without straining the relationship?

A qualification to this part of the discussion should be noted. The emphasis on meeting the needs for heterogeneity must not be exaggerated. In the metropolitan areas of the United States, heterogeneity of need is far more pronounced *across* jurisdictional lines than *within* jurisdictions. A major structural weakness in the governance of metropolitan areas is the separation of responsibility and fiscal capacity of the many municipal governments that constitute each metropolitan area. Little cooperation, coordination, or outright cross-subsidization occurs (see Chernick and Reschovsky, in this volume). This often results in serious jurisdictional mismatch between needs and fiscal capacity within a metropolitan area.

Fragmentation of local government in most metropolitan areas makes joint public-private arrangements *more* attractive. The fiscal distress of hard-pressed central cities generates a greater willingness to join with private developers in urban development schemes — a problem discussed below. Partnerships with private organizations can also help deal with public functions that have a natural impact or technology area wider than the individual jurisdictions that have responsibility for the function, yet lack special areawide governmental districts or other formal or informal entities to deal with them. As noted above, where new technology generates scale economies in the provision of a service far beyond a given jurisdiction's needs, the latter can contract out to a private supplier large enough to supply several jurisdictions at significantly lower costs than each jurisdiction would experience supplying itself. The same is true when special supply expertise is available to a large private organization but is beyond the capability of a single jurisdiction.

Stretching Collective Action in the Face of Severe Public Revenue Limitations

Partnerships are a technique for stretching the range or depth of collective action where governmental fiscal resources alone are inadequate, even when the service and its delivery are well within the substantive *competence* of government action.[9] The problem area in which this is likely to be especially severe is the redistributive functions of government. The problem is twofold: First, local governments are financially strapped due to a mix of demographic change, recession, retracted federal presence, and a climate of tax revolt; and second, there is often weak citizen commitment to dealing effectively with problems of poverty, deviance, and socioeconomic disability. These factors derive from decades of experience with serious attacks on poverty and its accompaniments, from which the following popular stereotypes have been distilled: (1) the problems are extraordinarily complex and have become increasingly difficult, (2) all or almost all of the approaches tried have failed, and (3) the targets, individual and group, of the various programs may not have done their share.

The result of budgetary "realities" and skepticism about results is that there are many deficits in the area of redistributional services, coverage in each kind of program falls far short of the need, and groups actually covered often receive inadequate help. The areas especially affected in this respect are low-income housing, social welfare services, drug abuse treatment, general education under adverse conditions, special education and job training, health care, notably preventive care, and community development.

For much the same reasons as presented under "Service Quality and Differentiation" above, these are especially attractive areas for partnerships. Many citizen groups have sought, over long periods of time and in various ways, to ease the lot of the less fortunate. A major portion of the resources brought to bear on efforts to help the disadvantaged do not have to meet market tests to justify their use. If a modest investment by government can help keep such efforts viable, a much larger and well-articulated effort by governments — local, state, and federal — toward amelioration of poverty may be mobilized, although this cannot be assured.

The character of partnership arrangements between public and private entities needs further discussion. Redistributional operations should be not only more extensive but also more effective. Much of the pessimism among the general public regarding social services is due to the perception that traditional ways of spending money on urban problems do not work. That perception can be modified at least in part by partnering with private nonprofit groups that specialize in dealing with particular kinds of problems, particular types of clients, or particular spatial locations, thus complementing the more mainstream efforts of government alone.

Another lesson of failed policies is that we have to learn more innovative ways of intervening. Private nonprofit organizations, and even profit-oriented organizations working in a nonprofit mode (e.g., "adopt a school"), have a better record of experimentation and imagination than do governments. Such a penchant for imagining and implementing better ways to attack urban problems, when carried out simultaneously by many small, independent agents, can represent an efficient laboratory for learning how to fight these enormously difficult social maladies. Public-private partnerships are a source of such experimental designs.

In all of this, local governments have an important role to play. They can take continuing stock of the panoply of new efforts, and provide a reasonable allocation of support to encourage innovative configurations of experiments while discouraging unwise duplication of efforts and repetition of already-failed approaches. Such a role is not easy. The partnership mode does not guarantee that resources will be well-directed and used effectively. Government, as a partner, may exercise some warranted oversight and planning over these privately implemented efforts, but must do so judiciously. Nongovernmental organizations are suspicious about having their mission and distinctive style preempted by government; they will take the government's money, but not if it has restrictive strings attached to it. Nonprofits must be allowed to fail and flounder in their own way. Only broad allocational criteria and responsive advice can be dependably exercised by government in these partnerships, but this may conflict with the need for active monitoring of output quality and distribution of services, as discussed above.

Partnerships between governments and nonprofits can pose further difficulty. In many of these functional areas the local government will be operating its own facilities, for its own purposes. If a local government gives its nongovernmental partner the impression that it is being accorded functional breathing space to implement its program, and if the government's own program then seems to squeeze it out, a souring of the partnership can easily ensue. This can make partnerships difficult to form and sustain even in areas beyond those under contention.

In sum, the redistribution function can potentially be greatly enhanced by use of the partnership mode. The arrangement, however, must be entered into with circumspection and tact on the part of the government, which must also recognize and accept responsibility for assuring comprehensive mutual understanding of what is being tried and how, and by what criteria performance will be judged.

The tasks for research here are much like those listed in the previous section of this essay, but two items must be added to the research agenda because of the special focus on poverty. First, one of the principles of effective intervention for the purpose of ameliorating poverty is the need to encourage a high level of participation on the part of clients themselves. That participation includes being parties in the intervention process. Still, little is known about how best to mobilize client participation. Research is needed about this, and on how achievement of the participation goal affects the working of the partnership itself—what potential strengths are added, what difficulties are encountered.

Second, the intervention must face the source of sensitivity of the clients served. They are likely to bridle at being patronized by those who seek to help them, feeling demeaned beyond the damage done by poverty itself. This feeling understandably weakens their willingness to cooperate maximally with the intervention effort. Policy makers must learn how to conduct interventions that maintain the dignity of their clients.

Major Reform of Complicated Systems

Two of our major service systems seem to be failing so badly, or at least seem so unequal to their tasks, that many critics have charged that what is needed is not more, nor even a different mix of elements, but a radical reform of the systems as a whole. These are public education and the criminal justice system (including drug use). (See the essays by Rosenbaum and Fagan, in this volume.) The welfare system is also profoundly troubled, but revision of that system deeply involves the federal government and is beyond the scope of the present discussion. (See, however, the chapter by Duncan, in this volume.) The partnership mode has potentially genuine value in dealing with these large system issues.[10]

Two things are clearly needed: fresh, imaginative thinking about new *integrated* organizational approaches, and a multiplicity of small-scale, flexible experiments embodying various organizational approaches. The public bureaucracies now responsible for these social service functions have serious disabilities for achieving these intermediate goals. They are likely to be defensive about the present system and, in questions of reform, they are used to thinking in incremental terms (what is the *least change* we can get away with?), rather than in large system engineering terms. Yet these bureaucracies are the repositories of the broadest and most intimate knowledge of the social problems and the complexities of administering services to deal with them. Reinventing systems and conducting numerous small-scale forays into rectification are initiatives that seem better suited to the private sector. Here, as with the redistributional system, it is non-profit groups from which fruitful activity can be expected.

The educational system is especially instructive in this regard. A fair portion of corporate America has "taken up" education.[11] Whenever a corporation or benefactor "adopts a school," or adopts a subsidy plan for changing students' incentives to stay in school or perform well, or links job entry and training to student school performance, this represents an informal experiment. What is critical for these experiments, but all too rare, is that they be closely monitored and their successes and failures noted, understood, and measured.

Many business-backed educational projects are currently under way.[12] In addition, a number of comprehensive reform schemes have been recommended by business groups.[13] The considerable public advocacy and discussion of goal-oriented schools is a notable example. Sometimes government is explicitly involved in these actions, but more often it is not, simply being passive.

Partnership would be most welcome in the education area. Cooperative, coordinated relations between government and these various private "doers" would permit more effective mechanisms for canvasing deficiencies and opportunities, suggesting functional and spatial areas where outside initiatives would be especially helpful, and systematically monitoring the purposes and records of these outside projects. The combining of experience would permit a more constructive attack on questions of overall reform. In a system of such complexity, ambitious reform must bring together the deepest, broadest, and most detailed information available about how the system operates.

The same types of considerations hold for the criminal justice system. While most of the limited experiments with respect to policing and incarceration are carried out within the state and local governments, projects connected with prevention of crime — treatment of drug use, alternative recreation for teenagers, school retention, job training programs, and so forth — are usually carried out by nongovernmental, largely nonprofit groups in the social welfare and health areas. The relevance of the partnership mode is the same as in its application to education. The knowledge base regarding how significantly to reduce crime is limited. Many interlocking components are involved: the criminal justice system, labor markets, the educational and welfare service systems, and low-cost housing markets. (Each of these is discussed in essays above, and their interactions are the subject of this entire volume.) A variety of approaches should continue to be utilized. The "cement" of selective government subsidization of private efforts can put local government at the center of the myriad of studies, tests, and trials, both to help rationalize who does what and to generate a clearinghouse of experimental results.

Thus, partnerships can provide an institutional structure that increases the efficiency with which relevant information is generated and mobilized into policy reform. Once again, success requires sophistication and tact on the part of government to make the potential mutual gains from linkage (including the subsidy) look better to the private groups than the possibility of co-optation by, and loss of independence to, government.

There are important implications for research. Above all, we need much more basic research on how the education and criminal justice systems actually work versus how they ought to work; and we need to understand how the partnership mode itself can aid that basic research by generating activities that can be utilized as a flow of hypothesis formation and laboratory experimentation.

Profit Making via Land Use Development, Revitalization and Growth, and Partnerships between Government and Private Enterprise

In some ways this category represents the highest profile use of partnerships. It is closest to the genuine partnerships that occur in a market system, and involves local government making deals with private, profit-making firms for private actions related to land use development. Examples include a developer participating in the large-scale redevelopment of a downtown area; a commercial or residential builder constructing a mix of housing for different income groups, and/or commercial buildings; or a business firm locating or expanding facilities in an urban area. In each case, the government obtains agreement from the firm to do one or more of certain things, which might be to undertake the development, or to locate in a certain area, or to build more low-income housing than the builder may have initially planned, or to locate the units in a different area, or to share in the profits of a private market action. For such a gain, the government might be willing to grant a below-market price land assembly; or zoning or other regulatory exceptions that enhance the market value of the project; or tax exemptions; or government below-market loans or loan guarantees; or outright government subsidies of one kind or another. There is potential in these various ways for trading advantages that are of great value to both the private developer and the city.

The factors leading to wide use of public-private partnerships are worth a brief review. Citizens of urban areas are disillusioned by local government and likely to block attempts to raise taxes to fund needed social services. This results in a de facto tax rationing of local government. Failure of the political jurisdictions within the metropolitan area to pool responsibility for services leads to gross inequalities in service delivery, with the central city government bearing the greatest strain. Recent and prospective federal cutbacks in welfare, health, and housing programs, coupled with new federal mandates, have added to the burdens of urban governments. And, finally, the worsening of crime, drug abuse, health, unemployment, and race relations over the last 15–20 years has pushed the resources of local governments to the point of exhaustion.

Overall, local governments are expected to do much more than they are doing to solve these problems, but they are denied, by their own taxpayers and the federal system of government alike, the financial means to do so. Measures that generate net increases in revenue capacity can make a significant contribution to the ability of local government to function better.

Three mechanisms are involved by which economic development deals can augment a local government's revenue capacity: (1) downtown vital-ization generates more business activity in the jurisdiction, thereby in-creasing real estate values and the sales tax base; (2) location of more businesses in the jurisdiction (indeed, probably anywhere in the same metropolitan area) increases employment and incomes as well as raises real estate values and the sales tax base; and (3) local government's shar-ing directly in the private developer's profits as an investor generates a direct financial return. These three routes have different time profiles and different magnitudes, but all have potential capacity for major enhance-ment of revenue capacity.

Such enhancement of revenue capacity, however, is likely to affect the mix and form of governmental activities, not simply generating revenue, and has the potential to cause significant problems. They arise from the specific details of the profit-making partnership arrangements, the riski-ness of the government's resulting situation, the redefinition of the proper role of local government, the impact on the redistribution function of government, shifts in the pattern of de facto representation for govern-ment decision making, and shifts in the locus of action initiative.

The partnership agreement specifies actions and responsibilities ex-pected of each party. In exchange for getting the project undertaken and a promised share of the profits, government must provide or improve public goods (usually infrastructure), release the developer from various regula-tory requirements, assemble land, forgive taxes in whole or part over a time schedule, and so forth. One direct consequence is a decrease in the extent or stringency of regulatory control.

Partnership in profit making generally requires government to bear some of the risks that such development projects inherently involve. Un-naturally higher degrees of risk may exacerbate the government's lack of experience. The egregious, but not unique, example of Orange County, California, is obvious, but lesser degrees of crisis can easily occur as well. The government must be able and willing to learn how to live in high-risk situations. Such adaptation is not easily achieved.

A third kind of problem for government is more subtle and speculative. The public perception from successful profit-sharing partnerships that there is an easy way out of the money bind could subtly and tacitly re-define the role of local government toward a bottom-line orientation: ac-tivities that "make money" are to be reached for, those that "lose money" are to be avoided. The resultant reshuffling of public goal priorities might well be very different from what the government intended to do through the partnership.

It is critical that the city not come to act as simply another private interest. Criticism of a recent New York City partnership illustrates the danger. The city's granting of a zoning exemption to a private firm in return for cooperation in the development of Columbus Circle led to charges of "abdication of regulatory responsibilities," as one writer put it. "If the city acts like a profit-seeking developer, who will then look after the public interest?" (Frieden 1994, pp. 12–13).

Most, but not all, past developments of the sort that are subject to profit-sharing partnerships have had mild to strong regressive effects on the income distribution: the low end of the income distribution has been on balance hurt, whatever the pattern of net gains higher in the distribution. If there is any implicit redefinition of the role of government toward bottom-line orientation as well, this effect could be aggravated: the poor typically "lose money" for local government. Thus, if there is no actual political intention to tilt the income distribution away from the poor, then special attention has to be given to compensatory programs. This requirement may be politically ticklish, especially at this time.

The actual process of partnership negotiations (Frieden and Sagalyn 1989; Frieden 1990, 1994) is likely to involve a narrower base of public representation than is involved in the more conventional kinds of government activity. An overall shift in the real balance of political representation might ensue if such partnerships come to be increasingly common. Once again, the rectification of such a change is not simple. Partnership negotiations require technical expertise and some degree of secrecy. To attempt to make them miniature cross sections of open representative government may be neither possible nor desirable. So the potential problem is a delicate one.

Finally, the locus of initiative for public policy might shift with a growing popularity of profit-sharing partnerships. Typically, it is private enterprise that discovers or formulates the proposal and approaches government. Government rarely has the resources or the know-how necessary to generate such proposals. Thus, the mix, timing, and important aspects of implementation will be largely initiated privately. This is not in itself a defect. On the contrary, among the attractions of public-private partnerships are those private-sector skill, information, and specialized resources. The potential problem is that increasing resort to joint projects could increase government passivity while increasing dependence on private dynamism, planning, and scheduling, with results unforeseen by government officials.

Little is known about the seriousness of these various side effects of public-private partnerships. The dangers, however, are great enough to merit hard research before governments move aggressively into the partnership realm for their financial salvation.

A Note on Partnership Form

Not much has been said systematically in this essay about the desirability of various forms of partnership. Some theoretical surmises can be made, but the lack of empirical research weakens their credibility.

(1) If a private advantage exists in the production or delivery of services, a division of labor between planning (government) and production/delivery (private group) seems warranted. If, in addition, (2) the production and/or delivery stages are technically separable from the planning function, and the product's quality and character of delivery are readily monitorable, then a contracting-out form of partnership may be most efficient. (3) If either nonseparability or inadequate external monitorability is present, a closer internal relationship is required—with each partner contributing the kinds of service it can render best.

(4) If the aim of the government's interest in a partnership is to take advantage of a private party's willingness to risk substantial resources on a novel technology or to target a beneficiary group, or to capitalize on a special set of circumstances, and if external monitoring is possible, then partnering with a for-profit organization is appropriate. The division of responsibilities between the partners, and the degree of closeness or separation of structures and operations, depends again on the degree of separability and the nature of the technology. Where external monitoring is impaired, and specialized tailoring of product type and/or quality to different targets is desired, partnership with a for-profit organization would have to be closed and tight. A looser, more open relationship could be attempted with a nonprofit because of its often presumed sense of mission concerning the product or service. Where the government has a strong interest in helping a given target group, in ways that meet specialized needs, an appropriate policy might be to select a subset of nonprofits known for dedication in particular services areas (e.g., church groups), subsidize their operation with funds, and then "get out of the way."

More combinations of circumstances can be surmised, with the same simple kind of plausibility as these, but those listed above are sufficient to indicate the kind of connection that might be expected to determine the form for each major type of partnership advantage discussed in this essay.

However plausible these surmises may seem, they are dimmed by the empirical record. In much of the literature to which I have referred is the repeated refrain that in each kind of partnership situation success or failure depends on very specific circumstances rather than on partnership form. This is not surprising. For one thing, partnerships are still a relatively new concept, with sparse research or experience on which to rely. Moreover, the problems addressed by partnerships are often complex. Also, initiation of the partnership is often not a matter of carefully planned strategy and timing by government, but rather one of opportunism: one or more private actors was/were ready, or indeed made the proposition to the government in the first place, with the partnership's character and timing based on private plans and urgencies. Finally, the identity of the specific people and groups involved matters greatly. In this area of novelty and uncertainty, boldness, adaptability, judgment, and other personal qualities in the actors can easily make the difference between success and failure. Partnership form is only one of a number of factors influencing the outcome.

Conclusion

Expansion of public-private partnerships is worth consideration by governments, both because of the fiscal plight of most cities and because traditional modes of local government action are inherently incapable of meeting the city's fiscal needs. There has been a wide range of applications of the public-private partnership idea, but little has been learned about the elements that determine "success" and "failure." Research is not a frill to satisfy curious academics; it is a critical element in the process of learning from experience. What we know now is that public-private partnerships as a class are serious candidates for helping meet this country's deep and troubling urban problems.

APPENDIX

MANY ARROWS IN THE QUIVER

The 36 alternatives we have found to standard service delivery by public employees range from the traditional to the avant-garde. We have arbitrarily grouped them in three categories.[14]

Traditional
1. Creating legal rules and sanctions
2. Regulation or deregulation
3. Monitoring and investigation
4. Licensing
5. Tax policy
6. Grants
7. Subsidies
8. Loans
9. Loan guarantees
10. Contracting

Innovative

11. Franchising
12. Public-private partnerships
13. Public-public partnerships
14. Quasi-public corporations
15. Public enterprise
16. Procurement
17. Insurance
18. Rewards
19. Changing public investment policy
20. Technical assistance
21. Information
22. Referral
23. Volunteers
24. Vouchers
25. Impact fees
26. Catalyzing nongovernmental efforts
27. Convening nongovernmental leaders
28. Jawboning

Avant-Garde

29. Seed money
30. Equity investments
31. Voluntary associations
32. Coproduction or self-help
33. Quid pro quos
34. Demand management
35. Sale, exchange, or use of property
36. Restructuring the market

Many of these methods can be used in combination. For example, when the city of Visalia helped create its nonprofit housing corporation, Visalians Interested in Affordable Housing (VIAH), it jawboned the private sector, catalyzed a nongovernmental effort, provided seed money, sold property to VIAH, and offered technical assistance.

NOTES

1. A wide literature makes these claims. See, e.g., Salamon (1987); Savas (1987); Wilson (1989); Bennett (1990); Ferguson (1994a, 1994b).

2. This was analyzed in Weisbrod (1975, pp. 171–95).

3. This section represents an amalgam of materials from Salamon (1987), Savas (1987), Wilson (1989), Bennett (1990), Osborne and Gaebler (1992), Kernaghan (1993), and Ferguson (1994).

4. Savas (1987, chap. 9) suggests a number of arrangements to facilitate increased competition.

5. This does not mean that universality can be obtained only via pure collective action. Contracting out for a basically uniform service, or for more complex ventures where government and private partners can furnish complementary components, which they are respectively best qualified to provide, can generate such universality if that is the goal of the partnership. Waste removal, construction of sports complexes, and some forms of urban development have such characteristics. See some of the references in the above section entitled "The Variety of Public-Private Partnerships."

6. There is a substantial literature on this. See, e.g., Chubb and Moe (1983), Stave (1984), Salamon (1987), Savas (1987), Osborne (1988a, 1988b), Wilson (1989), Bennett (1990), and Osborne and Gaebler (1992).

7. Weisbrod (1989).

8. Smith and Lipsky (1993).

9. The relevant literature here is much the same as that for the preceding section.

10. Among a large literature on education are the following: Chubb and Moe (1983), Kearns and Doyle (1988), Hornbeck and Salamon (1991), Marshall and Tucker (1992), Conference Board (1993), and Melaville and Blank (1993). This section of my essay refers most specifically to education.

11. See, e.g., Committee on Economic Development (1985, 1987); National Alliance for Business and the Business Roundtable (1988); Conference Board (1993). Also noteworthy in this regard is the Business Coalition for Education Reform, an ad hoc group of staff leaders of the major business associations (U.S. Chamber of Commerce, National Association of Manufacturers, American Business Council, etc.) that represents business interests in educational reform to Congress and the U.S. Department of Education.

12. A small sample includes (1) Corning, Inc.'s classroom "work ethic"; (2) Grand Metropolitan, Inc.'s workplace presentation for students; (3) Southern California Gas Co.'s training of parents for school leadership; (4) U.S. West Foundation's parents-educators communication; (5) Amoco's Science Enrichment partnership; (6) NEC-Apple's Science and Technology Integration; (7) Coopers and Lybrand's focus on mentoring; (8) Chevron Corp., Ford, and Coca Cola's school retention; and (9) Bank of America and Kaiser Permanente's (Honolulu) school-to-work transition. In addition, a number of comprehensive reform schemes have been recommended by business groups.

13. See n. 11 above.

14. This appendix is derived from Osborne and Gaebler (1992).

REFERENCES

Bennett, Robert J. 1990. "Decentralization, Intergovernmental Relations and Markets: Towards a Post-welfare Agenda?" Chap. 1 in *Decentralization, Local Governments, and Markets: Towards a Post-welfare Agenda*, edited by Robert J. Bennett. Oxford: Clarendon Press.

Bennett, Robert J., and Gunter Krebs. 1991. *Local Economic Development: Public-Private Initiative in Britain and Germany*. London: Belhaven Press. (Background reference)

Borins, Sandford. 1994. "Public Sector Innovation through Information

Technology: Recent Experience in the U.S. and Canada." Unpublished
manuscript. Toronto: University of Toronto. (Background reference)

Boston Housing Partnership, Inc. 1990. *Annual Report.* Boston: Boston Housing
Partnership, Inc.

Cerillo, Augustus, Jr. 1977. "The Impact of Reform Ideology: Early 20th Century
Municipal Government in New York City." Chap. 5 in *The Age of Urban Reform:
New Perspectives in the Progressive Era,* edited by Michael N. Ebner and Eugene
M. Tobin. Port Washington, N.Y.: Kennikat Press. (Background reference)

Chernick, Howard, and Andrew Reschovsky. In this volume. "Urban Fiscal
Problems: Coordinating Actions among Governments."

Chubb, John E., and Terry M. Moe. 1983. *Politics, Markets and America's
Schools.* Washington, D.C.: Brookings Institution.

Committee on Economic Development. 1985. *Investing in Our Children:
Business and the Public Schools.* Washington, D.C.: Committee on Economic
Development.

———. 1987. *Children in Need: Investment Strategies for the Educationally
Disadvantaged.* New York: Committee on Economic Development.

Conference Board. 1993. *Ten Years after "A Nation at Risk."* New York:
Conference Board.

Duncan, George. In this volume. "Welfare Reform and Employment: What We
Know, and What We Still Need to Know."

Ebner, Michael N., and Eugene M. Tobin, eds. 1977. *The Age of Urban Reform:
New Perspectives in the Progressive Era.* Port Washington, N.Y.: Kennikat
Press. (Background reference)

Fagan, Jeffrey. In this volume. "Legal and Illegal Work: Crime, Work, and
Unemployment."

Fainstein, Norman I., and Susan Fainstein. 1987. "Economic Restructuring and
the Politics of Land Use Planning in New York City." *Journal of the American
Planning Association* 53(2):237–48.

Ferguson, Bruce W. 1994a. "The Future of Non-profit Housing Development and
Federal Policy: Three Scenarios." Unpublished manuscript. Cambridge, Mass.:
Massachusetts Institute of Technology.

———. 1994b. "Towards a New Role for Local Government in Development."
Unpublished manuscript. Cambridge, Mass.: Massachusetts Institute of
Technology.

Frieden, Bernard J. 1990. "Center City Transformed: Planners as Developers."
APA Journal (Autumn).

———. 1994. "Dealmaking Goes Public: Learning from Columbus Circle."
Unpublished manuscript. Cambridge, Mass.: Massachusetts Institute of
Technology.

Frieden, Bernard J., and Lynne B. Sagalyn. 1989. *Downtown, Inc.: How America
Rebuilds Cities.* Cambridge, Mass.: MIT Press.

Hornbeck, Daniel W., and Lester M. Salamon, eds. 1991. *Human Capital and
America's Future.* Baltimore: Johns Hopkins University Press.

Kearns, David T., and Denis P. Doyle. 1988. *Winning the Brain Race: A Bold
Plan to Make Our Schools Competitive.* San Francisco: ICS Press.

Kernaghan, Kenneth. 1993. "Partnership and Public Administration: Conceptual and Practical Considerations." *Canadian Public Administration* 36(1).

Marshall, R., and M. Tucker. 1992. "Restructuring the Schools for High Performance: Tough Road to Excellence." Chap. 8 in *Thinking for a Living*. New York: Basic Books.

Melaville, Atelia I., and Martin J. Blank, with Gelareh Assayesh. 1993. *Together We Can: A Guide for Crafting a Profamily System in Education and Human Services*. Washington, D.C.: U.S. Department of Education and U.S. Department of Health and Human Services.

National Alliance for Business and the Business Roundtable. 1988. *The Role of Business in Education Reform: Blueprint for Action*. Washington, D.C.: Department of Health and Human Services.

Osborne, David. 1988a. "The First Agenda: Creating Economic Growth." Chap. 1 in *Laboratories of Democracy*. Boston: Harvard Business School Press.

———. 1988b. "Pennsylvania: The Economic Development Model." Chap. 2 in *Laboratories of Democracy*. Boston: Harvard Business School Press.

Osborne, David, and Ted Gaebler. 1992. *Reinventing Government*. Reading, Mass.: Addison-Wesley.

Ostrander, Susan A., and Stuart Langton, eds. 1987. *Shifting the Debate: Public/Private Sector Relations in the Modern Welfare State*. New Brunswick, N.J.: Transaction Books. (Background reference)

Rosenbaum, James E. In this volume. "Schools and the World of Work."

Salamon, Lester M. 1987. "Of Market Failure and Third-Party Government: Toward a Theory of Government–Non-profit Relations in the Modern Welfare State." In *Shifting the Debate: Public/Private Sector Relations in the Modern Welfare State*, edited by Susan A. Ostrander and Stuart Langton. New Brunswick, N.J.: Transaction Books.

Savas, E. S. 1979. "Public vs. Private Collection: A Critical View of the Evidence." *Journal of Urban Analysis* 6.

———. 1987. *Privatization: The Key to Better Government*. Chatham, N.J.: Chatham House.

Smith, Steven Rathgeb, and Michael Lipsky. 1993. *Nonprofits for Hire: The Welfare State in the Age of Contracting*. Cambridge, Mass.: Harvard University Press.

Stave, Bruce M., ed. [1971] 1984. *Urban Bosses, Machines and Progressive Reformers*. Lexington, Mass.: D. C. Heath.

Suchman, Dian R., with D. Scott Middleton and Susan L. Giles. 1990. *Public/Private Housing Partnerships*. Washington, D.C.: Urban Land Institute.

Weisbrod, Burton. 1975. "Toward a Theory of the Voluntary Nonprofit Sector in a Three-Sector Economy." In *Altruism, Morality, and Economic Theory*, edited by E. Phelps. New York: Russell Sage Foundation.

———. 1989. "Rewarding Performance That Is Hard to Measure: The Private Nonprofit Sector." *Science* 244(May):541–46.

Wilson, James Q. 1989. *Bureaucracy: What Government Agencies Do and Why They Do It*. New York: Basic Books.

PART III

Searching for Solutions

What Policy Makers Need from the Research Community

Views from the Front Line

An important feature of the Assembly was a panel discussion in which three leading representatives of the policy-making community expressed their views on their relationships with the research community and how the two communities can work together more effectively. The discussion was chaired by Burton A. Weisbrod, Director of the Center for Urban Affairs and Policy Research of Northwestern University.

CHAIRMAN WEISBROD: We continue to think about the kinds of tensions that exist between the world of research and the world of the practical. So we try in a variety of ways to see whether these two worlds can be brought together, whether we can understand each other in terms of language, but more importantly and more deeply, whether we can understand the ideas and the perspectives that we bring to bear on the problems that are of mutual concern. One of the things we have done is ask three people from the nonresearch community — what some of us like to call the real world — what they think the research community ought to be doing. We asked them not to pull any punches. If they feel that we researchers are going off in directions that are not useful, that what we are doing is counting the number of angels that can dance on the head of a pin, tell us. Let's hear what you really think. We have a very good triumvirate for this purpose. Let me tell you a little about them.

Jean Allard is president of the Metropolitan Planning Council and is of counsel for the firm of Sonnenschein, Nath & Rosenthal in Chicago. Jean serves as a director on the boards of Commonwealth Edison, ABN LaSalle Banks, and Axel Johnson Bank. She's a former vice president for business and finance at the University of Chicago, and served as research associate and assistant dean at the University of Chicago Law School where she received her J.D. degree. She's a former partner at Sonnenschein, Nath & Rosenthal, and has been an associate in the Chicago law firm of Lloyd, Bissel & Brook, as well as in a firm in Toledo. She serves on boards of the American Bar Association, the Metropolitan Chicago Information Center, and the Chicago Light Enterprise Center, and has been awarded honorary degrees from Culver Sackton College and Elmhurst College.

Vincent Lane has achieved national recognition for his work as chairman of the Board of Commissioners of the Chicago Housing Authority (CHA), which is responsible for 150,000 housing residents. In 1990, Vince was appointed by the Bush administration to serve on the National Commission on Severely Distressed Public Housing, and was elected cochairman. In 1992 he was appointed to the President's Commission on Model State Drug Laws, and that same year Mayor Richard Daley appointed him to the mixed-income, new Community Strategy Coordinating Council of which he became chairman. He served on Mayor Harold Washington's advisory council to the CHA and Mayor Eugene Sawyer's Navy Pier Development Corporation. Vince has an M.B.A. from the University of Chicago. Prior to joining the CHA, he was president and general partner of Urban Services and Development, and LSM Ventures Associates, managing close to 3,000 apartment units and developing commercial properties in Chicago neighborhoods. Before founding Urban Services in 1976, he served as senior vice president of the Woodlawn Community Development Corp. In 1986 he received a HUD regional award for minority developer of the year.

Finally, Neal Peirce. *Time* magazine has written that Neal is a journalist who got his career backwards. Most writers start at the local level, then graduate to the State House, hoping eventually to become a Washington correspondent. Instead, Neal started at the national level as political editor of *Congressional Quarterly*. He founded the *National Journal* in 1969 and remains as contributing editor of that publication. However, his interests turned to the cities and states of America, and he's done a lot of writing on that subject, culminating in *The Book of America: Inside 50 States Today*, published in 1983. For 19 years Neal has written the country's first and only nationally syndicated column on state and local government themes. Syndicated by the Washington Post Writers Group, his column has appeared in over 15 newspapers nationwide. Together with Curt Johnson, he's about to begin a project about the nature of Philadelphia's urban problems for the *Philadelphia Inquirer*. I'll begin our panel discussion by calling on Jean Allard.

ALLARD: I really took the title of our discussion group quite literally, and I want to answer what policy makers really need from the research community because I think we do need some things from the academy. More than anything else I think we need the outreach of the academy to us. You neglect us, you come around only when we're useful, you don't participate in our work, and you're not really very interested in what we're doing until we send you a publication. Many of us think that you could share in some of the agonies that the nonprofit, policy-making group tries to accomplish, because we think we are really laboring in the vineyards of the metropolis and the metropolitan area — what we're calling in this area the region. My organization, the Metropolitan Planning Council, historically has had a very good relationship with the academy. We've been around for 60 years and we've had long-term relationships with individual members — two or three from Northwestern, two or three from the University of Illinois at Chicago, the Illinois Institute of Technology, the University of Chicago, and some other academic institutions in this area. We've got probably 12–20 faculty members who are currently involved in the governance of our organization, either serving on the board — some of them are long-term board members — or busy on our work committees. We even have three university and college presidents who participate in our work, some of them of long-term standing.

But we don't see any young faculty coming around very much in terms of the work we're doing. We think we're in a kind of brave, new world as we extend our work from urban problems to those of the larger metropolis. And we don't see any of your young and eager research folks. These are the types who get their jollies, if you will, by dealing with the kind of policy issues that we deal with on a regular basis. And we see very few students. Those students we do see want jobs badly. If they can't find any other way to sustain themselves, they may intern for a summer. But we need those young faculty, and we need those students to participate in our work; we need them to help us think straight, to do some of the legwork for us, and also to learn what it is to be really working in the vineyard. But we need them to want to get involved in what we're doing and to also share with us some of the ideas they have about what needs to be done. Metropolitan Planning Council works almost exclusively through volunteers.

We have also noted that if the academy doesn't have a specific job to do, it has a general reluctance just to roll up its sleeves and help out. We don't see very many faculty who are at our doorstep, enterprising with us in terms of an agreed agenda with all of us involved in trying to solve the same problems. We think that the academy might want to look at its own civic obligation. Metropolitan Planning Council is made up of volunteers, people who volunteer their time and who think the kind of work that is being done, both in the city and in the larger metropolitan area, is important, and we need the academy to participate in this. So we need your help and your active and personal involvement in the work that we do.

Second, with not too much effort, even we can do what we call head counting and bean counting that we can rely on from a database. But we do need the academy very badly for causal interrelationships, an area we often don't have the depth of experience to deal with, and we do need the kind of intensive work that can be done at the college and university level.

I was shocked when I looked at the calendar today and recognized it was 3 years ago today that I started at the Metropolitan Planning Council after a long career in law practice. It was a shock especially to find that there was not the kind of electronic source of data that I had been used to in law practice, where I could plug into Lexis and get any case in the world at my desk for review.

In the fall of 1991, the 1990 census data were not yet out in totality. We had just a little idea of what was going on in the data that we were dealing with, which were drawn from 1980 and were used to make some informal predictions for the next census period. We had just decided to delve into what we've called our regional civic initiative, where we were focusing our program in terms of the larger metropolitan area. Never mind that the data weren't in fancy bar charts. Never mind that they really were not up on people's computers. Never mind that there weren't color graphs that we could work with, to talk about in terms of what was going on, even in the head-counting area. We didn't know very much about shifts in population. We didn't know very much about shifts in employment. We knew even less about changes in racial distribution. We had some idea that there was an aging population, but we had no idea what that meant. And we certainly were not aware of the extent of the multiworker households that we were encountering.

But let me tell you, this conference yesterday and today has put on the table the really important needs and relevance of the kinds of research that are being done regionally that I was not aware of. It's the trends of where we're going and what we think we can do about it that become the challenge in the interaction between the academy and the policy makers in this area and elsewhere.

So we need your help not only with data availability, when the census is not yet there, but also with its application. We also need your help with answers to particular problems that you're working on in your own research that we can work together to use.

Third, we need your help in understanding how complex things work. Let me give you a couple of examples that are hard for us in policy making to work with. Let's talk about the dynamics of coordinated actions — the process that brings together diverse people with their own interests to work collectively, rather than competitively — which we find so much throughout our region. One example is the dynamics of the intergovernmental agreements. Things are occurring with many of the people in this audience who have said it's easier to solve a problem if two or three communities work together on common problems than it is for each of us to set up our own organization. An example of this came from Rita Athos, who charmed us not long ago by telling us how the communities along the Wisconsin Central line are creating the first new suburban commuter train since 1923. That's a phenomenal kind of community involvement to turn a railroad line back into action and to help restore mobility within this region. We don't understand the dynamics of this. But we can do a lot of forward-looking work if we understand how to go about getting people together to work on such an enterprise. It is what I have come to call turf squared: how do we work with the trade-offs of turfs to begin to pull some of the dynamics of this region together in ways that say we're just a hell of a lot better off if we all get involved in it ourselves.

Another kind of thing happened today that reminded me of how little we really know and how sometimes even the academy narrows itself too much. It's not simply the racial implications of spatial mismatches that emerge when employment moves from the city where residents are to the suburbs where employment is. What about the mismatches — if that's even what you want to call it — for the modern multiworker household, and how does that "family" make locational decisions depending on multiple job circumstances? I think it is different than the analyses we talked about earlier and I think those models just don't work. But I think the academy has a lot to offer in taking it from the simple model in its analysis, from the racial/spatial misplacement to the kind of thing we're dealing with in the modern, complex family lives that we lead.

Fourth, and my last point: we need you to partner with us. We need to see you regularly. We need to get together like this regularly, where we're really rubbing off on each other, where we say, "You don't know what you're talking about." Where you say back, "You don't know what you're talking about." And somehow or other we pull things together and we begin a very sophisticated and complex new kind of relationship that will move each of our organizations 100 percent further than we might have been without the other. I think this conference has afforded us this opportunity, and thank you for putting us together.

LANE: I want to ditto what Jean says because, from a selfish point of view, I need your help. I'm going to be a little critical because I don't think we get the kind of help that you could give us. You really possess powerful tools. Right now public policy depends a lot on the news media to form public opinion, and our elected officials and public officials tend to set public policy by political expediency. And sometimes, like I do quite often, set policy by the seat of our pants. So it would be very, very useful if academia would hone in on a subject and really do a thorough job. We talk about fragmentation in government and services. Boy, are you guys fragmented! I mean, talk about turf—you never collaborate and you never hone in on one subject, and you never partner up in large enough numbers to use the major resource you've got, which is your students, to really thoroughly look at subjects. Then, of course, from your perspective, the question becomes, How do we fund it? That brings up the foundations, who've been criticized for years about having short-term viewpoints in terms of funding. Foundations want immediate results as well as whatever's hot for the moment. We should change all that. You guys have some meaty, meaty areas in which you really need to do thorough work that is long-term and consistent, such as cost-benefit analysis.

What we all talk about—and we've heard this for the past 2 days—is whether it's better to do prevention and treatment or hit them in the head and lock them up. All you have to do is do the research and put the numbers down, but do it in a manner such that it can't be challenged. That, in my opinion, would drive the media, which in turn would drive constituents and the elected officials to enact laws that reflect the numbers. It's a major piece of work that could be done right here.

Another issue is the disparity between the inner city and the suburbs. I know there have been studies, but again, it's the little, narrow sections of the problem that are studied. There's a direct relationship, I think, between the health of suburban communities and the health of the central city. And again, it's about showing people what their self-interests are. People understand that it makes sense to have a healthy central city that is going to impact their lives positively. Again, you begin to change public policy. That's the only way you're going to break this thinking of every man for himself. And if you talk about regional government, it's not going to happen unless you document the reasons why it ought to happen and why it's in the best interest of everyone to do so.

Also, what about some of the controversial issues that are out there? The spate of instances of child abuse that are occurring and discussions about welfare reform, for example? Do you cut the mother off after 2 years if she doesn't get a job, and what do you do with the kids if the parents are abusing the children? Somebody mentions orphanages, and everybody says, "Oh my God, that's a terrible thing." Well, maybe it is a terrible thing, but I'd like to know that it's terrible for some specific reason. Not because we just get this feeling that you can't take a child away from its mother. That's an area where you could do some significant research, and maybe we wouldn't have kids feeding into that pipeline and coming out the other end all emotionally screwed up.

Another thing is the debate on the crime bill, recreation or pork — pink pork as Alfonse D'Amato calls it — and whether that really makes any sense or not. You can document it. What happens to kids when they are in little league baseball or scouting or basketball? And the big thing: education. You know what happens in urban school systems? When they are in fiscal trouble the first thing they do is cut out art and music and sports. When I went to high school, I didn't go because I wanted to study history or algebra. I went because I wanted to be in concert band and I wanted to be in the ROTC. Those were the hooks that got me there and I knew if I wanted to participate in them I had to do well in class. We cut all of that out of inner-city schools, and then we wonder why we've got a 60 percent dropout rate. Schools are reimbursed based upon attendance, and it's crazy to cut out the things that are going to increase attendance. So why can't somebody document these relationships in terms of how boards of education spend their money?

Transportation. Is there a relationship between people having their own personal transportation and the ability to get a job somewhere out in suburbia, regardless of where they live? Is there a relationship between getting a job in the suburbs and ultimately moving close to that job? Maybe that's a way to get at racial integration. I'm just trying to make a point that you have the power because once you come out with a study people pay attention. The media pays attention. Elected officials pay attention. You can form and change public opinion if you engage in subject matter broadly enough and over a long enough period of time where it really provides us with a basis for making public policy decisions. I don't think you're doing that now.

PEIRCE: Since my two colleagues have been so "easy" on you, I'll just be a cotton puff and congratulate you on your distinguished departments. I hadn't planned to do that, but they've been pretty tough on you.

My basic belief is that there are immense opportunities and responsibilities but also fun to be had in the public policy arena, and that all of you, if you're not already in the swim, are ready for it and the public needs you. With Curtis Johnson, I've been doing studies of the metropolitan regions for the last several years. We've done eight regions so far. One of the last was Raleigh-Durham, and there we were looking for what's right and what's wrong with the region. There were these huge universities which had made a bundle of money and helped a lot of others make zillions on the Research Triangle Park, so we decided it would be interesting if those universities looked around at the social conditions in their regions. We began to develop a theory about the role of universities in a region or in our society today. We asked how much they look at racial and social divisions, and began to think that the entire university, not just individual departments, should have a responsibility and interest in that direction. Once you no longer think in terms of community service, you can recognize that the division in our society is really the central intellectual challenge of our time. And how could the academy, and every part of it, not want to be engaged in the central problem of our time, which we've been discussing here for the last couple of days?

Duke University, for example, is doing many good things. One is a great social service experiment where kids are taught in the first grade how to position themselves and think and act and talk in ways that will reduce violent and confrontational behavior. Duke's belief is that if they do this and trace it through the first five grades, they can create a group of alert and active youngsters who don't reach for violent ways of resolving disputes or won't be violent later in life because they've had this background. But this is going to take 5 years to begin to evaluate, and what about the other 55,600 kids who will go from first to fifth grade during that time just in that one region of the country?

So our thought was that there's a need for wide numbers of experiments and observations and variances, different ways of approaching the same problems happening at the same time. Multiple urban-related experience experiments. Engaged research. Looking for a critical mass of activity. Moving into experiential education. Trying to introduce students along the way to the real problems of the society around them as they learn to do research and engage in these areas. We were told, that's great, but there's the funding problem just mentioned. Our thought was that if you can do relevant and important research the funding will come, but you have to be willing to take a risk. Curtis and I are taking risks all the time. We're spending out of our own pockets to do things where we don't know if we're going to get business later. Everybody does this in private business, and I think the academy has to be willing to take some of those risks of personal time when it sees things to launch that are important to do.

I know there are a lot of good examples of this in this Chicago region of universities and faculties that are very committed and have done terrific things: Northwestern, John McKnight, Don Haider; Roosevelt University; the University of Illinois; and others along with many of you in this room tonight. I think that's really important because these examples set the example for others in the field.

In Baltimore, there's a new consortium of eleven or so universities beginning to form, or talking about forming, in relationship to their urban activities and their urban studies. Coordination is through the University of Maryland/Baltimore County. I think that kind of cooperation is tremendously important. I also think there's a role for universities to be keepers of the flame on regionalism.

One example is the State University of New York at Albany. Over the last 3 or 4 years Richard Nathan, head of the Rockefeller Institute of Government there, has sparked a major regional project which has engaged the local business community, a good number of academics, and citizen-based committees in a series of conferences on where the region ought to be going. They are working with a coalition of local governments, looking at the potentials for more effective forms of regional governance in an area that has hundreds of governing bodies, just like the Chicago region has. And it's beginning to bear fruit and some really positive projects like a new airport authority. But even more important, the New York legislature has just approved a new commission to look at the whole form of governance for the capital region — at what can be shared and what can't. This would never have happened if there had not been the university keeper of the flame, that was constantly saying, here is the place to come and talk about this.

Another example is the Center for the Study of Greater Philadelphia which Professor Theodore Herschberg runs at the University of Pennsylvania. Professor Herschberg is not into original research as much as he is into trying to make the region of Philadelphia work better. He's not very popular within the general university circles, but damn it, he's the glue for the Philadelphia region. Ted is the ally and the institutional memory. He's the person who brought together conferences of regional legislators with the business community, and he has done numbers of projects over the years so that it's possible to move a regional agenda forward. If the university hadn't at least tolerated that activity, and foundations in the Philadelphia region hadn't supported it, that capacity wouldn't be there. I think this kind of initiative is of immense importance.

This Nathan-Herschberg model may be way beyond detached research. But it's good to get one's hands on decision-making levers once in a while if you like that risky life. Of course most of you have the interest but not the itch. We do need more research, as you've been hearing, about what works and what doesn't. We know that to present the evidence without being able to show public policy makers the long-term consequences of letting contemporary trends persist will have no chance of changing public policy in many of the areas that Jean and Vince were mentioning to you.

Vince mentioned cost-benefit analysis and data. I'd like to see more research which puts together multiple findings and projections of the effects in any area of a whole set of alternative directions that public policy could go in. Vince alluded to criminal justice, and this is the example I was thinking of using, because in our group this morning we talked about this in the context of criminal justice policy. For example, the difference between policies for the state or for the region of continued high incarceration and mandatory sentences, with more and more young people getting a prison experience and becoming virtually unemployable for the next many years of their lives. The alternative would be a policy focused on alternatives to incarceration — community-based discipline and oversight, full or partial decriminalization of drug possession or minor drug dealing, and an emphasis on making young people, even those who have had a brush with the law, able to get back into society. We need studies like that because the politicians are going to be stepping in and just saying there's been another crime, lock them up and throw away the key. The policy will bring about incredibly negative consequences, human and financial, in the long run.

There can be a thousand and one permutations of those contrasting formulas. I'd like to see academicians individually and collectively taking on the challenge of combining the research and projections. Yes, Vince, that means making it as bullet-proof as you can in terms of criticism, but also being willing to say, "Hey, the science has only taken us this far but we can't want till the next century to make some decisions and some choices on public policy that will make immense differences to us." My gratuitous advice is to get out there and get into op-ed pieces, and into radio interviews, and into the public debate, and "just say no" to the culture within academia that says you never want to be caught out on a limb.

We're dealing with a society in real peril, and what we're talking about makes a difference — not just looking at something because it's of academic interest. Objective study is something that really matters because society needs your numbers, your charts, you evidence, and your best projections to use in the real world of serious social slippage.

For instance, there's that whole new area of civic or public journalism opening in the United States, beginning with election coverage where a number of newspapers and broadcast partners are going on National Public Radio in many cities, interviewing citizens about what they think the issues are, and then getting involved in a serious form of community dialogue about solutions. I think that's another area where selectively good academic research could be a lot of help, especially if it's not just on the election process, but takes on questions of what we do about major crime levels in the central city or welfare dependency or whatever.

Just three other things before I wind up. One is that for studies such as those that Curtis Johnson and I do, as well as for many other uses, we need more baseline research. If the current trends continue, given the demography of a metropolitan region, given the growth of poverty, given the racial and income divisions, where are we going to go? I think people need to have that knowledge, that it's very important that they have it. There's no motivation within government to create that knowledge, and therefore it has to come out of the independent academy if it's going to come out at all. Obvious questions out there: What are the early warning signs of major poverty or decline? What are the thresholds of significance? This is what David Rusk has been doing with his book, *Cities without Suburbs*. You quantitative types must love to see what David's doing. He's taken your techniques and made a popular trade out of it and scared the hell out of everybody in the process, because he talks about cities that go beyond the point of no return. I argued with him about it, but it's a good point and it gets attention. We need more of that kind of work done.

Second, regional econometrics. I'd love to see the availability of relevant research, so that when a significant or huge development is suggested in one part of a region, such as a major new freeway, a Disney project outside of Washington, D.C., or a new stadium here in Chicago, we can be told what the economic and social implications of that development will be over a period of time. Who will be winners and losers, and to what degree and how seriously will the existing conditions of the region be compounded? What does it mean in terms of future income potentials in central cities? There's good reason to have thought that the Disney project, if continued, would not only have had disastrous environmental consequences — increasing automobile usage and traffic congestion in the area by 11 or 12 percent just by the year 2000 — but that it also would have had air-quality repercussions across the region, plus impact on the Chesapeake Bay. It would also have had huge social significance because it would have moved the economic center of gravity west and well away from the most job-needy populations in Washington, Arlington, Alexandria, and Prince Georges County. So I'd like to see the ability to project what major development means within regions.

Finally, I think benchmarking is a really interesting new tool as applied outside of the industrial world, where it's most popular, into the future of regions. There seem to be two forms of it. One is the more accepted and understood form which Cleveland has now done through the Citizens League there. That form includes a whole set of indicators of how that region is doing compared to other regions, in every area from economic performance to culture and from the arts to the environment, social issues, and crime and justice, using obvious measures so that a region knows where it stands. I think that's an area where the academy has immense research capacity and should think of generating such a study within a region if no one else is willing to do it.

The newer and more interesting form, in my mind, which is the one that's been developed in Oregon, requires an immense amount of public participation. The process is undertaken on a broadly democratic basis to get the citizenry and business groups and every other kind of stakeholder in the society to think through where we want to go on major indicators. Teenage pregnancy for this year and 5 years from now and 10 years from now. The nature of commuting in terms of what percentage of all trips are made by people in one automobile alone, 5, 10, and 15 years from now. Economic performance measures on reprocessing versus exporting raw goods. They've been doing it in Oregon statewide for about 3 or 4 years. It's now being adopted in some other localities. Portland and Multnomah County are doing it jointly. And it's a way for people to be part of the process of seeing where their society goes.

This clearly can't be run totally from an academic base. But I think the academy can be tremendously helpful in being part of the consultative process, suggesting what the measures are, and then helping again to be keepers of the flame on what the standards are that people have agreed to, how valid they are, criticizing them as they're put together, and then watching them over a period of time. I think you all have enough to do.

WEISBROD: We have some time for questions and comments. Neal, what was it exactly that you said was the central challenge of our time or of our society?

PEIRCE: It's the economic and social division and racial division within our society into polarized camps.

AUDIENCE MEMBER ONE: I'd like to respond to Jean Allard. You may be waiting for the academics to come to your door. I think that if you invite us, we will come. But I've been waiting a long time to hear this kind of invitation. The academic community — certainly what I'll call the urban affairs academic community in the Chicago metropolitan area — is a great resource in terms of the research it is producing. I trust that everyone in this room knows that probably, pound for pound, the urban research being done in this city is better than any other place in the United States and maybe in the world.

ALLARD: I think you're right.

AUDIENCE MEMBER ONE: But there are a couple of realities. I think that in the 1990s professors in general are beleaguered by the demands that are placed upon them by our institutions and in terms of just surviving. But I think that this forum is a wonderful opportunity because the people who committed to this weekend and the people who organized this conference represent the people who want to join forces with the public policy community.

But there is a reality. The reality is that academic institutions are very envious of one another, and if you are going to get what you're asking for, you're probably going to have to find neutral ground away from Hyde Park, away from Evanston, away from Chicago Circle. You're going to have to create a mechanism whereby you bring urban researchers together in common cause to serve public policy and serve the training of future students as well, which is a major concern of ours. But again, I think if you created the mechanism, it wouldn't be expensive as these things go, and I think that you would find a very good response.

These things surely have been tried before in the history of urban studies in Chicago. I think Vince Lane is absolutely correct. It has to be done on a sustained and coordinated basis. But I think cutting-edge research is being done in this room and in this metropolis. I think you're absolutely right that we don't talk to one another enough. There's fragmentation among the social science disciplines themselves, but there is also a reservoir of good will among urban affairs professors. At least some and maybe even a majority, if that can be quantified, probably want to join forces with you to some degree.

ALLARD: I think we have a very good track record, and I don't mean to overchide the academy. Sometimes we don't really want you to do anything in particular. What we like is your judgment and your insight, your sense that we're on the right track. I'm really talking about the infusion of the academic community into the work of policy makers.

I serve on a number of boards or in an advisory kind of relationship with others. Nobody invites me other than to say, Hey, we'd like to have you come work with us. I don't do anything specific for them. That's the type of bringing yourself into the community that I'm talking about in part. Once that happens, we know some of the directions that the institution is taking. We read the literature and we use the literature as a way of saying we need somebody, and we use a lot of Northwestern people for that reason. We know your reputation, as we do the other academic institutions in the city. But I'm not talking about that. I'm not talking about furthering your career on a direct basis and getting you to do work for us. I'm talking about your participation in our policy making as coworkers with us in terms of being certain that we're doing it right.

AUDIENCE MEMBER TWO: I was at a conference a year or two ago, where one of the presentations was made by a professor who was rather dry. He gave a long talk about his study which indicated that plea bargaining in the criminal context closely matched the results of trials, which of course indicates that we have a very efficient system. Yet I knew that the general public perception is that plea bargaining is nasty, evil, and only done because you can't process these criminals fast enough, so we're giving them a break and they're getting off easy. I'm in the legal system and I had the same perception.

I went up to him afterward and said this is really exciting, who have you talked to about this, what have you done about this? He said, "Well, we published it." And it was in some journal that was on the shelf in academia. I said, "Have you talked to judges? Have you gone in and said, I'd like to give a little talk to your circuit, to your top judges to explain what's happening?" He said, "Well, no, that's not my table." I said, "Some of you know stuff about plea bargaining. Have you talked to legislators?" They said, "No, that's not my table, that's not what I do." This is the kind of involvement that I think Jean is talking about. That you have to do more than print in a journal that only colleagues read. You have to get involved with the real world so that we know about it too.

ALLARD: We know we're not the real world. We're policy makers. That's not the real world.

AUDIENCE MEMBER THREE: I'm a little reluctant to say what I'm going to say, but I'm going to say it anyway. I think there's some reality check that has to be done here by academia, and also about our exposure to you and the problems. The problem sets that you outlined are wonderful. Every one of them sounds interesting. But there is some reality. One, as Roberto Fernandez said today, is about getting into places like Sears, Roebuck. I used to do that sort of thing years ago. I wrote a book on how industrial democracy doesn't work, and the corporations never asked me back. The same thing is true in public policy work. I work in education policy, and school districts are very, very reluctant to give you the type of freedom that you need to explore the problems in their districts. They're political people. The superintendent's job is at stake and they cover up the data. They won't let you do it. They don't want the reports to come out. So there are problems on that side. But those problems can be overcome, at least in some cases.

More important is understanding the reward structure in most of academia. Most of the people in this room who are in academia are not in the center of their departments. Most good universities are run by strong departments. And those departments do not necessarily reward the applied type of work that you're asking for and sometimes they don't reward it at all. My university is more tolerant than most in that respect, but the reward structure in most universities means that it's hard to draw large numbers of people into applied research.

Some departments are worse than others. Economics has a very serious problem. I think the economists would agree that model papers with lots of statistics are the most important things. That's what is rewarded, that's where the top departments get their reputations. That's where the big money is made and that's where most of the research effort goes. The same thing is true to a degree in political science. What that means is, you've got to find the right people for the kind of work we're talking about here. You're not going to find them in large numbers. But you've also got to give something to those of us you do have. What we want and what we need are two different things. We do need to write those esoteric model papers that have statistics in them that you don't understand because that's what we get published in our journals that our colleagues then review us for raises and other increases.

ALLARD: I understand.

AUDIENCE MEMBER THREE: That has to be done. That means the translation problem is a serious one. It's an effort for us to do that without resources. It can be done and those translations are done all the time in institutes like this one. But you can't count on professors to do that kind of translation. And we've got to have the other stuff because we're interested in it, we think it's the way to get the right answers, and it's an incentive for us.

The other thing that I think is needed, which is harder, are theoretical questions we can work on. We've framed a lot of interesting policy questions at this conference, maybe 15 or 20. I run them through my mind and ask, is there an interesting theoretical question involved in any of those policies? Now, there might have been some, but it doesn't often happen that there's a larger theoretical body of literature and interest in those questions that draw us. Let me say it doesn't happen often because you need answers quickly, and these are likely to be relatively narrow. Maybe not narrow, because Vince said we should go broader in some cases and I think that's a good sign. That's what we like. But there also has to be a theoretical payoff of some sort. I studied educational choice because I'm very interested in the theory of market supply to monopoly structures like schools. There's a theoretical and interesting issue other than the dozens of other areas in educational policy that are really quite important but don't have that theoretical hook. I think that sometimes the practitioner community doesn't quite understand the incentive structures that prevail in most universities.

ALLARD: Well, here again it seems to me that you're taking it to the particular research design based upon a request. I'm not making that request. I can and do regularly hire a consultant to get me specific answers. We need help in analysis and identifying certain kinds of data that are available that we may not know about. For instance, I can say to you we've got a massive program going right now in our transportation study on market-based solutions to the automobile. We're also working on what is the true cost of the automobile to lay against our transit studies. We're not asking you to do anything except to help us try to figure out where to go and whether we are asking the right questions. You're a kind of steering committee, if you will, not a researcher. And I think this is the level where policy makers need the academy.

AUDIENCE MEMBER THREE: Well, that's much easier for us to do because it's hindsight. I don't want to throw water on academia for not doing policy research. I think it's wonderful and exciting. So I would say that we could do that and we could do some of the other things that were discussed here, but somehow there has to be a realization that we have access to information and freedom to use that information and let it fall out on a limb. We go out on a limb often and that's not what political activists want us to do, unless we go out on the right limb.

ALLARD: Well, we'll fight about that. I mean we think we're pretty tough. We've got an audience that will kind of crush you down, if we need help in that. However, we'll say we can't use it. But that's the give-and-take that we find in any practical situation.

AUDIENCE MEMBER THREE: That's not what we want to hear. We invest 6 months or 2 years in a study and all of a sudden we can't use it.

WEISBROD: I'd like to give somebody else a chance on this, too. Vince or Neal, do you care to comment on this?

LANE: Well, I think he's right about one thing, and that is that there are a lot of public institutions that don't want people to know what is really going on. I think you have to open it up. When I arrived at the Housing Authority, it was a black hole and nobody knew anything about what went on. One of the things I tried to do was to say, "Here it is, it's public, you own it and let the chips fall where they may." I think you're right. I think a lot of institutions that could use the help don't take it because they're worried about what the outcome might be.

PEIRCE: I think there needs to be much more leadership within the university community to look for where the resources exist for this kind of work. I would bet that we're dealing often with activists in your department. I think each one of you could point to people in your department who could be doing a lot more interesting and worthwhile work, but they're not being led and urged in that direction.

WEISBROD: I'm sorry, but we've come to the limit of our time. We've had a very interesting discussion, and I want to thank our panelists for their thoughtful contributions to our proceedings. And I want to thank those in the audience for their meaningful participation. This discussion has added materially to our understanding of the need for closer collaboration between the research and the action communities, and the means by which that collaboration may be enhanced. I thank you all for a most productive session.

An Urban Research Agenda

The following presents the broad understandings that were reached at the Metropolitan Assembly. All participants, however, do not necessarily agree with each of the points, and participants were not asked to endorse this report.

Consensus was achieved at three levels: on broad approaches and mechanisms for the research covering all six urban problem areas relating to jobs and coordination mechanisms; on research strategies; and on specific research questions.

Approaches to Examining Job-Related Urban Problems.
Assembly participants judged that in all six problem areas it is important that research include:

- Social experiments to test proposed initiatives
- Cost-benefit evaluations of these experiments
- Identification of benchmark cases of successes and failures.

Research Strategies.
There was also strong agreement that in each problem area we need to find more effective mechanisms for:

- Developing interdisciplinary team research
- Linking researchers, practitioners, and policy makers to facilitate understanding of the problems and solutions
- Communicating research results to news media, government officials, civic and private business leaders, and the public, both to discourage adoption of policies that have been found to be costly and ineffective and to encourage adoption of less costly, more effective approaches.

Research Questions for Public Policy Making.
We turn now to the questions identified as requiring further research. We consider, one at a time, each of the six public policy problem areas, begin-

ning each with a statement of overall direction and then listing the specific questions on which research is needed.

The Transition from School to Work

Overview.
More research is needed to understand how to motivate non-college-bound high school students, how to match school curricula to the specific needs of employers, and how to increase school and teacher accountability. More must also be learned about the best mechanisms for achieving employer-school linkages. Finally, there is a need for careful evaluation of the benefits and costs of various experimental programs.

RECOMMENDED RESEARCH QUESTIONS
 I. *Motivation and opportunity*
   A. How much would the motivation of teenagers to work hard and remain in school be increased if there were greater likelihood of a job at graduation?
     1. How important is the type of prospective job?
     2. How important is the initial pay? Prospects for increased pay?
     3. What is the impact on motivation of "career ladder" prospects? What types of career ladders exist for specific entry-level jobs? How can employers create ladders?
   B. How well informed are students about the potential rewards of hard work in school? About future job prospects?
     1. How effective is high school counseling for non-college-bound students?
     2. What new forms of information provision might be developed?
   C. How can incentives — financial and other — be altered for schools and teachers to increase their efforts to tie schooling to jobs, and how effective would such incentives be relative to their costs?
   D. What are the factors adversely affecting high school student performance?
   E. What, and how great, are the stigmatizing effects of dropping out of high school?

 II. *Mechanisms for change and their impact*
   A. What specific types of "formal linkages" between school and work would be most effective for various types of young people?

B. What, and how great, are the adverse effects of increasing the vocational orientation of schools?
1. What kind of balance between basic skills and vocational training is required to satisfy both employers and students?

III. *Employer behavior*
A. What is the extent of employer willingness to hire high school graduates and dropouts?
B. Why are employers averse to hiring high school students even at low wages? How can they be motivated to reverse this behavior?
C. Can small businesses offer career opportunities to high school graduates?
D. Why don't employers use high school grades as a hiring criterion, and can the usefulness of grades as information be increased?
E. What skills are both large and small businesses seeking in entry-level jobs? How can high school curricula be adjusted to meet those demands?

Welfare and Employment

Overview.
More work is needed to understand the nature of welfare recipiency, the costs and benefits of programs to move people off welfare, effective alternative programs both in the United States and abroad, and how to provide adequate and accurate information to public policy makers.

RECOMMENDED RESEARCH QUESTIONS
I. *Motivation*
A. How important are factors other than wages that make paid work an attractive alternative to welfare — for example, health-care insurance (including Medicaid), status, and form of pay (cash vs. tax credits)?
B. Does the "Hip-Hop" generation care more than previous generations about getting paid relative to getting jobs, and if so, why? How can this culture be reached?

II. *Nature of welfare dependency*
A. What motivates some welfare recipients to move off welfare relatively quickly and others to remain on welfare long-term?

B. What is the impact on the entire family as the transition is made from welfare to work, and vice versa?

C. What is the extent of the intergenerational transmission of poverty and welfare? What are the effects on individual family members?

D. What are the costs and benefits of programs that move people off welfare? What new approaches can be developed?

III. *Mechanisms for change*

A. What will be the effects of terminating welfare benefits after 2 years? What does this proposal say about the public policy-making process, and how consistent is it with the findings from research?

B. Are "draconian" measures required to influence teenagers not to have babies? What are the benefits versus social costs of specific measures? How else can teenage pregnancy be reduced?

C. What could cost-effectively reduce the number of people who get trapped in long-term welfare recipiency?

D. How can job mobility be promoted so people at the bottom of the labor market do not stay there?

E. Is the public willing to make the substantial investment required for the expensive training and related programs that are most successful in moving people off welfare?

F. Which other countries provide possible benchmarks for balancing social concern for the needy with recognition of adverse incentive effects?

G. To what extent do alternative forms of welfare support reduce costs to some level of government or agency by shifting it to another?

H. What role does the marginal labor market position of low-skilled males play in the likelihood and duration of women's welfare receipt?

Crime and Employment

Overview.

Interdisciplinary approaches should address the causal relationships among family circumstances, urban crime, incarceration rates, and unemployment. One major issue is how illegal activities can be made less lucrative while raising expectations that legal work will provide stable and family-sustaining wages. More work is needed on the factors that motivate young people to choose illegal over legal work, the effects of incarceration on future job prospects, and the costs and benefits of alternative crime prevention strategies.

RECOMMENDED RESEARCH QUESTIONS

I. Causes of opting for criminal activity

  A. What are the long-term interrelationships among crime, incarceration, and joblessness?

  B. What is the quantitative and hierarchical importance of labor markets (job opportunity and wage rates), social controls, and neighborhood and individual characteristics in affecting criminal behavior?

    1. What kinds of "socialization" processes occur within gangs in terms of prison experiences, attitudes toward work, and violent behavior? What are the roles of gangs and other street networks? Can these networks be adapted to guide youngsters into legitimate lifestyles?

    2. What is the quantitative impact of the declining influence of adult males on younger men's decisions to engage in legal relative to illegal work?

  C. To what extent is criminal behavior affected by young people's unwillingness to do legal work that is "beneath them"?

II. Intervention strategies

  A. Are the "turning point ages" at which people become significantly more or less likely to engage in illegal behavior changing? What is the nature of the "aging out" process?

    1. What events lead to these turning points?

    2. How can public policy hasten the aging-out process?

  B. What are the costs and benefits of various potential crime prevention and drug treatment strategies? Can they be evaluated through controlled social experiments?

    1. What are the costs and effects on crime of aggressively enforcing employment discrimination laws?

    2. What are the costs and benefits of training programs in terms of their effects on crime?

    3. How can police and social services be combined more efficiently?

    4. What are the costs and benefits of traditional jails versus alternatives such as increasing schooling services in jails?

5. How can the jail-to-work transition be improved?

6. What are the effects of very early intervention into high-risk situations of child abuse? What is the impact of group homes on welfare adolescents?

7. What increased role can churches play in crime prevention?

III. *Impact of criminal behavior*

A. How great are the stigma effects of having been in jail?

1. How do they affect job opportunities and recidivism?

2. How can offenders be directed into mainstream culture?

B. What are the quantitative costs and benefits of crime, as compared with legal work, to various groups of young people and under various conditions?

C. How large are the differences between public perceptions of the levels and forms of crime, and the true situation?

1. How do misperceptions affect individuals' actions (e.g., willingness to shop or live in particular areas)?

2. What are public perceptions of the economic determinants of criminal activity, and, particularly, perceptions of the effect of increased legal job opportunities on illegal activity?

3. How can people's misperceptions of criminal behavior and the effectiveness of various anticrime measures be corrected?

Spatial Mismatch: Housing, Jobs, and Transportation

Overview.

Much work is still needed to understand what drives employers to relocate in the suburbs, what keeps inner-city labor from following the jobs, and how the two can be matched through improvements in public transportation or other strategies. Data are lacking on the costs and benefits of improving public transportation, whether workers can be encouraged to follow jobs to the suburbs or employers can be enticed to move back to the city, and whether it is cost-effective to rebuild inner-city economies to provide new jobs contiguous to the labor supply.

RECOMMENDED RESEARCH QUESTIONS

I. *Employers*

A. What are the principal factors determining employer location, and how powerful is each?

1. To what extent is employer dispersal to the suburbs intended to avoid minority worker applicants?
2. To what extent is it motivated by other considerations such as transportation costs, shifting markets, and differential local government taxation?
B. To the extent that employer relocation away from central cities is motivated by technological and market forces, which can change rapidly, what kinds of flexible transportation mechanisms can be developed to facilitate movement of workers to jobs?
C. What costs are employers in the suburbs willing to bear to obtain workers from the inner city?

II. *Barriers to job seekers*

A. What are the barriers to workers, particularly blacks but also other minorities, who wish to relocate to areas of expanding job opportunities? How severe are those barriers, and to what extent are they becoming higher or lower over time?
1. To what extent are lack of knowledge about relocation options and individuals' preferences for the particular cultural values of a neighborhood, as distinguished from racial discrimination in housing markets, hampering geographic mobility?
B. What are the effects of job dispersal on information networks that affect workers' knowledge of job prospects?

III. *Impact of spatial mismatch*

A. How can spatial mismatch problems be understood in a family context, recognizing that it is not only the head of household who faces relocation decisions but also family members; that is, what are the long-run favorable and unfavorable consequences of worker relocation on workers, spouses, and children?

IV. *Interventions*

A. What are the relative costs and benefits of programs designed to:
1. encourage relocation of employers to areas of high unemployment (e.g., empowerment or enterprise zones);
2. encourage or facilitate relocation of workers to areas of greater job opportunity; and
3. improve the quality and/or reduce the private cost of transportation that would better link people with jobs?

Governmental Coordination

Overview.
Most, if not all, of the social problems we examined are best understood from a metropolitan regional perspective (i.e., solutions require actions that involve suburban as well as central city governments). Yet much more needs to be learned about the conditions under which intergovernmental cooperation is, and is not, likely to work effectively.

RECOMMENDED RESEARCH QUESTIONS
I. *Motivations affecting cooperation*
   A. Are there specific public services for which there is agreement that city and suburbs should finance them jointly? What is the potential for reaching agreement on additional shared-finance services, particularly schooling, transportation, arts, and culture?
   B. What are the dynamic forces affecting the appeal of regional approaches, that is, the factors affecting the formation, growth, and decline of regional cooperation? How can they be influenced through public policy?

II. *Forms of cooperation*
   A. How can the benefits to suburbs from alleviating particular problems of the central city be better identified, documented, and measured?
   B. What are the differences in costs and in quality of public services in cities and suburbs, in light of differences in populations and their problems? To what extent have innovative cooperative policy initiatives increased the efficiency of public service provision rather than simply changed their form and reduced their quality?
   C. Are municipal tax structures self-defeating by adversely affecting the location of people and firms? Should there be different tax rates on residential and commercial property?
   D. What is the evidence of the historical successes and failures of metropolitan regional governments and regional revenue sharing?
   E. How important is tax-exempt property as a fiscal problem in cities as compared with suburbs? Can a unified metropolitan area policy toward location of nonprofit organizations strengthen the metropolitan area, while balancing benefits with costs for each municipality?

Coordination between Public and Private Sectors

Overview.
To achieve cost-efficiency in dealing with pressing metropolitan area problems, we need to understand better which institutional form is most appropriate for each problem area. Among the institutional arrangements that are alternatives to purely government solutions are privatization (to for-profit firms or to nonprofit organizations), joint public-private ventures, and hybrid forms. How well does each function in each problem area?

RECOMMENDED RESEARCH QUESTIONS
  I. Forms of public-private coordination, and their records
  A. Under what conditions is government contracting-out of a particular activity socially cost-saving? Is the growing privatization of jails, schools, and hospitals desirable?
  B. What are the sources of cost-efficiencies for some privately provided municipal services?
  C. What are the potential forms of government and private-sector partnerships for providing particular services, and what are their benefits and costs?
  D. What is the record of community development corporations, and what are their strengths and weaknesses?

  II. Factors affecting successful public-private coordination
  A. Are there "benchmark" cases of successful coordination of government and private organizations? What factors contributed to the success, and is there consensus as to what constitutes "successful" collaboration?
  B. How important is lack of trust as an obstacle to effective partnerships between government and the private sector?
  C. What are the limits to partnerships between governments and private firms, in general and for handling specific problems? Can cost-effective partnership arrangements be extended?
  D. Can comprehensive benefit-cost analysis be successfully undertaken to evaluate alternative institutional arrangements — including public-private partnerships — for providing particular social services?
  E. Do government partnerships with profit-seeking organizations increase the probability of corruption or of a shift of incentives that threatens governmental performance of conventional functions?

Postscript

The ability of the Metropolitan Assembly to build broad agreement on this array of questions is testimony to the significant value of bringing together urban scholars and private and public policy makers to discuss issues of common concern. Indeed, the demonstrated ability of a diverse, experienced group to communicate with one another confirmed our confidence in the process. Not the least valuable outcome of the Assembly was the fact that within weeks of its conclusion a number of contacts were initiated among participants from several states who had not previously known each other. We hope that over time this network of scholars, practitioners, and government officials will continue to grow in both scope and value.

Burton A. Weisbrod & James C. Worthy

Epilogue

The enormity of today's urban problems is not in doubt. How to deal with them is very much so. The Metropolitan Assembly was organized in the belief that if society is to attack these formidable challenges effectively, it must understand their causes and know the costs and probable outcomes of alternative strategies for dealing with them.

The six background papers were commissioned not only to assess the current state of knowledge, but to define areas now lacking in information that is key to advancing the cause of sound policy development. More broadly stated, the Assembly was held to identify the obstacles to solving the problems of our cities. What are the specific information gaps? What do policy makers need to know in order to break the logjam of frequently ineffective and costly programs? How can the research community help?

The Assembly brought together leaders from government, the private sector, neighborhood groups, the press, and private foundations in the belief that what constitutes an "information gap" may appear differently from these various perspectives. Could the group reach consensus on what research is needed? As the six lists in the preceding chapter testify, the answer was yes. We now have an Urban Research Agenda, a call for answers to questions which, in the group's judgment, are consequential obstacles to the fashioning of more cost-effective urban public policies.

Now what? Will researchers choose to tackle these questions? Will funders be willing to support the research needed to answer them? If the research is done, and done well, will it reach policy makers in ways that are intelligible? Will they act upon it? Will they be successful in implementing new programs informed by the research? Will those programs be as cost-effective as promised by the prior research? These questions were beyond the scope of the Assembly, but the value of the Urban Research Agenda depends on how they are answered. The Research Agenda, in short, is part of a process, and unless the other parts of the process articulate with it the ultimate goal of helping make our cities and their people more vital, prosperous, and hopeful, it will die aborning.

Looking back on the Assembly contribution to the process, we see cause for satisfaction but also for caution. The satisfaction resides in the ability of the academic scholars to assess the state of knowledge in six major urban problem areas, and to convey that knowledge effectively not only to scholars from other disciplines but to persons whose perspectives are those of the business world, civic leaders, neighborhood development organizations, government agencies, the press, and, ultimately, the public. Most significantly, we were pleased that these heterogeneous groups were able to communicate meaningfully with each other and to reach a working consensus on what is needed from the research community if the cause of effective urban policy making is to be advanced. We found all that to be distinctly encouraging.

Caution, however, tempers our sense of accomplishment. Because the urban problem is complex, our decision to narrow the Assembly attention to employment-related issues, and to only a subset of those, had the advantage of concentrating attention and focusing discussion, but it also imposed a cost by limiting the scope of debate. It is abundantly clear that the plight of urban communities reflects not a set of independent problems that can be understood one at a time, but a web of interrelated issues. The background papers in Part 1 make clear that employment, which is of central importance, is entwined with poverty, schooling, crime, housing, transportation, and welfare problems, and that none of these can be dealt with without affecting the others. It is also apparent from the papers that solutions are inextricably enmeshed in the struggles among political units in metropolitan areas (Chernick and Reschovsky), and in the search for means of useful collaboration between local governments and the private sector (Rothenberg).

It is difficult to think of any of the plenitude of urban malfunctions that are not linked importantly with a variety of other malfunctions, since there is no such thing as an isolated urban problem. The interrelatedness of problems, each important in its own right, presents difficulties on both the research front and the action front. For good or ill, the academic world is divided organizationally into a series of specialized disciplines and, within each discipline, the work of individual scholars is further subdivided into still more specialized areas of attention. Urban problems, however, are not divided into a comparable set of neat categories, and a viable understanding of what is happening in the real world requires close cooperation among scholars working in a number of different fields.

On the action front, attempting to deal one at a time with closely interrelated problems is not necessarily hopeless but is at the very least sternly challenging and carries with it the heavy risk of unintended consequences.

Measures adopted to deal with one problem may exacerbate other problems. On the other hand, attempting to deal with many problems simultaneously presents another order of daunting difficulties.

This dilemma deserves serious attention. The economic, social, and human stakes are massive. If the various urban problems cannot be attacked effectively on an independent basis, a major rethinking of policy is called for. Efforts to improve inner-city schools, for example, could be doomed unless job opportunities for graduates are available. Those opportunities might hinge on reductions in crime in the area, which in turn could affect the location of employers, and on urban transportation systems that link workers with jobs. Study is urgently required of both the *need* for such integrated solution strategies and their *feasibility*. But here, as in complex situations generally, the challenge that confronts both the research and the policy-making communities is one of balance: finding a middle ground between all-encompassing strategies, which however attractive are operationally infeasible, and strategies that are so modest that lack of demonstrable results is virtually assured.

Can urban problems be broken into segments that meet the two requisites of combining operational feasibility with an acceptable probability of "success" in observable form over a reasonable period of time? Therein lies the twin challenge to both scholars and policy makers. Until a sufficient body of reliable knowledge is developed on effective means for integrating research and action, scholars and policy makers would be well advised to recognize at least the obvious linkages among those problems and the probable ripple effects of alternative courses of action (or inaction) on other elements of the urban system.

The challenge is actually greater. It is not sufficient that researchers and policy makers find ways to communicate and to resolve their different perspectives. The public must also be involved, must also have some understanding of what research has shown to be effective and ineffective urban policy, and from this learn to distinguish changes in the urban condition that would be *desirable* from those that are *achievable*.

In organizing the Metropolitan Assembly, we saw the need to initiate such a process of interaction that would contribute to information exchange — researchers communicating what is known about the cost-effectiveness of various mechanisms for solving urban problems, policy makers communicating to researchers what they see as the research they need, and journalists communicating to the public what is and is not likely to alleviate urban problems.

The knowledge gaps among the research community, political leaders who shape public policy, and the public that influences the course of events by approving or disapproving the manner in which public officials deal with urban problems are large. The essays in this volume make clear, for example, that the common view that incarceration of lawbreakers will significantly deter criminal behavior is not generally consistent with the findings of scholarly research, which indicate so decisively that the expenditure of large sums on jail construction and operation as a way of reducing urban crime is of questionable wisdom. Similarly, the development of welfare policy around the theme that most welfare recipients are capable of earning a reasonable wage but are choosing instead to live off public welfare is generally inconsistent with scholarly research: most long-term welfare recipients do not have the education or skills required to earn a socially minimum income.

Such cleavages between the assumptions of public policy and the evidence from research are counterproductive, and indeed are quite likely to lead to further public disillusionment with governmental leadership and academic research. Promises made to solve problems through programs that have been shown, with reasonable assurance, to be largely ineffective, very costly, or both have proved with bitter regularity to be unwise and unsupportable.

It is important that the transmission of knowledge be a two-way exchange between the research- and action-oriented communities. The panel of three users of research (Jean Allard, Vincent Lane, and Neal Peirce), who were charged to criticize the contributions of the research community, made this quite clear in the preceding panel discussion. In differing ways, all three pointed to their disappointments with the contributions of research and researchers to the quest for solutions.

The triumvirate of Allard, Lane, and Peirce represents distinct links in the chain connecting research with action. Allard's Metropolitan Planning Council relies on academic research to bring ideas from the research community to planners; Peirce, a syndicated columnist, connects the public with both researchers and leaders of action programs; Lane, until recently chairman of the Chicago Housing Authority, directed one of the nation's largest public housing programs. Each of these connects in a different way to the research community, and each therefore sees somewhat different needs from the researchers.

To Allard, the problem is that researchers are neglecting the policy world, not reaching out to assist organizations that are struggling to develop urban action programs. She said that her organization needs help in determining how things work in complex situations such as the development of intergovernmental agreements covering a new commuter rail line. She also pleaded that the academy should accept a civic obligation to become involved.

Peirce, seemingly recognizing the caution inherent in the scholarly research process, called for researchers to "go out on a limb," writing more op-ed pieces, for example, that highlight for the public the extensive knowledge base that exists. He urged researchers to show which action programs are "working" and which are not, and what progress is being made in metropolitan regional governance. More generally, Peirce called for greater involvement of universities in the process of dealing with the social divisions of society, which he termed the essential issue of our time.

Lane, whose operating responsibilities involved the most immediate of issues — housing, crime, drugs, and poverty — voiced a strong plea for help from researchers. He saw great need for cost-benefit analyses of program alternatives such as crime prevention versus incarceration of convicted criminals; for more adequate information about alternative ways, including orphanages, to protect children from broken or dysfunctional families; for evidence of the effects on children of cutbacks by the schools on athletics and music.

All three panelists, each in her or his own way, emphasized their dependence on research and expressed the view that they would like to see greater input from researchers. Perhaps to the surprise of many researchers, these three eminent panelists — who are outside the research community but see important relationships with it — emphasized that, as one of them put it, "the public, the media, and policy leaders *do* pay attention to research." The links between research and action, or at least the potential links, may be stronger than many researchers believe and weaker than many action leaders would like. More than that, the three advanced a number of valuable suggestions for more effectively integrating the efforts of the research and action communities.

Other questions remain, however. Are the perspectives offered by researchers too broad and too detached from feasible public policy? Is it the language of researchers, not the content of their research, that is the barrier to communication and implementation? What are the obstacles for the public and others outside the research community to conveying to researchers their notions of what they need to know? Are communications barriers severe, or is there lack of access to researchers who are willing to listen? Whatever the answers may be, the feelings of discontent and frustration with researchers were evident. So, too, however, was the eagerness of this trio to seek the attention and help of researchers.

In the United States, large cities beset by poverty and related problems are declining in economic importance, even while their metropolitan communities are growing and generally prospering. Elsewhere, in the developing countries of the world, cities are growing ever larger. Lessons from this country and other nations where urbanization occurred earlier appear to be lost, as the newly urbanizing countries experience the same quite predictable problems of poverty, crime, traffic congestion, noise and air pollution, and other ills of modern urban society. Once more we see the informational gap between what is known, with reasonable confidence if not with certainty, by the research community and what is known by the public and political leaders. We cannot be certain, however, that the basic obstacle is inadequate transmission of knowledge rather than inability of the political system to translate the knowledge into action.

We are chastened by the difficulty of advancing the process of urban development that is so crucial to alleviating the many and severe urban ills. These ills are different today than they were 50 years ago, when the end of World War II saw millions of rural people, largely black, move to northern cities in search of manufacturing jobs, which were growing in number. Today, urban America is in the midst of a long-run process of decline, accompanied by suburban expansion of economic opportunity and political influence, which together are creating central cities that are increasingly old, poor, and black — and desperately plagued by high, long-term unemployment.

A review of the papers and discussions of the Assembly highlights the overarching importance of employment as a necessary condition for effective progress. Welfare, fatherless families, crime in the streets — name it — would be far less important than they are today if *adequately remunerative* job opportunities were abundantly available, and — equally important — if the *job seekers* were properly prepared for the job market. The converse is equally true: if these kinds of opportunities are not adequately available, *and* if prospective workers are not work-ready, most of the problems identified by the Assembly will be exceedingly difficult to deal with, and solutions supported by even the most competent research are likely to be of only palliative value. This sobering conclusion points to the need to give priority attention to the tasks of economic development and educational preparation suited to the present and emerging needs of the economy and society.

The growing problems of our cities, the inability of urban and suburban populations to arrive at a political consensus on a metropolitan regional strategy for attacking them, and the social divisiveness of failure to attend to them formed the underpinnings of the Metropolitan Assembly. The essays in this volume, the consensus Urban Research Agenda produced by the Assembly, and the interactions that were fostered among influential participants in the urban policy process are cause for cautious hope.

The Metropolitan Assembly initiated a process by which further significant progress can be achieved. Of all the lessons learned, two are of primary importance:

  1. It is essential that public policy be built on a sound knowledge base, not on assumptions that research has shown to be incorrect nor on assumptions that are untested and of questionable validity.

If attacks on urban poverty and related problems are to be effective, they cannot be based on false premises, on mistaken assumptions about how people respond to particular kinds of rewards and punishment. Thus, to consider an example made clear at the Assembly, welfare policy should not be based on the assumption that large numbers of long-term welfare recipients — persons remaining on welfare for 2 or more years — are fully capable of earning wages above the poverty level. Research has determined that this assumption is false. Public policies based on false assumptions will not work.

  2. Communications ties between the research community and policy makers must be strengthened substantially so that the latter know what the research community has learned about what "works" and at what cost, and the research community learns what the developers of public policy believe is important to know.

Communication is a two-way street. Developing and nurturing these communications ties is not easy, but is an essential ingredient for success. Better communication is needed to overcome the facts that:

Planning horizons differ for people engaged in research and in political action. Policy proposals are typically made with little knowledge of their consistency with findings from research, and when they are implemented there is little time for researchers to test their likely effectiveness and costs.

Languages differ for researchers and policy makers. The words used and the styles of presentation of ideas are quite different for scholars and policy makers, and are serious obstacles to the interchange of ideas.

Analytic approaches differ for researchers and policy makers. Researchers demand evidence in forms and at levels of confidence that are frequently inconsistent with the kinds of evidence that policy makers regard as satisfactory. And while policy makers in a democratic society must be responsive to political pressures from citizens, researchers face the quite different but no less relentless pressures of the research community — yet another obstacle to effective interaction.

What can be done to bridge the chasm between the world of research and the world of action? Incentives have to be changed! Policy makers and researchers must come to see it as in their interest to work on communicating with each other. "Work" it is, for coming to understand the thought modes and perspectives of others is never as easy as talking to people who are like ourselves and think as we do. Thus, the challenge is to bring together in productive dialogue research people and action people, each group composed of individuals likely to be more comfortable interacting with others like themselves. New institutional mechanisms are needed as forums for such dialogue.

In that dialogue, it is vital to keep in mind that the formulation of urban policies is not an academic exercise and that the debate on urban issues does not take place in a vacuum. There are real people out there — flesh-and-blood men and women, young people with most of their lives ahead of them, helpless infants. If a policy proves wrong, the most vulnerable people in our society will bear the consequences.

The Metropolitan Assembly and the impetus supplied by the American Assembly illustrate the possibilities for responsible dialogue. It also illustrates the importance of external support, both financial and moral, from private foundations as instruments for change. Support from the John D. and Catherine T. MacArthur Foundation financed the Assembly, but it did far more. It permitted Northwestern's Center for Urban Affairs and Policy Research to commission state-of-the-art background papers from leading academic researchers, to bring a stellar group of nonacademic policy leaders to comment on those papers, to organize the panel of research *users* to challenge the researchers to be "more useful" — thereby confirming the question of what "useful" means and what the obstacles to its achievement are — and to demonstrate the willingness and ability of the diverse group to work at the process of advancing urban public policy. The challenge is not simply to sustain the process that has been launched, but to expand efforts to construct new instruments for policy development through engaging community and nonprofit sector leaders, government officials, researchers, and others whose ability and willingness to labor together constitute the links in a chain that needs to connect academic research to successful action.

The gulf dividing the research and public policy communities is highlighted by the very limited increment in knowledge about urban policy mechanisms that is being generated by the many and continuing urban initiatives. We are learning little from experience. Why? The answer, we suggest, lies in the communication problems we have emphasized. Seldom are action programs developed in concert with researchers. Without this, there can be little learning from experience.

Mechanisms for amalgamating experiences from the many hundreds of the world's cities and communicating the findings widely are virtually nonexistent. One reason is that without involvement by the researchers in the program design phase — rather than after the program has been launched, let alone completed — it is difficult to reach meaningful conclusions about the cost-effectiveness of specific approaches. A second reason is that there is no central clearinghouse for organizing such information as now exists or may subsequently be brought into being. And finally, there is little incentive to translate often technical research findings into forms that are both intelligible and of interest to the broad variety of audiences with stakes in stopping and reversing the escalating urban crisis.

Today's tragic urban problems should not be allowed to continue, let alone to grow. Inaction is indefensible. At the same time, we draw a sobering conclusion. Public policy makers, and ultimately the public, must come to realize that the state of knowledge severely limits — or, at least, should limit — the speed and direction of public policy initiatives. There is not a solution to every problem. Given the limited knowledge about the causes of urban problems and their solutions, action is not always warranted. Moving boldly to mobilize people and money, only to fail, seriously undermines support for research, disillusions the public, and further degrades confidence in government and the private institutions of society.

What is very much warranted is action combined with research so that there is *learning from experience*. Major national initiatives such as the new empowerment zones, and significant local initiatives such as community policing, can teach us much, but only if designed collaboratively by people of vision. Neither research without action, nor action without a sound research base, will reverse the process of urban decay.

Notes on Contributors

Howard A. Chernick is Professor of Economics at Hunter College and a member of the graduate faculty at the City University of New York. His research addresses the distributional effects of public sector expenditures and taxation, particularly at the state and local government level, with a long-standing interest in the relationship between fiscal federalism and the financing of welfare. Chernick's work has been published in a number of leading public finance and policy journals. His latest paper, in 1996, offers a review of the potential fiscal effects of the current proposals for block grants for welfare. He served as a staff economist for the Office of Income Security Policy of the U.S. Department of Health and Human Services from 1978 to 1982.

Greg Duncan is Professor of Education and Social Policy and a Faculty Fellow at the Center for Urban Affairs and Policy Research at Northwestern University. He has published extensively on issues of income distribution, child poverty, and welfare dependence. He continues to study neighborhood effects on the development of children and adolescents, and the consequences of income distribution for children and adults. The most recent of his five books are *Years of Poverty, Years of Plenty: The Changing Economic Fortunes of American Workers and Families* (1984) and *Panel Surveys* (1989). Duncan is a member of the Family and Child Well-Being Research Network of the National Institute of Child Health and Human Development and the MacArthur Network on Middle Childhood in At-Risk Settings.

Jeffrey Fagan is Professor in the School of Public Health at Columbia University and Director of the Center for Violence Research and Prevention. For over two decades his research has focused on the antecedents, consequences, and social control of violence. He has studied youth gangs, connections between substance abuse and violence, issues of juvenile justice, and the effectiveness of criminal sanctions in deterring drug selling and drug use. His current research examines neighborhood contextual effects on the social control of spouse assault, risk and protective factors for injury to women in domestic assault, economic decision making by young males on their legal and illegal "work" careers, and the situational contexts and dynamics of gun use by adolescents. He has published numerous articles on these issues, most recently in the *Journal of Criminal Law and Criminology*, *Law and Policy*, and the *Journal of Drug Issues*.

Roberto M. Fernandez is Professor of Organizational Behavior at the Graduate School of Business at Stanford University and formerly a Faculty Fellow at the

Center for Urban Affairs and Policy Research and Associate Professor of Sociology at Northwestern University. His research interests focus on skills retraining during periods of technological change, social impacts of firm relocations, and the effects of hiring channels on employee performance. He has served as a consultant for the New Hope Project in Milwaukee, and is a member of the Poverty and Race Research Action Council in Washington and the Panel on At-Risk Youth of the National Research Council of the National Academy of Science. His most recent research concerns the effects of industrial plant relocation on employment patterns, particularly those of minorities.

Andrew Reschovsky is a professor in the Robert M. La Follette Institute of Public Affairs and the Department of Agricultural and Applied Economics at the University of Wisconsin–Madison, where he teaches public finance, microeconomic analysis, and urban economics. He has also served as a consultant to several federal agencies as well as to state and local governments throughout the country. During 1994 and 1995 he served as an economist in the Office of Tax Analysis of the U.S. Department of the Treasury. Most of his research focuses on issues related to state and local public finance. He has written numerous articles in professional journals and is the principal author of *State Tax Policy: Evaluating the Issues* (1984). He is currently conducting research on long-run consumption tax burdens, on state government responses to block grants for welfare, on the design of school finance formulas, and on the impact on states of a balanced federal budget.

James E. Rosenbaum is Professor of Education and Social Policy and a Faculty Fellow at the Center for Urban Affairs and Policy Research at Northwestern University. For more than a decade he has studied the social and economic effects of relocating poor inner-city black families to the white suburbs of Chicago. He is also conducting several studies that examine the high school-to-work transition in the United States, Germany, and Japan. Rosenbaum has published three books and numerous articles on schools and work. His edited volume, *Youth Apprenticeship in America*, was published by the W. T. Grant Commission on Youth and America's Future in 1992. He is an advisor to the U.S. Departments of Labor, Education, and Housing and Urban Development.

Jerome Rothenberg is Professor Emeritus of Economics at the Massachusetts Institute of Technology and a faculty associate at the Joint Center for Housing Studies at Harvard University. Rothenberg's research combines his economics expertise with his concern for urban issues in areas that include the life-cycle theory of urban infrastructure services, urban housing markets and policy, urban environment and transportation, government and private sector cooperation, and the relationship between governmental structure and operation in the solution of urban problems. Among numerous publications is his most recent book, *The Maze of Urban Housing: Theory, Evidence, and Policy* (1993). He has taught at the London School of Economics, the University of California at Berkeley, and the University of British Columbia, and was a consultant with the RAND Corporation and the Brookings Institution.

Burton A. Weisbrod, Chairman of the Metropolitan Assembly, is the John Evans Professor of Economics at Northwestern University, and from 1990 to 1995 was Director of the Center for Urban Affairs and Policy Research. Weisbrod has published 13 books and more than 160 articles and papers focusing on public policy and benefit-cost analyses of the economics of education, health, medical research, manpower, the military draft, and public interest law. His most recent research examines the causes and consequences of technological change in health care; the comparative economic behavior of for-profit, government, and private nonprofit organizations; and the causes and consequences of the growing commercialism of nonprofits. Weisbrod served as a senior staff member of the Council of Economic Advisors to Presidents Kennedy and Johnson.

James C. Worthy, Director of the Metropolitan Assembly, is Professor of Management and Senior Austin Fellow at the J. L. Kellogg Graduate School of Management and Faculty Associate at the Center for Urban Affairs and Policy Research at Northwestern University. He has had a long and distinguished career in government, business, and education. He served as Assistant Secretary of Commerce and was a member of President Kennedy's Commission on Campaign Costs. During a 23-year tenure with Sears, Roebuck, Worthy rose to the position of vice president and later became a regional partner of the international management consulting firm of Cresap, McCormick & Paget. As a member of the Illinois Board of Higher Education, he played a key role in planning two new state universities, Sangamon State and Governors State.

Index

Note: Some page references include a *t* to indicate a table.

commuting, 209, 216, 236; from central city to suburbs, 91, 137; and spatial mismatch hypothesis, 88–89, 94, 95, 96n7

computers, use in management of municipal public services, 150

conflict resolution, education on for children, 212

Congress, U.S., 143, 144, 155–58, 168, 200n11

consultative public-private partnerships, 178

consumption tax, as replacement for income taxes, 168

contracts, city, competition between public and private sector for, 150–51, 170n13, 183, 185–86

"Contract with America," 22, 168

control, social, 51–52, 61–64, 69

Cook, Fay Lomax, 8

co-op programs, in high schools, 101, 102, 114–15

cost-benefit analysis, 210, 213, 226, 228, 236

cost-effectiveness, 230; of public-private partnerships, 185; of welfare-to-work programs, 12, 20, 21–22, 24

Crane, Jonathan, 139

crime, 5–7, 37, 58–59, 169n3, 188, 233

desistance from, 54–57, 67, 70

deterrence, 38–39, 40, 63–64, 71n6; research on incarceration, 235, 236; variables, 57–58, 61

doubling up with legal work, 49–50, 54, 71nn15, 16

drug dealing. See drug selling

early involvement in, 44, 50–54, 58–59; relationship to employment, 39–42, 49, 60, 61–62

enterprise zone incentives outweighed by, 146

fear of, 72n21, 147–48

income from. See income from crime

local governments' need to cope with, 131, 164

prevention, 69–70, 226, 236

relationship to unemployment, 33–34, 37–43, 233, 235; future research, 68–70; market incentives, 43–48; policies and interventions, 65–68; studies of, 57–65; temporal ordering of, 54

research agenda on, 225–27

rise in, 139, 194

See also work, illegal

criminality, 50–54; theories of, 30, 36

criminal justice system, 34, 133, 164, 214, 218, 226; public-private partnerships in, 192–93. See also incarceration

criminology, 33, 35, 37–38

cultural institutions, 132, 138, 140, 170n8

cumulative deterioration, as term for cycle of urban decline, 132

Dallas, TX, 170n12

D'Amato, Alfonse, 211

deindustrialization, 52–54

demand-side labor market, 17–19

Denver, CO, 170n12

deregulation of drugs, as means for reducing returns from selling, 72n23

determinism, view of relationship between crime and work, 34–36

Detroit, MI, 52, 82–86, 88–89, 95n2, 170n12

deviance, theories of, 35, 36

differentiation in public services, 187–

employment, 3–4, 5–7, 11, 14, 115,
136
agenda for research on, 222–29
as a cause of suburban residence,
87–88
continuing decline in central cities,
131, 132, 136
decentralization, reversal policies,
91–92
as focus of the Metropolitan Assembly, 233–38
formal work entry system not found
in the U.S., 114
of graduates of high school vocational programs, 110–11
job growth and loss in metropolitan
areas, 82, 83t, 85–86
measures of for economists, 33
of mothers, effect on children, 26–27
opportunities for linked with education, 6, 112, 234
patterns reproduced in succeeding
generations, 53
prospects for welfare recipients, 17–
19
public, inner-city programs for, 29–
30
public-private partnerships in programs for, 183, 185, 193
qualifications: of welfare recipients,
16; youth lacking in, 100
rates: high school vocational education effects on, 102; for Teen Parent Welfare Demonstration participants, 21; work-based programs' effects on, 103
and spatial mismatch, 81, 227–28.
See also spatial mismatch
urban structure changes, 137
See also labor market; unemployment; work, illegal; work, legal

employment discrimination laws, 68,
226
empowerment zones, 145–46,
170n12, 228
English skills, of high school graduates, 100, 106–7
enrichment strategies in central cities,
91–92, 95, 96n10
enterprise zones, 91, 95, 96n9, 145–
46, 170n12, 228
entitlement programs, means-tested,
cuts in, 140, 155–56
entrepreneurial government, public-private partnerships similar to,
181
entry-level jobs, 19, 223; skills needed
for among high school graduates,
106–8, 117
ethnic groups, 51–52, 53, 109, 110.
See also minorities
ethnographic research, 50–51, 60, 61,
64
Europe, 12, 42, 43, 60. *See also* Germany
evaluations, student, role in school-to-work transition: in Japan and Germany, 101, 104, 114, 118; in the
U.S., 115–16, 118
ex-offenders: studies of work-crime association based on, 58; studies on
effects of unemployment on
crime, 41–42, 71n7; work programs for, 65–68
extortion, commercial, 51, 52

Fagan, Jeffrey, 4, 5, 33–80
fair housing laws, 92, 94
families, 1, 7, 22, 26–29, 55, 237; effects on youth, 60, 65, 69; parents'
influence on school achievement,
109, 112; programs for provided

vocational education. *See* vocational
  education, in high schools
See also school-to-work transitions
Hines, James R., Jr., 145
hiring practices, 112; racism in, 68;
  and school-work transition, 105–
  9, 119–21
Hispanics (Latinos), 52, 71n18, 84t,
  85, 95n3, 96n10
Historic Rehabilitation Tax Credit,
  145
Holzer, Harry J., 44, 86–87, 88,
  95n6
homelessness, 131, 139, 156, 158–59,
  183
homeownership: tax subsidy for, 144–
  45. *See also* housing
home relief, paid by New York City,
  171n19
hospitals, as tax-exempt entities, 138
"Hot Idea" program, in Indianapolis,
  170n13
housing, 1, 6, 28–29, 144–45, 194,
  233
  affordable/low-income, public-
    private partnerships dealing with,
    182–84, 190, 193, 199
  age of, effect on fire safety, 140
  antiurban bias in federal policies on,
    143–45
  construction, tax incentives for,
    144–45
  discrimination in, 139, 144. *See also*
    segregation, residential
  dispersal strategy, 92–93, 94
  prosuburban bias in federal policies
    on, 135
  See also public housing; spatial mis-
    match
Housing and Urban Development, U.S.
  Department of, 29

Houston, TX, 170n12
Hughes, Mark Alan, 93, 97n12
Huizinga, David, 72n20
human services. *See* social services
human/social capital, 42, 46, 58,
  71n11; deficits in, 40–41, 54; as
  protective factor, 54, 60–61
Huurne, A., 43

Ihlanfeldt, Keith R., 87–88, 96n7
immigrants, elimination of welfare
  benefits for, 22
incarceration, 37, 59, 69, 72n23, 158,
  214; as a deterrent, research on,
  235, 236; effects on later employment, 34, 40–42, 48, 54, 71n7;
  jobs programs for youth prior to,
  66–68; research questions on,
  225–27
income, 30, 33, 37, 58, 89, 196; central city and suburban differential,
  137, 164; legal and illegal compared, 35, 44–48, 71n13. *See also*
  income from crime; wages
income from crime/illegal work, 43–
  48, 58, 68–69, 72n20
  drug selling, 44, 45, 46–48, 71nn12,
    13; compared with pay for legal
    work, 60, 63; role in motivation
    for detaching from, 55–56
  seen as incentive for illegal work, 60,
    62–63
income maintenance program, EITC
  as, 27, 30
income taxes, 20, 137–38, 153, 165–
  66, 171n25; consumption tax as
  proposed replacement, 168; exportation to nonresidents, 153–
  54, 170nn14, 15; treatment of
  owner- versus renter-occupied
  housing, 144–45

mismatch hypothesis applied to, 86; in urban neighborhoods, effects on children and adolescents, 19–30; variables of, connection with crime, 38–43; for welfare-to-work transitions, 11–12, 17–19. *See also* employment; unemployment

labor unions, 108, 134–35, 150, 170n13

Ladd, Helen F., 134, 136, 156, 159–60, 169n4

Land, Kenneth C., 39

land use development, public-private partnerships, 194–96

Lane, Vincent, 5, 206, 209–11, 213–14, 217, 219, 220, 235–36

language of legal work, used to describe illegal work, 51

Latimer, George, 5

Latinos (Hispanics), 52, 71n18, 84t, 85, 95n3, 96n10

Laub, John H., 38, 41, 65

"legitimate means," concept of, 70n5

libraries, 138, 140

Liebow, Elliott, 71n15

longitudinal research, 42, 54, 60, 65, 88, 148

Los Angeles, CA, 170nn12, 14

Lowell, MA, 182

low-income population, 27–28, 131–32, 139, 161
  federal programs assisting, 155–58, 170n17. *See also* welfare housing. *See* housing, affordable/low-income; public housing
  See also poverty

McCall, Patricia L., 39

MacCoun, Robert, 46, 49, 70n2, 71n12

macro-level interventions, role in jobs programs, 67–68

macro-level studies, 39, 61

magnet schools, 149

managerial and professional jobs, 82, 83t, 85

managers, attitude toward academic skills, 105–9

mandates, federal and state, effect on cities, 158–59, 168, 194

manufacturing, 107
  employment decline, 50–51, 59, 71n17, 136, 137; effect on choice of illegal work, 53–54
  facilities: property tax abatements for, 170n6; and tax-exempt financing of industrial parks, 145

marital status, of welfare recipients, 15t

Marks, Laurence R., 135, 169n5

marriage: as reason for exit from welfare, 14; teenage pregnancy's effects on prospects for, 26

Martinez-Vazquez, Jorge, 136, 169n4

Massachusetts, 143, 159, 182, 184. *See also* Boston

Massachusetts Housing Financing Agency, 184

math skills, of high school graduates, 100, 106–7

Mayer, Susan E., 86, 95n6

mayors: policies designed to address fiscal problems, 152–54. *See also* government(s), city

media: and public policy, 209–10, 213; roots of "no penalty" attitude, 122n2

Medicaid, 157, 159, 171n19

Memphis, TN, 170n12

mental health care, 159, 183

mental retardation services, 183

Merton, Robert K., 70n5
metropolitan areas, 6, 188–89, 194, 215, 233
cooperation between suburbs and central cities, 162–66, 229
fiscal disparities, 135–49, 169n4; policies designed to address, 149, 152–62
regional governments, 161–62, 171n23, 210, 213, 229
tax-base sharing, 160–61, 171n21
See also central cities; suburbs; *individual cities*
Metropolitan Assembly on Urban Problems (Northwestern University, 1994), 1–8, 81, 177, 232–40; panel discussion, 205–21; urban research agenda, 222–31
Metropolitan Planning Council, 205, 207–8, 235
Meyer, R., 102
Miami, FL, 170n12
middle class, 145, 151–52; migration to the suburbs, 131–32, 136, 148–49, 167
migration: selective, 86, 87–89, 96n7. *See also* in-migration; out-migration
Milwaukee, WI, 47–48, 150, 170n12
Minneapolis, MN, 160–61, 170n12, 171n21
Minnesota, 169n4, 170n12; Twin Cities metropolitan area tax base sharing, 160–61, 171n21
minorities, 84t, 85, 87–88, 93, 131, 148; hiring avoided by business relocations to suburbs, 89–90, 228; housing. *See* housing; segregation, residential; political objections to suburban annexation, 165; spatial mismatch effects on,

81, 89, 94, 228; youth, gains from school-employer linkages, 118. *See also* African Americans; Hispanics; nonwhites
mobility: lack of among low-income households, 143–44. *See also* in-migration; out-migration
mobility, job, 19, 30, 107–8, 225. *See also* advancement, job
Moore, Joan W., 51–52
municipal government. *See* government, city
Murphy, Patrick, 46, 49, 70n2, 71n12
museums, 138, 140
music, future in dreamed of by high school students, 112, 122n2

Nashville, TN, 161, 165, 170n12
Nassau County, NY, 170n7
Nathan, Richard P., 155, 156, 213
National Crime Victimization Survey (NCVS), 43–44
National Latitudinal Survey of Youth (NLSY), 40–41, 45, 49–50, 102
National League of Cities, 169n1
National Research Council, 69
neighborhoods, 11, 34, 51, 53, 69, 151–52; effect on public-service costs, 139; effects on welfare reform efforts, 28–30; federal housing policies' effects on, 143–44; processes as deterrence variables, 61
Nelson, Karen, 110
Netherlands, studies on effects of unemployment on crime in, 43
networks, job, 53, 62
networks, social, 49, 51, 55–56, 61, 67, 226. *See also* gangs
Netzer, Dick, 152
Newark, NJ, 170n12, 183, 184

New Orleans, LA, 170n12

New York, NY, 47, 82–85, 135, 170n12; Chinatowns, 52; local income tax, 137–38, 170n15; metropolitan area, 82–86, 136, 138, 162, 164; property tax rates, 151, 153; public-private partnerships, 182, 186, 196; shares of AFDC and Medicaid paid by, 171n19; state aid to, 143, 170n11

New York (state), 138, 170n7, 213. *See also* New York, NY

NLSY (National Latitudinal Survey of Youth), 40–41, 45, 49–50, 102

NOJOBSCHOOL group, study of, 45, 49

nondiscrimination, bureaucratic emphasis on, 179

nonprofit organizations, 138, 155, 180–81, 207, 229

partnered with local governments, 186, 188, 190–91, 197; criminal justice system efforts, 193; for human and social services, 183–84, 187–88

nonresidents, 134, 137–38; provision of services to, 132, 139, 140–41; tax exporting to, 136, 153–54, 170nn14, 15; user fees exported to, 151

nonwhites, 53, 60, 72n22, 84t, 85. *See also* African Americans

"no penalty attitude," toward school performance, 110–13, 121, 122n2

Norquist, John, 150

North Carolina, 71n7, 211–12

Northeastern Illinois Planning Commission, 161

Northwestern University, 207, 212; Center for Urban Affairs and

Policy Research, 1, 8, 239; studies on work-school linkages in the U.S., 105–18. *See also* Metropolitan Assembly on Urban Problems

Oakland, William H., 131, 140n9

Oakland, CA, 91

Ohio, 136, 171n25, 183; Cleveland, 162, 170n12, 215–16

Oklahoma City, OK, 170n12

Omnibus Budget Reconciliation Act (OBRA) of 1993, 145–46

open admissions policies, in community colleges, 112

opportunity structure theories, 64–65, 69

optimization models, and decisions on legal and illegal work, 35, 50

Orange County, CA, 195

Oregon, 216

Osborne, David, 185

out-migration (from cities to suburbs), 85–87, 131–32, 169n2, 171n20; of businesses, 87–90, 131–32, 145, 169n2, 227–28; and fiscal disparities, 135, 147–49, 164, 169n3; of high- and middle-income households, 136, 143, 147, 148–49, 167. *See also* spatial mismatches

Pack, Janet Rothenberg, 139, 151–52

Padilla, Felix, 52, 71n18

Papke, Leslie E., 146

parking fees, suburban commuters affected by, 151

paternity establishment, punitive provisions for in welfare reform proposals, 26 peer group effects, on school-age children, 109, 169n3

Peirce, Neal, 5, 206, 211–16, 220, 235–36

Pennsylvania, 182, 213; Pittsburgh, 162, 171n25, 183. *See also* Philadelphia

Persky, J. J., 91–92, 93

Peterson, George E., 145, 155

Philadelphia, PA, 82–86, 91, 134–35, 162, 213; empowerment zones, 170n12; public service spending cuts, 150, 151, 152; studies on relationship between crime and employment, 39–40

Phoenix, AZ, 183

Pirog-Good, Maureen A., 39–40

Pittsburgh, PA, 162, 171n25, 183

plea bargaining, 218

Ploeg, G. J., 43

police services, 133, 164, 226

politics, 156, 159, 196; as barrier to implementation of dispersal strategies, 93, 97n11; role in views on annexation, 165

Popkin, Susan J., 96n8

population: central cities' losses, 136; state aid to local governments based on, 141; trends in large cities, 84t, 85

poverty, 1, 7, 28, 183, 233, 238; in central cities, 138–39, 143; intensification of, 33, 50–51; intergenerational transmission of, 225; spatial concentration of, 51, 54; transition out of and welfare-to-work programs, 25. *See also* low-income population; welfare programs; welfare reform

poverty line: and income for unskilled full-time workers, 18; and wages

of women making welfare-to-work transition, 12, 21

pregnancy prevention, knowledge of needed for welfare-to-work transition programs, 24, 26–28

private for-profit organizations. *See* for-profit organizations

Private Industry Councils, 183

private sector, 180
use for public services, 4, 150–51, 170n13, 184–86, 230. *See also* public-private partnerships
See also for-profit organizations; nonprofit organizations

property taxes, 136–37, 141, 148, 149, 165–66, 229; abatements, 152, 170n6; exemptions, 138, 145, 151; exportation to nonresidents, 153–54; limitations on in Massachusetts and Wisconsin, 143, 159; rates in New York City, 151; sales taxes replaced by, 170n17; tax-base sharing, 160–61, 171n21

Proposition 2½ (Massachusetts), 143

public assistance. *See* AFDC; welfare programs

public employment programs, 29–30

public health services, 150, 164–65. *See also* health care

public housing, 2, 11, 12–14, 96n8, 143, 156; programs for moving residents to private housing, 28–29; scattered-site in suburbs, 92–93. *See also* housing, affordable/low-income

public policy, 1–7
designed to address city fiscal problems, 149–62

and the research community, 232–
40; agenda for, 222–31; panel discussion on, 205–21
welfare-to-work experiments, 19–
22
public-private partnerships, 177–78,
192–93, 197–98, 230, 233; alternative provision of public services,
184–86, 198–99; in land use development, 194–96; municipal
use of, 150–51, 170n13; relevance to local government problems, 180–81; service quality and
differentiation, 187–89; used for
redistributive services, 187, 189–
91, 195; variety of, 181–84
public services, 132, 133–35, 179
financing, 132, 138–41, 166–68,
169n3; federal funding for, 155–
58; metropolitan area cooperation on, 163–64, 229; spending
cuts, 149–53, 164
provision, 135, 147–49. *See also*
public-private partnerships; *individual services*
public transit, 94, 169n3, 171n22; federal aid to, 143, 155, 158
public works projects, ARA focus on
in 1960s, 91
Puerto Ricans, 71n18

quantitative studies, 54; longitudinal
research, 42, 54, 60, 65, 88, 148
quasi-privatization, as form of public-
private partnerships, 181

race, 1, 5, 164–65, 209; role in hiring
preferences, 34, 60, 68, 72n22;
role in out-migration, 148–49; of
welfare recipients, 12, 14; worsening relations, 33, 194. *See also* Af-

rican Americans; segregation, residential; whites
Rafuse, Robert W., 135, 169n5
Raleigh-Durham metropolitan region,
NC, 211–12
random allocation, of families to
welfare-to-work experiments, 19–
20
Reagan administration, welfare-to-
work experiments encouraged by,
20
real estate: development, public-
private partnerships in, 181–82,
194–96; white-collar jobs in, 137
reality: high school students' perceptions of, 122n2; information on
given by teachers with links to employers, 117
recessions, economic, 13, 91
recreational facilities: public-private
partnerships in provision of, 181,
187, 193, 200n5; use by nonresidents, 132, 138, 140
redistributive services, 155, 157, 158–
59, 161, 181; public-private partnerships used for, 187, 189–91,
195
redlining, efforts to eliminate, 144
regional econometrics, 215
regional (metropolitan) governments,
161–62, 171n23, 210, 213, 229
Regional Transport Authority (metropolitan Chicago), 94, 171n22
regulatory exceptions on land use development, granted by local governments, 194, 196
Rendell, Edward, 150, 151
rent subsidies, 92, 143–44
Republicans, 168; "Contract with
America," 22, 168; welfare reform proposals, 11, 22–23

Reschovsky, Andrew, 4, 6, 133–76, 233

research
ethnographic, 50–51, 60, 61, 64
and public policy, 232–40; agenda for, 222–31; panel discussion on, 205–21

residential settings, jobs programs in, 66–67

Reuter, Peter, 46, 49, 70n2, 71n12

revenue-raising ability of municipalities, 134, 135–38, 169n5; expansion of, 151, 159–60, 171n20; and use of public-private partnerships, 189–91, 194–96. *See also* taxation, state and local

rewards, intrinsic, role in abandoning crime for legal work, 55–56

Risk Management Division, in Philadelphia, 150

robbery, 45, 71n16, 72n20

roles, social, changes in, 51, 56–57

Roomkin, Myron, 8

Rosenbaum, James E., 4, 6, 28–29, 96n8, 100–128

Rosett, Richard N., 138

Rothenberg, Jerome, 4, 7, 177–202, 233

rural areas, ARA's focus on public works projects, 91

Rusk, David E., 133, 161, 215

St. Paul, MN, 160–61, 171n21

sales taxes, 171n22, 195; exportation to nonresidents, 140, 153–54; replaced by property taxes, 170n17

Sampson, Robert J., 38, 41, 65

Sanchez-Jankowski, M., 52, 64

sanctions, 55, 56; and crime-employment relationship, 37, 38–39, 70n4; as deterrence variables,

57, 61; use in welfare-to-work experiments, 21

San Diego, CA, 20–21

San Francisco, CA, 162, 170nn12, 14, 182

Schill, Michael H., 144

school-based enterprises (SBE), 102

school performance, 101, 105; "no penalty" attitude, 109–13, 121, 122n2; perceived relevance to future careers, 109–13, 118, 122n1; teachers' links with employers as motivation for, 116, 118

schools, 1, 2, 6, 7, 211, 234; approach to school-to-work transition based in, 102–3; attendance, 40; class size, 133; middle-class out-migration effects, 169n3; place-based formula for funding, 95. *See also* education; high schools; school-to-work transitions

school-to-work transitions, 67, 69, 100–102, 200n12
approaches to improving, 102–4, 118–22
in Germany, 6, 101, 103, 104
high school teachers' role in, 113–18; proposed improvements in, 118–22
in Japan. *See* Japan
and relevance of education to future career, 109–13, 118
research agenda on, 223–24
See also high schools

Seattle, WA, 170n12

Section 8 subsidies, 92

segregation, residential, 89, 90–92, 94, 96n10, 139, 143; effect on choices about income, 51, 54, 61

self-perception, role in desisting from crime, 56–57

self-reported crime incomes, 48, 58, 72n20

self-sufficiency, skills needed for, support for development of, 27–28

sewage disposal, 140, 169n3

shelter for the homeless, 139, 158–59

shoplifting, 71n16

short-term receipt of welfare, 14–15

Sickles, Robin C., 39–40

Sjoquist, David L., 87–88, 96n7, 136, 169n4

skills. *See* academic skills; job skills

social networks. *See* networks, social

Social Security payroll taxes, increases from welfare-to-work programs, 20

social services, 155, 190, 194; block grants for, 146, 168; combined with police services, 226; public-private partnerships for providing, 180–81, 183, 190, 193. *See also* welfare programs

socioeconomic status, 26–27, 40, 109–10, 153. *See also* income; middle class

sociology, 4, 62–65

solid waste disposal, 182–83, 185

South Carolina, 182

spatial mismatches, 34, 81–90, 209, 211; effect on choices about income, 51, 54; policies addressing, 90–95; research agenda on, 227–28. *See also* housing; transportation

sports complexes, public-private partnership use to develop, 181, 200n5

State University of New York at Albany, 213

status, 38, 51, 54–56, 61–64, 109–10

Stinchcombe, A., 109–11

stratification in job opportunities, influence on work-crime decisions, 38, 70n5

street cleaning, public-private partnerships in, 181, 182–83

structural fiscal problems, 132, 133–35, 169n1

subsidies, 27, 192; for housing, 92, 143–44; for industrial-business growth, 152, 182; for land use development, 194; for mass transit, 143

suburbs, 5, 6, 92–93, 179, 210, 237; African Americans in, 81, 85–86, 87, 92–93, 94, 96n8; annexation of, 161–62; cooperation with central cities, 162–65; fiscal condition, 135–36, 167, 169n4; high school seniors' attitudes, survey of, 110–13; high school vocational teachers interviewed, 113–18; low-income housing in, 28–29, 92–93, 144; under metropolitan area governments, 161–62; public service costs, 138, 140–41; as source for state tax increases, 158; spillovers into of central city problems, 164–65, 167; suburban exploitation thesis, 140–41. *See also* government(s), local; metropolitan areas; outmigration; spatial mismatches

success stories, roots of "no penalty" attitude toward school performance, 122n2

Summers, Lawrence H., 145

TARP (Transitional Aid Research Project), 41–42, 69–70

ventions, 65–68; research on, 57–
62, 68–70; theories on, 62–65
See also employment
uniformity, bureaucratic emphasis on,
179
universality in public services, 187;
provided by public-private partnerships, 200n5
universities. *See* colleges and universities
University of Maryland/Baltimore
County, 213
University of Pennsylvania, 213
Unraveling Juvenile Delinquency
(Glueck and Glueck), 41
unskilled labor, 39, 62, 66–67, 69,
72n21; decline in jobs, 53, 59;
wages for, 18, 64–65
"Urban Research Agenda," 3, 8, 222–
31, 232, 237–38
user fees, 140, 151, 153–54

vanpools, for reverse commuting, 91,
94, 95
verbal expression, basic skills in
among high school graduates,
106–7
violence, 1, 52, 59, 61–62, 139
Visalia, California, 183, 199
Visalians Interested in Affordable
Housing (VIAH), 199
Viscusi, W. Kip, 44–45, 48, 72n20
vocational education
in high schools, 101, 102, 109; and
future relevance attitudes among
students, 110–12; teachers' role in
school-to-work transitions, 113–
22
public-private partnerships in, 187
See also job training programs
Voting Rights bill, 165

Wachter, Susan M., 144
wages, 17–19, 21, 59, 66, 72n21, 103;
assumptions on welfare recipients'
ability to earn, 235, 238; credits
for in empowerment zones, 146;
dispersion from central city to
suburbs, 137; effects on crime participation, 45–46, 71nn8–10;
high school students' unrealistic
expectations about, 114; high
school vocational education effects on, 102, 110–11; in New
York City subject to local income
tax, 137–38; for public employment under Clinton's reforms, 23,
103; public opinion on subsidies,
27; reducing returns from illegal
work to match, 72n23; spatial
mismatch studies of, 96n7; for unskilled workers, 64–65. *See also*
income
wages, illegal. *See* income from crime
War on Poverty, 96n9
Washington, DC, 46–47, 170n12, 215
water treatment, 169n3; private management of, 170n13
Ways and Means, Committee on,
Green Book, 13, 16
Weisbrod, Burton A., 1–32, 205–9,
216, 220–21, 232–40
welfare dependency, 11–12, 131, 224–
25
welfare programs, 2, 6, 139, 233, 235,
237–38; AFDC, 155, 157,
170n16, 171n19; benefits, 20, 23,
25; demography and dynamics of
caseloads, 11–17; income options, 5–6, 34; length of time on,
11–16, 22–23; public opinion on,
27–28; public-private partnerships, 180–81, 183, 187, 190,